Chancellor Engelbert Dollfuss, an official portrait ; 'the huge mild eyes of a quite startling blue, infectious smile, the almost child-like simplicity of manner . . .'

DOLLFUSS

GORDON BROOK-SHEPHERD

MACMILLAN & CO LTD
NEW YORK · ST MARTIN'S PRESS
1961

MACMILLAN AND COMPANY LIMITED
London Bombay Calcutta Madras Melbourne

THE MACMILLAN COMPANY OF CANADA LIMITED
Toronto

ST MARTIN'S PRESS INC
New York

PRINTED IN GREAT BRITAIN

Dedication

This Book is dedicated, with permission, to my old friend
LEOPOLD FIGL
Federal Chancellor of Austria 1945–1953 ;
Austrian Foreign Minister 1953–1956,
and now President of the National Assembly ;
like Dollfuss, a Lower Austrian peasant politician ;
and, like him, the embodiment of the Austrian spirit
in a time of desperate struggle

CONTENTS

ILLUSTRATIONS

Dollfuss

INTRODUCTION

I HAVE slim qualifications for talking about the art of biography, for this is my first and possibly my last venture in the field. But perhaps that is all the more reason for explaining what led me to write the life of Engelbert Dollfuss.

There seems to me little point in writing anybody's biography unless one admires or dislikes him ; unless the ground has not been properly covered before or fresh evidence has come to light which justifies a new approach ; and, in the case of a historical personage, unless one wants either to 'debunk' him or do much-needed justice to his memory. In Dollfuss's case, one or the other of all these motives were present and strong.

He was not a commanding figure in a Europe over-shadowed by Hitler and Mussolini, by an emergent Stalin and a somnolent Baldwin. But of all this company he took the noblest character into high office, faced the most impossible odds with the greatest courage, and met the most tragic end.

He is also the most maligned. For the little Austrian Chancellor who was a better practical Socialist than any of his opponents has gone down in the domestic history of his country as the 'murderer of defenceless workers'. And the patriot who gave back to his nation that self-respect and sense of identity on which seven million Austrians — Socialists and Conservatives alike — nourish themselves today, has been portrayed on the international stage as a 'Fascist traitor' who sold his country into Mussolini's bondage.

This distortion has taken place because what passes for the story of his troubled times is, in fact, history by default.

With the notable exception of Dollfuss's successor, Kurt von Schuschnigg, hardly any of his followers has put his case, which was the Austrian case as opposed to the democratic case (and the two *were* at that time in opposition). But nearly all of his former opponents have spread their rival arguments against him in the West, with that fluency natural to Left-Wing intellectuals and that nervous energy understandable in refugees.

Indeed, for many of these people, the destruction of Dollfuss's reputation was something more than an ideological necessity. It became vital to their own self-esteem. True, they had many qualities which he lacked, or deliberately set aside. But he had much for which they yearned. The four-square solidarity and the dynamism of his fatherland love, for example, showed up the airy-fairy world of their Socialist International in a sickly light. Furthermore, he was a man of action and they were men who fled from action. Despite their equal idealism and their greater cleverness, I suspect that some of them envied him, and with the envy went the spite — fully matched on the other side, I may say, by the unreasoning hate of the 'Clericalists' for the 'Austro-Marxists'. It is this venom which, as an outsider, I have tried to remove from the story. But his case must be left to argue itself in the following pages, and not be advanced here.

This is not, of course, just a portrait of Dollfuss. It is also a portrait of that Great Dictators' age which encompassed and crushed him. After all, it was his Austria which kept Hitler and Mussolini apart in the mid 'thirties ; and Dollfuss himself has the immortality of being Hitler's first foreign challenger and his first foreign victim. The abortive Nazi *putsch* in Vienna on July 25, 1934, which cost Dollfuss his life, was the beginning of Hitler's long trail of foreign aggression which, five years later, plunged Germany and the rest of the world into disaster.

In view of all this, it is remarkable that no proper biography of Dollfuss should exist in any language — not even in German. The handful of works about him were written almost exclusively in the two-year period 1933–35, and are either brochures published during his brief term of office or uncritical panegyrics produced hurriedly by the impact of his murder. Soon afterwards, Hitler's shadow fell over Vienna ; the name of Dollfuss became a fatal one to mention, and at least one Austrian far better qualified than I to write this book died in a Nazi concentration camp.

Yet, precisely because the gap has yawned so long and so wide, it has now been possible, in an attempt to fill it, to draw on a whole mass of completely new material. The general reader as well as the student might be interested in a summary of these fresh sources which have been used.

First, a word about the various original documents which somehow survived Austria's seventeen years of war and foreign occupation, and were made available to me. Frau Alwine Dollfuss, the Chancellor's widow, has kindly supplied some valuable papers, both personal and political, which followed her round the world in her war-time exile. Prominent in the latter category are the full secret reports drawn up by Dollfuss's State Secretary for Security, Baron Karwinsky, on both the Austrian Civil War of February 1934 and the Nazi *coup d'état* five months later.

I am indebted to Dr. Karl Maria Stepan, who paid under the Nazis for the privilege of being the leader of Dollfuss's 'Fatherland Front', for his own unpublished record of the period. This six-hundred-page private diary has the supreme merit of being a spontaneous account of events and impressions — full of doubts as well as convictions — and it has been handed over to me just as it was written years ago, without any attempt at editing or re-touching. I must also thank the widow of Field-Marshal Lieutenant von Bardolff for letting me see her husband's papers, which give a fascinating glimpse into the mental perplexities of a pan-German Austrian aristocrat after the First World War. Dollfuss's successor as Chancellor, Schuschnigg, and one of his former colleagues, ex-Minister Ludwig Strobl, have both supplied valuable original documents about the Austrian domestic conflict.

In a class by themselves as new and unused material on the 1934 Nazi *putsch* are the so-called 'Weydenhammer Report' and the so-called 'Holzweber papers'. The first is a long secret report made to Hitler about the abortive Vienna *coup* by one of the principal German conspirators involved. For access to this document, I must record a special debt of gratitude to Univ-Dozent Dr. Ludwig Jedlicka in Vienna, who very generously allowed me to make use of this and other connected material before the publication of his own special study on the subject. The Holzweber papers represent about everything that has survived in Austrian political police files on the 1934 *putsch*. In the year 1960, these could not be made officially available in Vienna, due to regard for German susceptibilities. I must thank a very highly placed Austrian friend for spiriting them away from the bureaucratic machine for me during two precious weeks. Needless to say, he wishes to remain anonymous.

A veritable mine of information on all aspects of the secret diplomacy of Hitler and Mussolini towards Austria is contained in Volumes 1 to 3 of the Series C of *Documents on German Foreign Policy*, published by Her Majesty's Stationery Office. The last of these three volumes, which cover the period January 1933 to March 1935, happened to appear just as I was concluding my own researches, and together they saved me from many an error of emphasis and fact. This is the first time that the plentiful material on Austria contained in these three thousand pages of diplomatic telegrams has been used. It only remains for me to express to the joint British and American editors of the project my admiration for the way they have tackled their giant task.

But all these documents represent only half the help I have

been given. Owing to the fact that, for twelve years, Vienna was the base for my travels as a foreign correspondent, I have been able to talk at length to nearly all of Dollfuss's surviving friends and opponents, both political and private. This book might almost be called, in fact, an experiment in history written 'from the running-board'. I have used both the documents and the actors who wrote or lived those documents, confronted the one with the other, and learned more from the resulting reactions than from either source taken in isolation.

Under this second general heading of eye-witness help, I must again thank Dr. Schuschnigg, who devoted two or three days of his last stay in Europe to answering my questions; the ex-Ministers Czermak and Ludwig, former confidantes of Dollfuss; the late General Dr. Emil Liebitzsky, Military Attaché in Rome during the Dollfuss era; Dr. Leo Mueller, a former agricultural colleague of Dollfuss; and all those like Dr. Stepan and Dr. Strobl who also provided documentary help. Others who have provided me with useful reminiscences on the political side include all three Austrian Chancellors of the post-war period — Dr. Figl, Herr Raab and Dr. Gorbach; the former Austrian Minister of Defence, Ferdinand Graf, and the present Governor of Lower Austria, Dr. Gleissner.

To another good friend, Dr. Theodore von Hornbostel, I am heavily indebted. Dr. Hornbostel held the key post of Political Director at the Austrian Foreign Office during Dollfuss's Chancellorship. He has not only described for me events like the private Dollfuss-Mussolini meetings, of which he is the only surviving witness. He also devoted the whole of one springtime's leisure to studying the neat mountains of German diplomatic documents referred to above and comparing them with his own records of the time.

Obviously, in dealing with the domestic scene, I have not confined myself to Dollfuss's friends. Many of his principal Socialist rivals — above all Otto Bauer and Karl Renner —

are dead. But I have been able to spend several stimulating hours with Dr. Julius Deutsch, Bauer's right-hand man and Commander of the Left-Wing paramilitary *Schutzbund* which fought in the Civil War ; and with ex-Minister Oskar Helmer, who played an important role twenty-five years ago in the vain negotiations for an Austrian domestic truce. I have also had several long talks with the present Austrian Foreign Minister, Dr. Bruno Kreisky, about the Dollfuss era, which he saw and suffered under as a young Socialist student leader. These talks have altered neither our respective stand-points nor our personal friendship — another small sign, perhaps, that those passions which once plunged Austria into Civil War are on the wane.

As regards Dollfuss the man, I must again thank his widow for many unpublished anecdotes ; also his surviving step-brothers for their help and hospitality on a memorable visit to his Lower Austrian peasant home — still being farmed by them today. Much valuable material about Dollfuss as a schoolboy and a student has been supplied by two of his former class-mates — Ing. Bruckner and Kons.-Rat. Toifl, now the parish priest of Niederkreuzstetten. Dr. (now Sektions-chef) Egon Krisch, who was once Dollfuss's secretary in the Chancellery, and Frau Alice Ruppel, who supervised the various private charities that Dollfuss started up, have helped me greatly in their respective fields. Hofrat Dr. Rischanek, Dollfuss's one-time law teacher and lifelong friend, has pro-vided many an illuminating reminiscence. But the list of these assorted personal contributors is endless.

Finally, a special word of thanks to two irreplaceable 'back-room helpers' on research and collation of material : Herr Karl Zronek, Librarian in the Austrian Parliament, and my former assistant in Vienna, Annelise Schulz, without whose devoted spare-time labours this and various books before it would hardly have seen the light of day.

A word about arrangement. I have deliberately separated

the account of Dollfuss's foreign policy struggle between Hitler and Mussolini from the story of his domestic political troubles. I am of course aware that the two were interrelated, and, at the vital connecting points, cross-references will be found. But the Austrian domestic imbroglio is such a confusing tangle by itself that, in order to preserve some basic simplicity of narrative, I have kept it apart from the parallel and almost equally complicated tale of Austria's diplomatic dilemma. This may distress one or two scholars who are steeped in the period ; but I feel sure that the general reader will get a clearer picture by reading these chapters in sequence and remembering the points at which they interlock, than in trying to follow both confusing stories at once.

It might be worth adding that this particular book really concludes a trio (trilogy is altogether too pompous a word) of works on Central Europe that I started on nearly ten years ago. They are connected like concentric circles, each covering a related field, but each narrowing down in time or space. The first, *Russia's Danubian Empire*, described the incursion of Soviet power into the whole area and the problems this raised. The second, *The Austrian Odyssey*, dealt with one of the keys to these problems, the existence of an independent Austria and the emergence of an Austrian state-patriotism over the last hundred years. And lastly comes the story of Dollfuss, who is himself the key to the re-birth of this specifically Austrian patriotism in that savage Central European jungle of politics between the two World Wars.

His spirit is at the centre of this last and smallest circle, and therefore at the centre of all three. That is the meaning of his life's work for all Austrians, and all Europeans, today.

GORDON BROOK-SHEPHERD

CHAPTER ONE

Peasant and Soldier

THAT rich, tranquil wedge of land between the Wachau
Valley of the Danube and the foothills of the Alps was
the right soil to have bred Austria's first patriot.

For this is a rib of the green cradle of the nation. No
foreign borders can be seen here, or even sensed. There are
no pockets of Slav or Magyar settlers to recall that patchwork
Empire of a dozen peoples over which the Austrians once
ruled. It is an enclosed, compact, homogeneous and, above
all, a deep-rooted countryside. The great river shuts it off
to the north, sending down two blue-green arms, the Pielach
and the Erlauf, to embrace it on the east and west; and, in
the far south, where those arms nearly join, the peak of the
Ötscher stands sentinel, making an abrupt end with its barrier
of ice and granite to the softer forest slopes.

There were many others who rightly called themselves
Austrians in the rump Republic of $6\frac{1}{2}$ millions which was left
in 1918, sitting amputated and helpless on the crossroads of
Europe. But the affinity was nowhere else the same. Far
over to the west, the Vorarlbergers looked instinctively across
their Alpine frontier to Switzerland and to the common
Alemannic ties which have always linked these stolid folk
as closely to Valais as to Vienna. Their neighbours, the
Tyroleans, lived as always for their own province first and
for Austria second; what fascination could a new Federal
Republic have for a race who had regarded even the Habsburgs as the Princely Counts of Tyrol rather than as Imperial
and Apostolic Majesties? In Salzburg, the German influence

I

was physically so close that its pull could be felt in the air like a magnet, then as now, anywhere further than a thousand yards from the utterly native shrine of Mozart's birthplace. Carinthia and Styria, precisely because they bordered on the newly-independent Slav worlds, had that exaggerated Teutonism of a racial bulwark which is also non-Austrian in its essence. Vienna was a disenchanted cosmopolitan lady, always complaining she had seen better days ; and the Burgenland, which only came to the Republic in 1921, still had one foot in the Hungarian *puszta*. The herons poking out of the reeds, the storks nesting on the chimney-tops, the regiments of geese waddling between the 'back-to-front' Magyar-style houses, the heaths, the feathered grass, above all the stupefying flatness and exposure of this dried-out sea-bed : none of this is Austrian.

If any one area can claim therefore to justify the existence and the continuity of an Austrian people as such, it is those hilly plains which border the central Danube. Indeed, it is here that the heart of Austrian history beats. This was the home of Gudrun and the Nibelungs, or Hagen, the terrible one-eyed tyrant ; this was the centre of that original 'Eastern Mark' with which the Babenbergers were enfeoffed in 976 to begin the story of the *Ostarrichi* ; and, for the Habsburgs who succeeded them in 1273, this became the core of the feudal *Erblande*, the lands on which that family's dynastic power ultimately rested. They were too close to this part of their domains ever to be crowned formally as its rulers. The Habsburgs became Kings of Hungary and Bohemia ; but they stayed to the end simple Archdukes of Austria.

In the middle of all this Austrian history, a history that he was himself destined to make, the future Austrian Chancellor Engelbert Dollfuss was born, on the 4th of October, 1892, at a farmhouse in the village of Texing near Mank. The name is his mother's, Josepha Dollfuss, then 25 years old, and it was the only one which the village priest Joseph Feyber could enter in the church registry when the infant was brought to him to be baptized two days later. For Engelbert was an illegitimate child. His father, according to the general verdict of the villagers, was one Joseph Wenninger, a local labourer, who had been rejected by Josepha's parents as a totally unworthy suitor.

The Dollfuss family were old-established independent peasant-farmers whose roots went deep into the rich soil they ploughed. Their *Stammbaum*, or table of ancestors, is still being embellished today. It is an impressive chart the size of a hearth rug, eight feet long by three feet wide, covered with name-squares in blue and gold like a coloured quilt, and backed, somewhat incongruously, with flowered kitchen linoleum so that it can be rolled up tidily after the privileged visitor's inspection and stored again in the great oak cupboard.

At the very top, in a square thickly bordered with gold, stands the first Dollfuss to be traced in the church registers of the neighbourhood — André Dollfuss, who died in 1588, already working the land of Lower Austria as a free man. By the time little Engelbert opened his eyes on to this same landscape, therefore, his mother's family had been settled and respected there for over 300 years. Like all conservative peasants, it was more cattle and green acres they wanted for their daughter in marriage and not a landless town labourer. The obscure Joseph Wenninger thus disappears from the picture almost before his famous son is born.

His place is soon taken, when the infant is barely a year old, by a candidate right after the Dollfuss family's heart — Leopold Schmutz, a peasant with thirty acres of land in the nearby village of Kirnberg. In such isolated agricultural communities, a healthy son born out of wedlock was scarcely an embarrassment and certainly not a grave handicap to matrimony, for indeed its very existence gave welcome premarital proof that the woman concerned could breed good male stock. So, however relieved Josepha's parents may have been, nobody in Texing was particularly surprised when, in 1893, Leopold Schmutz married the attractive young mother and took her with the infant to his own farmhouse three miles away.

It was under this roof, Sattlehen Number 4, that the Dollfuss child lived and slept with scarcely a night's break until 1904, the year when he left home to become a scholarship boarder at the Catholic 'Gymnasium' in Hollabrunn. His childhood was frugal, hard-working but happy. Three sons and a daughter came of Schmutz's marriage with Josepha, so the little Engelbert was never short of playmates or workmates. Yet though the five children grew up as a single family and felt themselves as such, the Dollfuss boy somehow remained, as he had begun, a child apart from his step-brothers and sister. Leopold Schmutz was a kindly man, but taciturn and severe, with a rather shuttered-up look about his gaunt features. Something of this spirit of withdrawal passed into his own children, over whom he ruled with unchallenged patriarchal authority. But Josepha Dollfuss had not only given her own name to her love-child. She gave him also her dwarf-like stature (they were both exactly the same height), her luxuriant dark hair, her large expressive eyes and, above all, her own gentle and sunny nature. Whatever he was doing about the farm — feeding the pigs, tugging at the grain-sacks or scrambling up the fruit trees — the diminutive Engelbert must always have looked rather like some elf from a gayer and more luxuriant world, as though some itinerant Oriental pedlar had deposited him there on the grass in a silver filigree basket and forgotten to call for him again.

At all events, this air of belonging yet not belonging, coupled with his lead in age and his own infectious spirits, soon made him the central figure in the Schmutz household — the first and smallest of the many life-circles he was destined to dominate. His mother, of course, had a special affection for him, for he was the one living link between her romance and her respectability. Indeed, a strange intuitive bond always existed between these two tiny people. (On 'Mother's Day' in May 1934, just as the famous Austrian Chancellor was leaving the old farmhouse after his last visit, Josepha Dollfuss suddenly dipped her fingers in holy water and made a cross on her son's brow, as though seized by some stark premonition of evil. Ten weeks later Hitler's assassins shot him down in the Vienna Chancellery.)

But almost equally for the others, 'Engl' was the beacon light of the family, and even today his stepbrothers can remember that sense of emptiness which came over the house when he left it for school after the holidays, and that air of vibration when he ran into the courtyard again after another ten weeks spent with his priests and his books. Already as a child he showed a gay but passionate attachment to life that stayed with him always, and made his own fate doubly ironic.

His was a stiff, spartanic upbringing, to be sure. The turn of the century was no easy time for the small farmer in those parts. To eat another egg apiece called often for a special decision, while a new pair of shoes for the ceremonial Sunday walk to church was a major item in the monthly budget. Even with the hired labourer and the dairy-maid which his stepfather then employed, there was no shortage of manual work for the young Dollfuss from the moment he could walk steadily on his short legs.

The lessons of these childhood hardships, and particularly of the common struggle by which the household overcame them, under the stern eye and hand of Leopold Schmutz, remained with Dollfuss throughout his life. Once when, as Chancellor, he was out driving with a friend and discussing the many problems which beset his country, he passed a road leading to his home village, he paused to point out the familiar landmarks, and then added : 'This was where I saw, from my childhood onwards, the battle against want. And if today I take such an interest in these things, it is because I learned it all here. We never had anything to spare and always had to slog away for what we got. That gave me understanding and sympathy for the economic troubles of the people.'

But though he grew up well knowing what it was to wring out a hard livelihood in sweat, there was nothing sombre about those early days. The man Dollfuss carried with him that precious stamp of serenity on his brow which, all the world over, only a happy childhood can implant.

The purely physical environment of his first twelve years must have played a big role in this. Kirnberg belongs to that part of the Danube Valley which was settled in the 6th century by the Bajuvars, and the mark of their free way of life can be seen on these hills today. For, 1400 years later, Kirnberg is still a Bajuvar village. That means it is not a village at all in the compact market-square Austrian sense so much as a sprinkling of farms, a mile or more apart from each other, scattered about the country with no pattern except the haphazard one dictated by suitable sites on clearings or hill-crests. There is no trace here of the serfs' cottages huddling in the shadow of the feudal castle. It was an unfettered exist-ence, calling for strong independence from the tribal family units who lived it.

The farm Sattlehen Number 4 is a typical survival of these ancient 'open settlements'. It sits quite by itself on a small grass plateau, enclosed on all sides by the softly-rucked green blanket of the forest slopes. The only approach from the road is a cart-track with deep wheel-ruts four feet apart which winds up and down for the best part of a thousand yards before the farm comes in sight. In summer, everything around sings and vibrates with colour. Yellow fields of wheat and rye, splashes of blue flax and red poppy, the pink and white blossom of orchards and, behind it all, the dark sheen of the pine forest — such was the setting in which the boy Dollfuss worked and played every year. There is precious

little around that God did not make, and not even a glimpse
of a street, town or factory.

The house itself also betrays the four-square foundations
of a Bajuvar dwelling — though, as an inscription in the main
ceiling beam shows, it was built in its present form in the
year 1661, the home of one Steffl Wanger. In this dark-
beamed 'best' room the ceremonial life of the Schmutz
family was, and still is, enacted — birthdays, Christmas and
other festivals and, above all, the entertaining of visitors.
Then, as today, the octagonal corner table under the crucifix
would be laden with jars of *Birnenmost* or pear cider, loaves of
dark brown sweet-scented 'house-bread', baked with a cross
in the centre and shaped like an enormous discus, and slices
of home-cured peasant ham. The old walls of the house,
three foot thick, deaden both the summer blaze and the winter
frost. Even in this mechanized day and age, the room, and
the whole house, give out an air of solid tranquillity, a feeling
of belonging to the soil around and to the disciplined communal routine with which the soil is worked.

It is to try and convey something of this *genus loci* that
we have lingered so long, in a political biography, on the very
sights and smells of Dollfuss's home. For to know his environment as a child is not merely helpful but absolutely vital in
understanding his actions as a man. Many statesmen turn
their backs on their humble beginnings; some genuinely
grow away from them; some take constant and savage
revenge on them. But for Dollfuss, the whole of his tragic,
meteoric and controversial career was a projection of those
first twelve years.

He could never jump away from his shadow — the strong,
short shadow of his peasant piety and discipline. Indeed, he
made no attempt to, for he was proud always to walk in it.
This pride of attachment had its good and its seamy sides.
The knowledge that the shadow was there gave him strength
to stand his ground, even when the earth was rocking around

him. But, at times, it also prevented him from enlarging that ground.

For better or for worse, however, the child lived on in the man, to such an extent that even his politics became basically a sublimated childhood. Most of the qualities and achievements for which Dollfuss was adored or reviled are directly rooted in these early years, as his own speeches reveal : the courage, endurance, industry, humility and utter personal integrity of the man ; and also the almost mystic medievalism (no other word will do) of the statesman. His attempt to purify the corrupt and embittered political life of his day by refounding the Christian and socially disciplined order of the past — 'Austriam instaurare in Christo' — this was essentially the dream of a pious peasant-thinker bred on an ancient Bajuvar farm. Subconsciously, Dollfuss would have liked to have turned the whole of Austria into an open-settlement Kirnberg, run just as his stepfather had run Sattlehen Number 4.

*　　　*　　　*

Dollfuss's way out — and up — into the world, as with countless generations of gifted peasant boys before him, was through the Catholic Church. Apart from his strong, gay personality, the only sign of anything exceptional about the child had been his insatiable appetite for reading. The moment he had mastered the mysteries of print, he lived with a book in his hand, either tending the cattle on the meadows during the long summer days or squinting under a petroleum lamp up in his room during the even longer winter nights. The problem, on that isolated farm, was to find something to read ; and it was a great moment when he discovered a heap of old Austrian 'Peasant Calendars' which, in the days of the Emperor Franz Josef, were the staple literature, often the only literature, of the farm-dweller.

He himself later described to a friend how he had first

learned about the problems of the country around him from this hoard of well-thumbed annuals, just as his first geographical notions of the greater world beyond that came from the novels of Karl May.

'It was the custom in our house', he related, 'to store up the old Calendars, and by a lucky chance I once stumbled on the chest in which they were kept. I used to take three or four of them at a time out with me during the grazing weeks and just read and read. You would never believe how much knowledge and self-education one can get that way. From those Calendars I learned the lesson that the peasant must be ready to help and advise everyone, even those people who stand outside his own circle and field of work.'

It may have been the Bible stories and Saints' days with which those Calendars were plentifully sprinkled ; it may have been those solemn moments at table when stepfather Schmutz, the Crucifix in the *Herrgottswinkel* above his bowed head, called for the Lord's Prayer before the whole family — hired help and all — dipped their spoons into the common bowl of 'Stohsuppe' or sour cream soup. Whatever started it off, when 'Engl' was eight or nine years old, he began to play at being a priest. He built a little makeshift altar in the house, and read Mass and preached sermons in his piping voice just as he had learned in the local church. The household was too close to God to find this either exceptional or blasphemous.

Kirnberg church, which now begins to play a dominant role in his life, is just as untypical of picture-postcard Austria as the village, though in quite the opposite way. If the village stands wide open to the skies, without a square or a centre, the 14th-century Gothic church is unusually aloof and enclosed. It stands, not among the scattered houses, but up on the crest of a small steep hill, completely surrounded like a fortress by high yellow walls and a screen of trees. One is not surprised to learn from the priest that it once served as a hermit's settlement in honour of St. Hieronymus, though at the time when young Dollfuss was trotting in and out of it, dressed in his dark green Sunday best, it had already entered on a more cheerful existence as the summer seat of the Suffragan-Bishop of Vienna. With its elaborate baroque chapel, its frescoes, its gilded angels, and its fine altar painting of the Holy Family (which somehow got there from the great Carthusian Abbey at Gaming when the Emperor Leopold dissolved the monasteries), it is an impressive church for such a humble community.

The Dollfuss boy fell completely under its spell. A single ambition surged in his tiny breast — to assist at Mass. He first tackled the sacristan Fiala, who protested that the smallest robes he had in the vestry were far too long. But, even in those days, Dollfuss was not one to give up the chase. He resumed his attack through the village priest, Simon Veith, a kindly man who anyway had a soft spot for the child. And, in the end, Fiala was persuaded to take six inches off the children's vestments (black for ordinary occasions and red for Sundays), and the diminutive Engelbert had his great day, swinging the incense-burners before the assembled farmers of Kirnberg and their Sunday-polished broods.

It was when an even greater day arrived, and he was allowed to perform the same service for no less a personage than the visiting Suffragan-Bishop Doctor Schneider, that the Dollfuss boy made up his mind. He announced to his step-father that he would like to become a priest.

As it turned out, it was a false sense of vocation. What was really driving Dollfuss was simply the impulse to go and meet the great world and put his mark upon it somewhere. And the Church, represented by that glowing baroque altar at Kirnberg and the ornate Sunday robes, just happened to be the first part of that great world to touch him.

But the decision was none the less firm for being short-lived, and it placed the Schmutz household in a quandary.

As we have seen, there was barely enough money for the necessities of life ; to finance a costly education was out of the question. As soon as the difficulty became known, however, everyone of standing in Kirnberg got together to solve it. The head of the village school, Helmberger, pronounced confidently that his small pupil was quite capable of mastering the hard training ; his deputy, a certain Niemetz, offered to supply any extra coaching gratis during the intervening months. But it was the priest Simon Veith who solved the vital problem of payment : an eloquent plea to Bishop Schneider promptly produced a free place in the archiepiscopal boys' seminary at Oberhollabrunn, on the other side of the Danube, some 30 miles north of Vienna. It was here, in the autumn of 1904, that Engelbert Dollfuss presented himself, after a last excited summer amid the pear trees and rye-fields of Kirnberg.

Peasant boy students were nothing new to the priests at Hollabrunn. Indeed, they rather specialized in them, looking among all this rustic chaff for a few grains of precious seed for Mother Church. Yet, for Dollfuss, the beginning must have been a special ordeal, since the challenge was to his courage no less than to his brain. He could not have been more than a tennis net high at this stage and, for the first time, he had to defend himself against the mockery and bullying, not of a handful of familiar village lads, but of two hundred complete strangers drawn from all corners of Austria.

On the whole, his courage did better than his brain. Indeed, the diminutive scholar from Kirnberg failed in his *Prima* or first year's test and had to repeat the class studies as an external student before he could rejoin the seminary. And though there was never again any such disastrous setback, his whole academic career seems to have been marked by industry rather than by brilliance. (A school list which has survived for one of his early years shows him only 23rd out of 26 in his class.) One of his teachers at Hollabrunn has summed up the general impression he made on the staff in these words : 'Dollfuss was certainly among the good students. But I cannot remember him ever standing out especially in his work. He was an industrious scholar, even very industrious, and he made steady progress ; yet he never threw off any sparks.'

The sparks were reserved for outside the classroom. The boy found himself instantly absorbed by the other human beings around him, their problems, their weaknesses, their opinions. It was at Hollabrunn that he first discovered his own passionate interest in people and practical issues ; and then, as ever afterwards, he greatly preferred them to books. It was here also that he first proved, to himself and to others, that his strength of character and his sunny nature were more than enough to make up in the world for his lack of inches. Without arrogance, and apparently almost without effort, the smallest pupil in the school soon commanded respect from the biggest.

He took a full part in the school's life, was a keen clarinet performer in the school band and an even keener gymnast and football player in the school team. But the picture which most of his comrades will have taken away is of Dollfuss, standing on tiptoe or upon a chair to make himself seen and heard, organizing petitions or protests, reconciling two heated disputants in an argument, or drawing the essentials out of some general debate. The politician in him was, in fact, already awakened, and it was significant that, during his later years at Hollabrunn, young Dollfuss was already devoting far more time to political problems than was natural in a candidate for holy orders.

Many of the actual characteristics of the statesman seem to have been discernible in the schoolboy. One of his classmates,[1] who sat next to him for eight years, has described how sociological problems came to absorb Dollfuss when he was still in his early 'teens. Even at this age, he was deeply interested in the Catholic reforms of München-Gladbach and saw the Christian faith as the only worthwhile impetus for political regeneration. One of the few places in the school where Dollfuss shone academically was in the voluntary rhetoric classes, and that self-reliance and sense of responsibility he was soon to show as an Army officer came out clearly enough in the debates. In one such discussion on the duties of a deputy, for example, Dollfuss stoutly maintained, against the general view, that, once elected to Parliament, a politician must represent the people according to his judgement and conscience, and should never allow any 'dictation from below'. Both the Catholicism and the paternalism of his later political programmes were thus foreshadowed in his school days. So also was his pronounced individuality and his steady determination to make the best of what he had got. That same class-mate tells how Dollfuss would practise his signature for hours on end so that it should properly reflect his personality.

The Church was still his choice when he finally took his *Matura* in 1913, however, and he devoutly elaborated on the reasons for it in his qualifying essay : 'By what principles should I be guided in my choice of vocation ?' (The earnestness of his arguments so impressed the priests that the essay was exhibited by the school for its ethical content.)

It was when he moved on to Vienna, to complete his studies at the Theological Faculty of the University there, that the religious ecstasies he had been filled with in front of the altar at Kirnberg ten years before began quietly to leak away, like air hissing out of a punctured tyre. Nothing had changed in him. It was merely the true self which was coming to life in the new setting. For here, at last, was that great world of action and ideas which he once thought to have glimpsed in the Church.

He was lucky to have seen Imperial Vienna just before the

cannons of the First World War blasted away both her gaiety and her glory. Those were its last months as a peaceful *Kaiserstadt*, the end of its long reign as one of the four proud capitals from which the destinies of a continent were decided. But, like so many cities and so many empires which have stood, half-knowing, on the brink of disaster, the Vienna of those immediate pre-war days had an almost feverish brilliance. This was the climate for which the restless peasant child from Kirnberg had longed ; he could scarcely be blamed for not realizing that it was, in fact, only the last brief Indian Summer of his great fatherland.

Yet, as regards his own career, he was driven by a growing inner emptiness to call a halt within a few months of entering the University. He took the bitter decision to abandon his theological studies, telling his friends, with characteristic bluntness, that he would 'rather stay a good Christian than become a bad priest'. In January 1914, he went, cap in hand, to his Rector, Prelate Gustav Müller, and was relieved to find only sympathy and good wishes.

A far greater ordeal was to break the news to his stern stepfather back in Kirnberg ; and this task he tackled with a pounding heart a few days later, falling down on his knees on the floor as old Leopold Schmutz came in from the fields. That worthy had already been forewarned and partly disarmed by his weeping wife, and the contrite Engelbert finally escaped with the following admonition : 'As far as I'm concerned you can become whatever you want, and if you can find people to help, then you can go on studying something else. There's only one thing that matters — grow up to be a decent person and not a rogue.'

Dollfuss was to manage both ; but the first thing which the overjoyed ex-candidate for the priesthood did was to hasten back to Vienna, where he had already put out feelers for his further studies. 1914 was now advancing, and there was not much time to go before the old world fell apart.

Dollfuss's birth-place at Texing (Lower Austria)

Dollfuss's family — ancient and sturdy Lower Austrian peasant-farmer stock. In the centre his mother, who was exactly his own diminutive height. Second from left, step-father Schmutz

Dollfuss as a student in Hollabrunn

Chancellor Dollfuss as a much-decorated
Lieutenant of the famous Austrian *Kaiserschuet*

The Chancellor with his wife and children in their happy and unpretentious
Vienna home

However, in those final months of peace, the young student took three steps which were vitally to influence his future. He decided to take up law — a broader gateway to office than the Church, even in the highly clericalized Austria of the day. He joined the German Students' Union of the 'Franco-Bavaria' and thus became a member of that powerful sworn Catholic brotherhood, the 'Cartell-Verband', or 'C.V.' This was a link which was to give him strong political and moral support throughout his life, though its uncompromising political creed may well have robbed him, as a statesman, of some of his flexibility. And finally, he started out, within the framework of the Christian student societies of the University, on social welfare activities, spending many of his free evenings in the Workers' Home of the 3rd Vienna District, teaching the labourers and factory hands stenography. This was in the tradition of that great Austrian Catholic politician Karl Lueger, who had discovered practical Socialism long before Vienna's Socialists claimed both the patent and the credit. And, like the 'C.V.', it was a honeymoon for life. As a soldier, as an agrarian expert and as a Minister, Dollfuss never ceased to be a social reformer whose heart was with the humble of this earth. The dreadful paradox that, five months before his death, he was to order the guns to fire on Vienna workers' tenements can only be fully measured against that irrefutable fact.

There was one other odd twist of fate about Dollfuss's time in pre-war Vienna, which had begun with regular visits from Hollabrunn a few years before. For among the other poor young students who were tramping the same streets and arguing in the same cafés in the Austrian capital of the day was another future Chancellor. This was none other than Adolf Hitler, who was trying in vain to get his pictures accepted by the Fine Arts Academy and acquiring in the process a lasting hatred for Vienna's Habsburgs, her Jews and her Marxists. One wonders whether, without knowing it,

Dollfuss ever brushed shoulders or exchanged words with the man who was to murder him less than twenty-five years later.

*   *   *

On June 28, 1914, the dreams and ambitions of the law student Dollfuss, like those of his colleagues throughout Europe, were shattered by the thunderclap from Sarajevo. On the 28th of July, exactly a month after the assassination of the Austrian Crown Prince, Austro-Hungary declared war on Serbia and the Juggernaut started to roll.

As much as patriotism, it was the instinctive determination of his not to be left out of anything which impelled Dollfuss to the nearest recruiting office to volunteer. There was nothing remarkable about this : in Hanover and St. Petersburg, in Lille, Sheffield and Kragujevac, young Germans, Russians, Frenchmen, Britons and Serbs were doing the same. Yet there were not all that many who, despite such a physical handicap, managed to talk themselves into such a crack regiment.

Dollfuss was now almost fully grown and that made him, to return to our earlier comparison, about one and a half tennis nets high — or, to be precise, 4 foot 11 inches. When this miniature would-be defender of the fatherland presented himself to a Military Selection Tribunal in Vienna, the answer was a broad smile and a polite refusal. 'My little fellow,' the inspecting doctor grinned, 'you have time to grow a bit ; the war may last quite a while yet !'

Undeterred, Dollfuss took the next train out to St. Pölten, the metropole of his home province of Lower Austria, hoping for greater indulgence there. His dismay can be imagined when he encountered at the recruiting station there the same military doctor who had turned him down the day before in Vienna. What was worse, there was nothing wrong with the doctor's memory.

'Haven't we seen you already and rejected you for being undersized ?' he frowned.

'Yes, sir,' replied Dollfuss unabashed, 'but since then I've been concentrating really hard on growing!'

And, as he spoke, he rose on tiptoe under the corporal's measuring stick, to reach the extra inch which his Emperor required for the minimum.

The tribunal came to the unanimous conclusion that such ardour should not be analysed by centimetres. Dollfuss was pronounced fit for service, and for him too the World War now began. It was to range close behind the farm at Kirnberg as the second formative influence of his life.

He started off his training with a Vienna Infantry Regiment of no particular renown. But not for long. Partly because of that same desire to be in the thick of things and partly, no doubt, because of a subconscious wish to compensate for his size, Dollfuss searched for a more resplendent setting. He found it when he saw a field battalion of the Tyrol Rifles marching through Vienna on its way to the Galizian front. The air of comradeship and panache which this élite regiment exuded went straight to Dollfuss's heart, and never left it. He got his transfer to the Tyrol Rifles the next morning and was sent down to their training garrison at Bozen. It was, as we have said, an attachment for life. Had he been asked, Dollfuss would probably have admitted in later years that he was as proud of becoming a much-decorated officer in the famous *Kaiserschuetzen* (as they were later called) as of becoming Chancellor of Austria. Indeed, during the two troubled years he held that loftier post, when the political front was often every bit as perilous as the military front had been, he took every chance to put on his cherished uniform again. No parade in those days was complete without the little Chancellor as a *Kaiserschuetzen* — the edelweiss symbol and the two stars of a First Lieutenant stitched on to his collar, the black cock's feather jutting from the soft field cap, and the Emperor's eight medals for bravery clinking across his narrow chest.

The Army proved in Dollfuss the man what Hollabrunn

had proved in Dollfuss the boy : that he was born to lead those comrades around him who were a head and shoulders taller than himself. Hoots of mirth greeted the arrival of the diminutive recruit at Bozen, struggling into the barracks like an ant, under his mountain of rucksacks. ('Omnia mea mecum porto.') But though the jokes went on, the teasing slowly died down, while the ridicule stopped completely before the first week was out.

To begin with, 'Dolli', as he was soon known, showed that he could endure, better than the next man, eight or ten hours a day of manœuvres under the blazing South Tyrol August sun. His good humour, calm intelligence and the huge parade-ground voice which he managed to squeeze out of that small body marked him out from the first. Within a few weeks he was made 'Commander' of his barrack-room ; by the autumn he was leading his section in manœuvres up on the Schabser Plateau ; and by Christmas of 1914 he had passed out with distinction from the Brixen Officers' School. After a few more weeks of training and wine-swigging in the cellars of South Tyrol, Cadet Dollfuss was posted down to the Italian front in command of a machine-gun platoon. It was to be the start of thirty-seven months' almost unbroken active service in the Dolomites and the 'Sette Commune'.

When Italy declared war on Austria-Hungary, on May 23, 1915, there was barely one Austrian soldier for every hundred yards of this southern line, and defence works were completely lacking. Steady endurance spiced with heroism were needed to hold the new front, and Dollfuss produced his share of both.

The most remarkable of his exploits during this bitter three-year mountain battle was his successful defence of the so-called 'Schrimmlerjoch' in October of 1916. This peak was the key to the whole divisional sector, and the right-hand spur allotted to Dollfuss and his machine-gunners was in turn the key to his regiment's position — a flanking fire and observa-

tion post from which the approach of the Italians up the steep
Val di Calamento could be controlled. As such, it had been
pounded by the shells of 28-centimetre Italian howitzers
throughout the summer of 1916 (one of which, mercifully a
'dud', rolled right into the tiny command cavern Dollfuss
had hewn out of the mountain-side) ; and in the autumn the
long-awaited ground attack was launched. The Italian commander sent up wave after wave of crack *Alpini* and *Bersaglieri*
troops, confident that their steel would impale whatever
Austrian resistance the artillery had left alive in the rocks.

He had reckoned without the smallest subaltern in Franz
Josef's service. Dollfuss hung on to that shattered Dolomite
crag with something that was more than bravery : the peasant
tenacity that impelled him, as always in life, to finish whatever
he had set his mind on or pledged his word to. His force
was reduced at one point to 45 able-bodied men, and those all
weary and shell-dazed, in the face of 600 fresh attackers. But
the right wing of the 'Schrimmlerjoch' was held. It was duly
christened, for the rest of the war, the 'Dollfuss Breach'.

The row of medals can be taken as testimony for Dollfuss's
other exploits. More interesting for our purpose than his
valour are two other characteristics which began to blossom
in this testing climate. One was his personal popularity, based
on that charm and resourcefulness which became a Regi-
mental (and later a national) byword. The other was the
sheer humanity of the man, which seemed to flow, deep and
spontaneous, from some rich, uncontaminated spring in his
nature.

As to the first, it is enough to cite the evidence of his
comrades that the 'M.G.A. Dolli', or Machine Gun Section
Dollfuss, had the longest waiting-list of transfer volunteers in
the battalion. Everyone wanted to get under his command,
for reasons of comfort as well as prestige. For Dollfuss had
the knack of getting the best out of his surroundings as well
as the best out of his men. Up in the Dolomites, he managed

to turn those bare holes scratched out of granite in which they lived into homes, equipped even with a makeshift chapel. And down on the dusty wilderness of the Isonzo Plain (where, in the summer of 1916, Italian aviators used to fire sheaves of steel-tipped arrows into the marching Austrian columns!) his soldiers were among the few who could always reckon on their daily one-litre ration of water, or even better. And if there was a chamois or two to be had in the mountains or a few chickens in the plains, it was usually his unit which got them.

Yet many of the good deeds which now started to spread the name of Dollfuss around went far beyond these conventional requirements of the 'good officer'. They revealed the devout Christian in action. Once, for example, when there was a breathing and a burying space in the fighting, Dollfuss was making his way down to the valley with his batman to buy supplies in Bozen for the unit. They had almost reached the valley when they overtook an ominous little group : four men with fixed bayonets escorting an unarmed infantry-man. 'Deserter !' returned the corporal-in-charge abruptly to his query. The shivering captive must have seen a glimpse of salvation in Dollfuss's compassionate, questioning look, and poured out a passionate appeal for help. He was 18 years old ; two of his brothers had already fallen ; and when yesterday, in his first day of front-line service, his best friend had been killed standing next to him, he had lost his head. But even then, he hadn't meant to desert.

The boy was a raw mountain peasant, a type Dollfuss knew at a glance. He also knew that once the escort had marched him down as far as Brigade Headquarters, nothing could save him from a firing-squad. The only hope was to find his battalion commander and persuade him to alter his decision. Yet — the matter was absolutely none of his concern ; the commander in question was bound to be several ranks his superior ; the mountains were a five-hour climb away, retracing the weary route he had just descended ; and the wine-cellars of Bozen were waiting for him down the road.

Not many junior officers in any army of the world would, in those circumstances, have done what Dollfuss did. He ordered the corporal to about-turn and then, followed by the astounded escort and their incredulous prisoner, climbed all the way back up to the front-line. It took him till dusk to find the boy's commanding officer, an elderly major with the reputation of a martinet. It took him five minutes to find his opening — the major's contempt for the poor training system of the General Staff, and indeed everything connected with the rear echelons ; and another twenty minutes of eloquent pleading to save the boy's life as a 'worthy but badly-trained recruit'. Dollfuss not only got his request granted but was pressed to stay the night. The next morning, after break-fasting on those rare front-line luxuries — coffee, butter and marmalade — he was despatched by cable railway to the valley where he found the major's horse waiting to get him speedily into Bozen. The gruff old battalion commander could scarcely have imagined that he had been dealing with a future Chancellor ; but he clearly regarded the little reserve lieutenant as something quite out of the ordinary.

There were many such incidents. On a tactical with-drawal after the great spring offensive of 1916 his unit was trapped under heavy Italian artillery fire when camping in open ground on the slopes of Zugna Torta. A salvo fell among the men, killing several outright and maiming others. Among the seriously wounded was Dollfuss's favourite N.C.O., a Tyrolean called Ploner. Only a speedy operation could save his life, yet there was not a Red Cross vehicle in sight. Dollfuss commandeered a full ammunition waggon which happened to be passing, off-loaded its shells onto the ground despite the driver's vigorous protests, and strapped his wounded corporal into this improvised ambulance. He then drove to the valley himself with his already delirious comrade, transferred him, at the first village, to a motor-car, also requisitioned on the spot, and did not rest until he was under the surgeon's knife at Calliano, where the retreating Field Hospital had been set up. Late that night, a weary Dollfuss rejoined the remnant of his unit, having been under constant fire for both halves of the journey, and having exposed himself to an even hotter fire of reprimand from his own superiors. After two weeks on the ridge between life and death, Corporal Ploner lived to tell the tale.

Nor was Dollfuss concerned, in these harsh days, only for his own men. Once, during the autumn offensive of 1917 down on the plains, the whole brigade lost touch with its supplies train somewhere in that stony wilderness between the Tagliamento and the Piave. The troops, as they marched, were forced to feed off the countryside. Somebody produced a jocular requisitioning note left by another unit at a roadside farm :

> This chit is yours ;
> Your pig is mine (weight 450 lbs.).
> Dear Fatherland, rest on in peace.

Dollfuss laughed with the rest when he read it ; and then the bony finger of stepfather Schmutz seemed to reach out from Kirnberg and tap him on the shoulder.

'The joke's a good one,' he declared, 'but the man who made it does not seem to have realized that the peasant will suffer if this is all he has to show for his loss.'

And after a vain attempt to identify the unit in question, Dollfuss wrote out a proper official receipt of his own in the faint hope that it might indemnify the peasant for his precious pig.

Such is the picture of Dollfuss growing into manhood as a soldier of the old Austria. It must be remembered when we come to judge him as a statesman of the new Austria. For the character it reveals shows decency and compassion well above the normal measure, without a trace of that harshness or intolerance of which his political enemies were so often to accuse him. Did power change the very essence of the man? Were his foes, blinded by their own bitterness, unable to see it? Or were circumstances too much for them both?

*   *   *

At all events, it was those last months of war which completed the transition in Dollfuss's own mind from officer to politician. After the Emperor Charles's clumsy if well-meaning armistice attempts in the spring of 1917, and particularly after President Wilson's Fourteen-Point peace programme announced the following January, diplomacy began to dominate the soldiers' discussions in the most isolated outpost of the straggling, subsiding Austrian front.

Dollfuss was one of the many to whom, at that time, the dismemberment of the Empire still seemed unthinkable, whichever way the fortunes of war fell out. Not that, as events were soon to show, he was an uncompromising Monarchist. Far from it. As a Lower Austrian peasant-farmer, he had been born and bred to the outlook of a democratic yeoman rather than that of a feudal retainer; and indeed, when the old order which he had served so well did collapse beyond repair, he was one of the first to recognize the reality of the new.

Until that turning-point came, however, he did his duty without reserve as an officer of the Emperor — less perhaps out of emotion than out of plain loyalty and habit. After all, for centuries the double-headed eagle had brooded over the fields of his childhood like the winds in the sky — something so accepted and inevitable that one got beyond questioning the good or the bad of its ways. And now, for over three years, he had fought for that same omnipresent emblem in the Dolomites. Discontent and mutiny had begun, it is true, to weaken the ranks even of that loyal Alpine army. But, until the horror of the final collapse, this 'Bolshevik agitation' was regarded by the front-line soldier as just another excrescence of that civilian world with which he had lost real contact. Like profiteers or faulty cartridges, it might help to lose a war ; yet it could surely never carry away a fatherland.

Dollfuss reflected the general mood when he declared, in one such officers' mess discussion, in 1918 :

'As far as I'm concerned, let's give Italy the South Tyrol up to the Salurner Klause. But the rest of Austria-Hungary must stay as it is in its historic frontiers. It's an economic entity formed over the centuries and it's the heart of Europe. If the pulse gets blocked here, the whole continent will fall sick.'

He was equally emphatic — and prophetic — when a comrade asked him about his own future :

'I certainly shan't stay in the Army. The country also needs men out of uniform. I intend to finish my law studies and then I have a strong inclination to go in for a political career. Our politics must not be allowed to go wrong, and it's we men from the front who must see to that. The main thing is that we keep up our comradeship, a true comradeship, throughout our lives.'

A few weeks later, politics caught up with them all. The ancient walls of the Austro-Hungarian Empire finally caved in, their great motley stones loosened from within and pounded from without. When the Armistice was declared, Dollfuss happened to be on a three-day leave of absence in Innsbruck, a chance which saved him from the months of imprisonment which befell his surrounded regiment. The news broke just as he was about to board a train to return to Rovereto. Instead, he got on the next train eastwards for Vienna, and set about putting his front-line declarations into practice.

CHAPTER TWO

Climber in the Ruins

WHEN Dollfuss left that train at Vienna ten hours later, he stepped out into a city which was somehow suspended in time. The past had been pulled from under its feet. The future could not yet be glimpsed. And the present was confused, clamorous and bitter. The capital had saved its bare bones, but it had lost its soul.

Even today — from the perspective of nearly two generations — it is hard for us to grasp what the sudden end of the Habsburg Empire meant to the Austrians, and above all to the Viennese. Some great capitals, like Carthage, perished with their peoples. Some, like the Fatephur Sikri of the Moghuls, were just abandoned by their builders. And many others, like ancient Rome, were at least lived in by their conquerors. But Vienna in that autumn of 1918 was a mutilated city condemned by its very assailants to linger on in isolation.

There seemed little to live for. It was more than a war that had been lost, or even vast domains that had been abandoned (both had happened often enough before in the six and a half centuries of Habsburg rule). The disintegration of the entire Empire — which, only a few weeks before, had still been a great ponderous entity in war and politics — destroyed at a blow the Austrian way of life and even the Austrian *raison d'être*. The spirit of the nation as well as its pride, the roots as well as the blossom, had been swept away.

The suddenness had been as numbing as the completeness. Only three weeks before the young lieutenant's homecoming, his Supreme Commander, the Emperor Charles, had been proposing from his throne sweeping eleventh-hour reforms designed to put his ancient Empire on a modern footing. The famous Imperial Manifest of October 16, 1918, had appealed to the peoples of the Danube Monarchy to cling together as a federation of independent states, and had expressly authorized the creation of 'National Diets' representing those peoples to act as the new federal organs. The offer turned out to be a case of 'too much too late' which, if anything, is even worse in politics than 'too little too late'. The Czechs, Hungarians, Serbs and Croats had got the fashionable bit of parliamentary democracy too firmly between their teeth to be side-tracked by any more desperate pulling on the reins from the Vienna Hofburg. One by one and in rapid succession the peoples of the Empire used the Emperor's authority against him. The National Diets proclaimed their total independence and, all along the Danube, new nation states tried to found their separate existences — an attempt that was to land them all, after twenty years, in the newer and harsher empires of Hitler and Stalin.

On the 12th of November the German-speaking Austrians, who had been left 'a people without a state' by these hectic developments, themselves followed suit. Their deputies in the old Reichsrat or Imperial Parliament gathered in Vienna as the new National Diet of the Austrian people and proclaimed the 'Democratic Republic of German-Austria'. In a bid to find some shelter — any shelter — in the storm, they went one further and declared themselves an 'integral part' of the new German Republic which their blood brothers and war allies had founded across the border.

Thus the constitutional prop with which the last of the Habsburg rulers tried to shore up his Empire was used instead as a pick-axe to complete its demolition — the final irony of a dynasty never poor in ironies. And the Austrians, by trying to unite with Germany in their understandable desperation, did some extra demolition work of their own. For that one

act hindered the growth of a new Austrian Republican consciousness even before their old Imperial consciousness had
faded. The ease with which Hitler overran Austria in 1938
is partly to be traced back to the panic and muddled thinking
of Vienna in 1918.

These troubled times left at least two marks on Dollfuss
whose effects can be seen in his later political life. In the first
place he shared to the full, at least in the early years of the
Republic, the widespread view that Austria's loyalties, and
even her destiny, should have a basically German alignment.
This put him, in those days, firmly in the camp of the so-
called *Nationalen* — those Austrians for whom the common
blood-tie with the Germans was the most important fact in
their cultural and political lives.

Thus Dollfuss, immediately after his return to Vienna
University to complete his interrupted studies, threw himself
whole-heartedly into reorganizing the German-Catholic
students' group 'Franco-Bavaria', which he had joined just
before the war ; indeed, he was soon elected its 'Senior' as a
reward for his energy and talents. And the 'Franco-Bavaria',
under Dollfuss's early leadership, seemed inspired more by
the German race than by the Austrian nation. How far
Dollfuss himself had slid down that slippery racial slope can
be judged by his behaviour at a Catholic Students' Congress
in Regensburg in August 1920, when he and the Cistercian
Professor Father Schloegl helped to push through a rule
excluding from membership all students 'tainted with Jewish
blood'. Among the minority who opposed this 'racial paragraph' was a rival Catholic student faction from Vienna, the
so-called *Nibelungia*, who were led by that Don Quixote of
the Austrian legend, Ernst Karl Winter.

Racial tolerance was not the only aspect of the old Austria
which the *Nibelungia* tried to salvage from the wreck of 1918.
Monarchism was another : in contrast to most of these
Catholic student groups, who had removed the Imperial

eagle from their crest and the oath to the Emperor from their pledge, the *Nibelungia* hung on — defiantly and archaically — to both. And with their monarchism went automatically an opposition to all the current ideas of *Anschluss* with Germany, whether Republican or not. At the closing festivities of the Regensburg Congress, it was Dollfuss who thundered 'Deutschland, Deutschland über alles', while E. K. Winter, sitting opposite him, sang to the same Haydn music the words of the old Habsburg anthem 'Gott erhalte'.[1]

Little more than ten years afterwards, after another great upheaval within that mobile temperament of his, Dollfuss was to become the first Austrian to discover state-patriotism without these nostalgic monarchist overtones. He became the first, in fact, to separate the nation from the dynasty as an object of veneration. But it is interesting to note that, in 1920, Dollfuss had moved a long way from both. At that time it was incorrigible monarchists like Winter who were the only guardians of a truly Austrian spirit. The vessel in which they sheltered the flame may well have been the cracked and useless shell of the Empire ; but it was from this flickering flame that Dollfuss himself was later to kindle his fire.

For the time being, however, he was consumed with a pan-German ardour. He played a prominent part in founding a new 'German Students' Union' in Austria, and was in contact with the so-called 'German Community' grouped around Field-Marshal von Bardolff, a former Military Secretary to the murdered Archduke Franz Ferdinand.

Bardolff's circle was a quasi-secret society, embracing influential Austrians in all walks of life and representing, at that time, pan-Germanism in its most rabid form. For this former servant of the Habsburgs, the colours of the Weimar Republic seemed the only emblem worth looking up to in a sky suddenly and mysteriously devoid of double-headed eagles. His group came out uncompromisingly for the *Anschluss*, or complete political union with Germany, and his own words, written on the 11th of July 1920, can be taken as typical of a temporary emotional surge which had young Dollfuss strongly in its tow : 'In the great confusion of the collapse of the Monarchy one fixed pole remains firm — that we are no longer "Austrians" but "German-Austrians", with the accent on "German". Through the passing of the old Monarchy we are freed at last from the nightmares of Dualism and the quarrels of the nationalities. For many who, up to then, had proved themselves good Austrians, this was the only consolation in their grief. If they could no longer be Habsburg yellow-black, at least they could be German black-red-gold.' [2]

We shall see how, later on, this type of sentiment was to be twisted out of recognition in many Austrian breasts when Adolf Hitler grasped the black-red-gold banner across the frontier. But even then, the *Nationalen* — Dollfuss included — did not so much abandon their theories as find a new post-Hitler basis for them. Quite apart from being dishonest, it does no service to his memory to play down this background, as many of his blind admirers later tried to do. For the true merit of Dollfuss's subsequent defiance of Germany can only be measured against this early attachment to the German ideal, an attachment which remained so strong that he never abandoned hope of reconciling his Austrian patriotism with it. Even after 1932 Dollfuss did not change national coats, but rather turned the coat of pan-Germanism inside out, with the Austrian lining showing.

The second mark left by these early post-war years was Dollfuss's first experience of the 'Austro-Marxists'. These were, even in those days, among the oddest and most unsatisfactory of Lenin's disciples to be found anywhere on the continent. They were too international to be patriotic yet, at the same time, too Austrian to be revolutionary. And, throughout the twenty years the First Republic was to endure,

they remained suspended between these two stools of fatherland and World Socialism. Their own national roots, however hard they tried to burn them out, still pulled one way.
The cosmopolitan ardour of their largely Jewish leadership
pulled the other way. But for the narrower choice they lacked
the humility and for the broader choice they lacked the
courage. A long flirtation followed with violence, which they
finally embraced with reluctance in the brief Civil War of
February 1934. For the rest, their great achievements in the
fields of social welfare and municipal housing, of which they
were justly proud, came to represent for them more and more
a sort of emotional escape-hatch by which they avoided the
challenge of responsibility. Thus Breitner's Vienna tenement
houses and Bauer's universal pipe-dreams *were* Socialism in
the end ; there was nothing in between.

This, however, is to look at them in retrospect. In those
first post-war years, with Communist *coups d'état* crackling
away across the frontiers in Bavaria and in Hungary, Austria's
Social Democrats were not short of fiery words. Indeed,
they could afford to cook their ideological soup so hot precisely because they were never prepared to eat it. In this
situation the radical orators and leader-writers were in their
element, and it is only fair to point out that this radicalism,
combined with the solid conservatism of the peasantry,
probably saved Austria from Communist experiments.

Already, during the death-agony of the Empire, a clear
split had appeared in the Socialists' ranks. On one side stood
men like Karl Renner, that tireless pragmatist throughout
forty years of Austrian politics, who were prepared to give
the federal reform ideas of the Emperor Charles a chance.
Opposed to him were the Jewish intellectual wing under the
leadership of Otto Bauer, determined with one giant step to
break with the past and move into the future ; the future,
as he also saw it then, being a union with the new Germany
as a 'union with Socialism'.

In the confusion of 1918, which seemed to call for desperate remedies, Bauer and his followers triumphed. It was not until 1933, when the thunder of the Civil War could be felt in the air of Vienna, that the moderates gained enough resolution to push him into the background, and gave Renner the hopeless task of trying to halt events at the very brink of disaster. Bauer, a slave to his own outstanding dialectical brilliance, thus had a long reign ahead of him in 1918, and he began it in savage style.

Inspired by his passionate rhetoric, the Socialists tried to trample into the ground the thousand years of Austria's history. They reviled everything that the Babenbergers and the Habsburgs had achieved or represented in the world and tried to start all the clocks of Austria ticking anew from the 12th of November, 1918. Even today the record of those Socialist speeches, pamphlets and articles in the party paper *Arbeiter Zeitung* makes a rather sickening sight : it is the spectacle of a whole nation being invited to start a new life by committing *hara-kiri* against itself.

And what the journalists and orators declaimed, the 'activists' of the party put into practice in the streets of Vienna. It was no uncommon occurrence in the capital in those days for officers straight back from the abandoned fronts to have their rank-badges and decorations torn by hooligans off their uniforms as the detested symbols of Empire. The heirs to the Habsburgs tried to muster faith in the present by shutting out the past.

The effect of all this on the political fortunes of the First Austrian Republic is examined below. What needs to be recorded here is its impact on the young Dollfuss — a highly-decorated war hero from a crack regiment of the old army who had been brought up, both on his native farm and on the battlefield, to put loyalty and comradeship before all else. Ten years later, as a young agrarian reformer, he was to strike up polite relations with Bauer and his circle for a brief period.

Yet, in private, it is doubtful if Dollfuss ever completely forgot the memory of Austria's Social Democrats running amok in the first post-war months. It was not so much his sense of tradition which had been outraged — for he soon accepted the inevitability of the Republic — as his sense of decency. To him, always concerned with human beings first and theories second, this was a sad exhibition of character rather than of ideology. And it may as well be said here and now that the failure of the First Republic, as regards the guilt on both Left and Right, was to some degree a plain failure of character.

*   *   *

This has been a necessary anticipation of events. For the moment, all Dollfuss was conscious of was bewilderment and disgust at what he saw going on around him, coupled with a typical urge to roll up his sleeves and get to work in the ruins.

His basic problems were to find a roof to put over his head and a job to fill his pockets while he completed his studies. He was lucky in both quests. A shrewdly-worded advertisement he inserted in the Vienna *Reichspost* : 'First lieutenant with provisions seeks furnished room' produced a prompt reply in the hungry capital of the day. A few days later, First Lieutenant Dollfuss moved into a furnished room in the Vienna apartment of a certain Frau von Fath. This good lady belonged to the minor aristocracy of that antimacassar world which had disappeared, as if through a trapdoor, only the month before. One of her brothers was a general, another an admiral, while she completed the orthodox family picture by trying to earn a genteel living as a portrait painter.

In his landlady, Dollfuss was to find not only a useful guide to the customs of Vienna society (which grew even more refined as it became more impoverished) ; he found as well a devoted friend for life. Like that gruff battalion

commander up in the Dolomites, she fell completely under
Dollfuss's charm, and under the force of that serene personality
which seemed to mark him out for great things in life. The
rent had been fixed at thirty crowns a month, and for a long
time the only 'payments' were the parcels of food sent in
periodically from Kirnberg. But even when the bill for
board and lodging had risen to the respectable sum of two
thousand crowns, Frau von Fath never doubted her little
boarder's promise to pay her back in full, nor the wisdom of
her voluntary investment in his future.

In due course Dollfuss was to justify her faith in both
respects, and the good woman could be pardoned for regarding his appointment as Austrian Chancellor a bare thirteen
years later as something in the nature of a personal triumph.
Brief and bitter though that triumph was, she seems to have
relished it to the full. Pictures survive of carefully-posed
family groups taken in the courtyard of the Schmutz farm in
1933, when it was fast becoming a sort of national monument.
In the centre, gazing phlegmatically through the gateway, are
a couple of Herculean bulls in harness. They are flanked on
the right by the Chancellor's stepfather and some hired
labourers (carrying scythes and pitchforks), and on the left
by his mother and sister (self-consciously holding a rake and
a sickle respectively as the instruments of their calling). On
the fringe of the group, leaning on some unidentifiable farm
implement as though it were a shooting-stick, stands Frau
von Fath. Her long black town robes and white lace *jabot*
form an odd contrast to the rough working clothes of the
peasant family around her and, for all the homely smile on
her face, she still contrives to look just like Royalty who has
dropped in for a cup of tea.

His more immediate debts Dollfuss began to pay off when,
after brief employment in the War Invalids Compensation
Commission, he got a permanent post in the Lower Austrian
Peasants Union. Few squarer pegs have ever gone into such

a square hole. The work was his past, his present and his future rolled into one. It was as a Lower Austrian peasant child that Dollfuss came into the world and it was as a Lower Austrian peasant leader that he was now to make his name and enter into politics.

Like many such vital turns in life, it was a pure fluke. On the 5th of August, 1919, Dollfuss was attending a church festival at Plankenstein, near his birthplace, with a group of other 'Franco-Bavaria' students from Vienna. In the afternoon, after the usual round of songs in the local inn, a serious discussion started up. Dollfuss soon had the sawdust floor to himself and spoke at length with his usual fluency and common sense. The then Director of the Peasants Union, Dr. Sturm, who happened to be sitting at the next table, got up on the spur of the moment as the young student finished and offered him a job as his secretary. After a moment to collect his wits, Dollfuss gave a solemn answer which was to decide both his immediate prospects and his whole career : 'Sir, I am a peasant's son from Kirnberg, down there in the valley, and it would be the dream of my life if I could serve my own peasant folk'.

A few weeks later, Engelbert Dollfuss took up his post in the Vienna Headquarters of the Peasants Union. This low-arched doorway in the Schenkengasse was the threshold of his road to power ; the Chancellery building, where it ended so brutally, was a bare three hundred yards away. The new sphere of work determined Dollfuss's private as well as his public life. The usual first reaction of his colleagues, ironical amazement at his size, was followed by the usual second reaction, admiration for his intelligence and his industry. As a peasant intellectual, he seemed to his superiors the ideal man to study the new agricultural theories of the day and advise on their applicability to the Austrian countryside. Accordingly, after a few months in Vienna, the Lower Austrian Peasants Union sent their promising new official to Berlin, to attend the lectures of the well-known German agrarian specialist Professor Seering. To provide him with a livelihood, they also found him a temporary post in the Berlin Preussen-kasse Bank, and it was here that Dollfuss met and fell in love with Alwine Glienke. He proved as resolute in matters of the heart as in matters of the mind ; on New Year's Eve, 1921, soon after his return to Austria, the couple were married before that resplendent altar at his native Kirnberg church which had played such a role in his early childhood.

Their union was one of those happy things which spring from the right blend of contrasts and similarities. There was never the exciting but exhausting tension of being complete opposites, nor the soothing boredom of being complete duplicates. As the daughter of a small Pomeranian land-owner, the wife was born several steps higher than the husband on that social ladder which — fortunately — did not matter to either of them. She had a retiring, almost reserved, disposi-tion as compared with his bubbling gaiety and passionate interest in the world. In fact, when she first moved down to Vienna, Alwine Glienke was as much the typical North German as Dollfuss was the typical Austrian, and the differ-ence in outlook led to a great deal of good-humoured teasing between the two. Yet, quite apart from the fact that she largely adapted herself to his temperament and his surround-ings, there was always far more to link them than to set them apart. Both had the same deep and unaffected piety ; both had the same unshakeable sense of duty ; both had the same devotion to their home and family ; and both — a lucky chance — were of much the same small stature.

The thirteen years of their marriage produced three children, of whom the first died when still young, and the others — a boy and a second girl — survived to grow up, after 1938 in exile. The loss of their first daughter was to be the only shadow on their time together. Alwine Dollfuss provided her husband with the second greatest gift an ambitious man can have (counting health as the first) : a harmonious and well-run home. He returned this service by never, even during the days of the heaviest bitterness and strain, bringing the worries or irritations of his public life back into his family circle. With the one exception of the Civil War of February 1934, the political agony of Austria never poisoned the atmosphere of their modest flat in the Stallburggasse ; though, as we shall see, many a vital secret discussion was to be held there.

To his wife, the Chancellor of Austria remained essentially the same man as the unknown peasant official she had married in 1921. Whatever Messianic visions it may have brought him, power made him neither pompous nor covetous nor suspicious as a human being, nor did it succeed in corrupting his own personal life by one iota (a tribute his worst enemies would not quarrel with). Indeed, looking back today across more than a generation of war-smoke and suffering, Alwine Dollfuss can still only find one fault in her husband as a family man : that he regularly gave away to needy friends and war comrades so much of his Chancellor's salary that, after the twentieth of the month, the Dollfuss household often had to borrow itself to keep going until the next pay-day. This was not exactly a serious failure, especially in an age when the Danube at Vienna sometimes stank worse of political corruption than all the Venice canals in August put together.

Inspired by what he had learned in Berlin, and with his academic studies finished at last (in 1922 he had joined the magic company of the 'Herr Doktors'), Dollfuss threw himself like a miniature whirlwind into the task of reorganizing Austrian agricultural life. Interest in the broader field of politics was always there ; but for the next ten years it became completely submerged, or sublimated, in his work for the peasants.

Had he not died a martyr for his beliefs, had he never become Austrian Chancellor or even entered an Austrian Cabinet, Dollfuss would still have left a mark and a monument behind him as an agrarian reformer. To this task he brought all that sympathy for the underdog and talent for improvisation which had marked him out as an officer, with that added confidence and devotion which sprang from the knowledge that he was working with and for his own folk.

His administrative ardour soon found a worthy target. The first years of the Republic were hungry years. The granaries of Hungary and Moravia, which had fed Imperial Vienna, no longer paid their golden tribute and, instead, the new state was thrown back on its own undeveloped agricultural resources to feed itself. As part of the drive to raise home food production, a Lower Austrian Chamber of Agriculture was established, to provide the peasants in the fertile plains around the capital with up-to-date advice and help. As a junior official of the Peasants Union, Dollfuss had played a leading part in founding the new Chamber, and in explaining the importance of such newfangled methods to the conservative peasantry in hundreds of village assemblies. In July 1922, soon after its creation, he moved in as its Secretary, and was promoted Director exactly five years later.

From his room in the Chamber's imposing offices in the Loewelstrasse, whose three tall windows looked out onto the back of the lyre-shaped Burgtheater and the broad, graceful sweep of the 'Ring' beyond, Dollfuss revolutionized the whole basis of Austrian peasant life. Seed culture, fertilizers, dairies, distilleries, vineyards, cattle-breeding, poultry-farming, forestry — every aspect of agriculture was modernized and rationalized by the stream of ideas and regulations which he poured out during the 'twenties. His social reforms were even more revolutionary than the technical ones. Following the doctrines he had learned in Berlin, he helped to develop that type of modern, free agricultural co-operative which still flourishes in Austria today, in contrast to the regimented variety planted across her eastern borders.

Even in his own day, when forced land collectivization in Europe was confined to the brutal but remote Russian experiments three frontiers away, Dollfuss seems to have sensed the dangers threatening the Danube Basin. In one of the last major speeches of his life he said : 'We are indeed deeply convinced ourselves that the system which deprives the peasant of the right to dispose freely of his land and which transfers to the state the whole organization of agricultural exploitation — in other words, and to speak frankly, Bolshevism — is a very bad, indeed the very worst, basis for agriculture and therefore for feeding the world.'

He went on to condemn the other extreme — 'unrestrained economic liberty' — and recommended, as the golden *via media*, the free co-operative. 'The co-operative is the first large-scale organization which does not operate by taking from the individual what he has, but through preserving his independence and guaranteeing his existence by marketing his produce in common and thus regulating his prices.' After developing this theme, Dollfuss again returned, like a preacher to his text, to the necessity of leaving the natural foundations of the peasant's existence undisturbed : 'For who stands closer to nature, and who shall more readily find the natural laws of economic co-operation than the peasant or the agrarian ?'

It is not without irony that this speech, delivered on June 14, 1934, to an International Agrarian Congress, was made in Budapest which, fifteen years after his death, was to justify all his sombre warnings about the destruction of peasant life.

While we are in the year 1934, it is worth noting in passing that, whatever else changed in Dollfuss's political thinking, his loyalty to the co-operative ideal as such remained unaltered. In the spring of 1934 he resisted the strongest pressure from his extreme Right-Wing colleagues to dissolve the whole consumer co-operative movement as a 'Marxist stronghold' ; instead, he appointed as its special 'Administrative Commissioner' Dr. Ludwig Strobl, a lifelong friend who was also a strong critic of his new authoritarian doctrines. The co-operative organization thus became one of the last common meeting-grounds where Left and Right worked together in relative harmony in pre-war Austria. More than that : until his death, Dollfuss constantly urged Strobl to keep democratic principles working to the full inside the co-operative movement, which, he said, he soon intended to restore to complete autonomy.[3] This was one of the many contradictions in Dollfuss as a statesman — contradictions which can only be explained by the difficulties which he never overcame and the hopes which he never lived to realize.

The greatest single achievement of Dollfuss during these early years as an agrarian reformer was undoubtedly the intro-duction of a unified social insurance scheme for the agri-cultural community. Before entering the Chamber, he had grasped the fact that, if the drift of labour from the land to the factories was ever to be halted, farm workers would have to be given the same security and social benefits as those en-joyed by their comrades in industry. Between 1922 and 1927 he used the whole weight of his steadily growing influence to bring about the necessary innovations. A land-workers' sick-ness insurance law was the first step, to be followed by other systems covering accidents, unemployment and even old-age pensions. Dollfuss's main concern was for the rural 'pro-letariat' — the hired labourers in the fields and the domestic servants in the farmhouses. But nearly all the insurance legislation he pushed through contained clauses by which even the richest independent farmer could join the scheme and claim its full benefits. This reflected his desire, even in these pioneering days, to instil a strong sense of communal pride and separate identity into the peasantry as a whole, which in turn could serve as a model for other sectors of Austrian cultural and economic life. His 'Agricultural Insurance Institute', an organization embracing more than half a million peasant subscribers of all types in Vienna, Lower Austria and the Burgenland was more than a rural revolution of the early 'twenties. It was the basis and pattern for that extraordinary corporative state which Dollfuss tried to impose upon the whole country in the early 'thirties. As he himself declared at a rural meeting in Upper Austria on October 3, 1932 : 'I am personally convinced, and I am ready to admit this openly, that I regard agriculture as the foundation of the whole economy. I stress, it is the foundation and not the only fully legitimate corporative element ; but the development of almost every other branch of the economy remains not merely strongly influenced by, but even dependent upon, the agricultural situation.' And in a speech made at Klagenfurt the month before, he revealed his almost metaphysical attitude to the peasants when he referred to them as the 'primary force and the primary cell of human regeneration'.

His social reforms showed Dollfuss as the practical Christian and the practical democrat in action. They were personal triumphs in the truest sense of the word : more than once, he staked his whole future on their realization in the face of indifference and opposition both from the agrarian pundits of Parliament and from his own immediate superiors. His pro-posal, for instance, to introduce compulsory unemployment benefits for hired farm labourers was opposed by no less a personage than Reither, the all-powerful President of the Lower Austrian Agricultural Chamber, of which Dollfuss was a mere official. Reither was a huge, heavy-jowled, hard-drinking farmer from the Tullnerfeld plain west of Vienna who was later to play a significant role in Dollfuss's political life. He adminis-tered his Langenrohr property there like a benevolent despot, often making free gifts of land to his peasants when they married. But the idea of making even his humblest milk-maid economically independent by a compulsory insurance scheme, to which he himself would have to contribute, was anathema to this conservative farmer-squire. Dollfuss stood his ground, however, and finally won the day by offering his resignation unless the reform were passed. Reither must have sensed that the whole building stood behind his indomitable secretary ; Dollfuss had indeed mobilized that Chamber of Agriculture, just as he had mobilized the school class, the machine-gun company and the Students Union before it, into a phalanx of willing and enthusiastic followers.

The paradox of Dollfuss's later career is, incidentally, well illustrated by his relations with Reither. Less than ten years after this battle in the Agricultural Chamber, the secretary had become Federal Chancellor and the President, by now Provincial Governor of Lower Austria, had played a leading part in his nomination. For a while, their friendship remained untroubled, and it flattered the burly farmer to regard the little statesman as his *protégé*. But the apprentice rapidly grew mightier than the sorcerer, and started dabbling with experiments of which his master had never dreamed. The roles now became reversed in more senses than one. For when Chancellor Dollfuss embarked on his authoritarian course, it was Governor Reither who, among other of his friends, took a stand for the rights of the individual and opposed him. In this switch both men were consistent, and yet neither was. Both were democrats at heart, yet neither was a full 20th-century democrat in practice. For Dollfuss, democracy consisted basically of social reforms ; for Reither it consisted basically of Parliaments. Again, in pointing this contrast, we touch on the medievalism of Dollfuss's thinking : his politics remained largely the 'Good Works' of the mystery play. And the foundations for that whole structure of stern Christian state paternalism which he tried to construct later on were laid in these early peasant reforms. He fought proudly under the motto :

Am bäuerlichen Wesen wird Österreich genesen !
(Austria will heal herself through the peasant way of life.)

*   *   *

By the time Dollfuss was promoted Director of the Lower Austrian Chamber of Agriculture, in July 1927, his own personal reputation as Austria's leading agrarian spokesman was firmly established. Parliamentary expert committees working on agricultural legislative measures had long made it a habit to consult the dynamic young official who sat just across the Ringstrasse, and from now on, with Dollfuss holding the office which matched his influence, they began to leave the initial drafting entirely to him.

His name and voice also began to be heard during the next three years throughout Europe : wherever the agrarian problems of the day came before an international forum, the little figure from Vienna in the black suit, his large eyes and ready smile gleaming softly above the stiff white collar, became a familiar and welcome sight. Dollfuss represented Austria at the International Agrarian Institute's meeting in Rome in 1928 and at the Agrarian Congress in Bucharest the following year. The Economic Committee of the League of Nations appointed him as its agrarian expert, and lecturing trips followed to a dozen European capitals and industrial centres. It was during this period that Dollfuss began to expound his doctrine of bilateral protective tariffs concluded between neighbour states whose economies were basically complementary. He saw in such carefully restricted preference pacts one method of protecting Austria from the economic ills of the time and, as usual, it was the interests of his peasant compatriots that he had most at heart.

Soon afterwards, during his fourteen-month spell as Minister of Agriculture and the twenty-six months which followed on as Austrian Chancellor, he was able to put some of these ideas into practice. Austria's timber exports to Italy and Switzerland received a badly-needed boost, while Austria's grain and dairy farmers got the protection they wanted from Hungarian or Jugoslav dumping. In the so-called Rome Protocols of 1934 between Austria, Italy and Hungary (by which, politically speaking, Dollfuss strove to anchor the leaky Austrian ship of state in the teeth of Hitler's tempest)

these 'good neighbour preference tariffs' made their diplomatic debut. They came to be echoed in all the vain schemes
hatched by Mussolini and the French Foreign Minister
Tardieu for an economically integrated Danube Basin under
Italian or French patronage respectively. The Nazi *Gross-
raumwirtschaft* of Messrs. Schacht and Funk, followed by the
tighter post-war autarky of the Marxist 'Comecon', put
an end to all these bilateral and regional ventures in Central
and South-Eastern Europe. But, judged by their restricted
possibilities in time and space, these efforts of Dollfuss to heal
the economic wounds of his day had a deep if transient influence. And, like most of his theories, they were simply peasant
logic put on paper.

Dollfuss's upward way had been such an agrarian one that
it seems strange to think of him entering power by anything
but the homely rural path. Yet it was his six-month spell
as President of the Austrian Federal Railways which first
brought him to the notice of the general public and first commended him to the politicians as a candidate for something
other than a purely agricultural office. The new appointment
was, indeed, a stern enough introduction to the financial and
moral plight of the nation.

Throughout the twenty-years life of the First Austrian
Republic, the nationalized railways remained the country's
economic Cinderella, Ugly Duckling and Bad Fairy rolled
into one. The only things that the tiny state had been allowed
to inherit in 1918 from the past were the debts and obligations
of its resplendent forebears. This burden crippled the railways
from the start, for to be a pensioner was always a favourite
career for Austrians, and no branch of the Empire's economy
had been as prolific of them as the Imperial railways. The
administration thus had to start up again after the post-war
collapse with tens of thousands of retired or unemployable
officials on its books who had once punched tickets or mani-
pulated level-crossings everywhere from Bohemia to Bosnia.

And this army of drones had to be paid out of a revenue from a decimated network, operated with out-of-date rolling stock. Worse was to come. Within a few years, what little money there was in the till had been reduced further by financial corruption on a large scale (several of the Directors were accused of supplementing their handsome salaries by regular contributions from a 'special fund') so that, after a decade of misfortune and mismanagement, the whole organization threatened to fall apart at its shabby seams.

As an official of the Agricultural Chamber, Dollfuss had already served a short spell on the Federal Railway Board, rapidly advancing to become Vice-President ; and on the 1st of October, 1930, at a time of crisis in the Board's affairs, he was elected to the Presidency. His well-known zeal as a reformer, added to his equally well-known pair of clean hands, seemed to make him the saviour needed to wield the whip of scorpions among all these unruly railwaymen.

The Chancellor of the day — the Christian Social ex-War Minister Vaugoin — was not disappointed in his choice. When Dollfuss entered the Railway Directorate building in the Schwarzenbergplatz, he found a headquarters in uproar and a staff in semi-mutiny. Declaiming against the department's scandals occupied far more of the officials' time than running the trains ; and, as the notorious 'secret fund' was known to be pumping money into the Socialist Party's treasury as well as into various private pockets, the constant protest meetings had a strong political flavour. There was, in fact, neither loyalty nor discipline, neither purpose nor honesty : a pretty accurate microcosm of the current state of the Republic itself.

Dollfuss, who had never faced a task of this magnitude or delicacy in his life before, rolled up his sleeves and waded undaunted into the mud. Within a few weeks, he had achieved a minor miracle of reclamation. He named Dr. Strafella as the new Director-General (a controversial appointment in

view of the scandals linked with the good doctor's name in
Graz, but, as things turned out, a successful one) ; several
directors were replaced, all on a heavily-reduced salary scale ;
the political penetration of the Social Democrats was checked ;
and steps were announced to bring dismissed corruptionists
to justice. The new President operated just as much through
his own charm and personal example as through his authority.
He took over eight executive and administrative sections himself, working fourteen hours a day and more ; he was ac-
cessible to everyone and vindictive towards none.

He not only won the hearts of his staff, turning them from
a rebellious mob into a devoted team of comrades, but he
rapidly grew into a legend up and down the rickety railway
lines of the country : his waiting-room became filled with
station-masters, signalmen and even greasy shunters, awaiting
their turn alongside the white-collared bureaucrats for a few
words with the chief. As with the crowds who began to
collect barely two years later in his antechambers at the Chancellery, they often had to wait for hours in vain and resume
the vigil another day. But, like all his visitors, if their patience
only held out, they eventually found themselves putting their
successors in the queue to despair. Dollfuss lived only for the
moment and for the man opposite him, and seemed to regard
time-tables as an invention of the devil designed to lure
politicians into frivolity.

Before the winter of 1930–31 was out, the name of Engelbert Dollfuss had become one to conjure with in the capital.
His relatively tranquil days as an official now belonged to
the past ; he had become a man of mark, and the constant
tumbling of short-lived Cabinets in those months presented
frequent openings. It caused no surprise, therefore, and
general approval when, on the 18th of March, 1931, he was
asked to lay down his duties as Railways President and enter
the Cabinet of the day (now presided over by Dr. Ender) as
Minister for Agriculture and Forestries.

Not that Dollfuss himself had gone out of his way to seek office. The news of his appointment reached him when he was relaxing with a round of friends at a coffee-house in the Vienna Prater, and one or two of them still alive today testify that this first step on the road to political fame caught him unprepared and even in two minds.[4] The Chamber of Agriculture, whose affairs he had continued to run even while reforming the railways, had absorbed him to the exclusion of everything else for the previous ten years. He had lived for his Lower Austrian peasants and was reluctant to undertake anything which might sever his close contact with them. Yet, on the other hand, he had always chafed under the knowledge that, as Director of one Provincial Chamber — however powerful — his reforms were restricted to a regional framework. As Federal Minister, he might hope to realize his dream of welding the whole of Austria's peasantry, on the mountains and in the plains, into one social community with a common pride and conscience ; and, after all, the post itself was difficult for anyone bred in Kirnberg to resist. Thus, in the spring of 1931, Dollfuss entered on his last amazingly short and steep stretch upwards, to a goal of total power and total tragedy.

In his fourteen months at the Agricultural Ministry, Dollfuss was able to consolidate the doctrines he had already applied in Lower Austria and expounded throughout Europe. It was a busy and happy term of office, and many of the measures he launched as a Minister he went on to complete as Chancellor. One aspect of his services to Austria's agriculture were those preference tariff agreements which, as already mentioned, he concluded with various neighbouring countries. From June 1931 onwards, he was compelled to devote as much of his energies to promoting Austria's position in the world as to promoting the peasants' position within Austria. In that month he was confirmed in his old office when the Austrian kaleidoscope was given another shake and yet another Cabinet pattern emerged. But the new Chancellor, Dr. Buresch, detached the Forestries Department from Dollfuss's control and placed him instead at the head of the important joint Ministry of Agriculture and Commerce.

In the fresh stream of reforms which followed, his new responsibilities were harnessed to his old interests and loyalties. A revised customs law was drawn up which finally broke away from the semi-free trade position adopted by the earlier regulations of 1924 and 1927 and brought Austria into line with the highly protective systems already in force throughout the continent. Having erected these sheltering tariff walls, Dollfuss proceeded to boost home food production behind them. The wheat yield was raised as a first priority because, as he told a peasants' meeting in November 1932, in words which had an unusual patriotic ring, 'whoever neglects to ensure a bread supply within his own country sacrifices a portion of the nation's political and economic freedom'. He increased butter output by the introduction of a special export subsidy — a novelty for the times ; he expanded Austria's live-stocks by creating compulsory centralized markets which guaranteed minimum profits to the cattle farmers who supplied them ; and, above all, by vigorous state intervention, he managed to keep prices for all agricultural products fairly stable in times of both shortage and surplus. That 75 per cent level of self-sufficiency in food which the First Austrian Republic reached in 1937 (the last pre-war year for which independent statistics are available) was due not the least to Dollfuss's continuous fifteen-year struggle for the peasants' interests — first as a provincial official, then as a Federal Minister, and finally as Chancellor.

This final rung of the ladder he climbed on the 10th of May, 1932, when still under forty years of age. As with every post he had assumed in life, his entry into the last and highest office was clouded with difficulty and danger. And this time the problems were of an order that no mere crusading zeal or administrative talent could resolve. Indeed, the new Chancellor, probably the youngest Head of Government in the Europe of his day and certainly the shortest in both stature and experience, had been summoned to rule a country which seemed politically, morally and financially bankrupt beyond hope of repair.

The causes of this mortal sickness were largely rooted in that Empire from which the new Austria had been forcibly torn in 1918 ; but, by her own mistakes and mishaps, the young Republic had steadily aggravated her case. This background is set out separately below to provide some outline of that political tangle which Dollfuss inherited in 1932 and to illuminate the desperate steps he took to unravel it during his first two years of power and his last two years of life. All that need be mentioned here is the general picture of government which Vienna presented when he took office.

It was that of a creaking merry-go-round, revolving wearily in some deserted corner of the fair. Almost all the figures on the different Cabinet horses had been riding the merry-go-round for the past fifteen years, one hand stretched out in front to try and unseat the passenger ahead and the other stretched out behind to ward off similar attacks against themselves. For some time it had been of little importance which rider was up and which rider was down, since the whole apparatus was anyway revolving in the same fixed and vicious circle of intrigue. But, by 1932, not even this monotonous circular motion could be guaranteed. The motor was running out of fuel, the organ was running out of breath, and the real interest in the Vienna fairground had already shifted to the lusty side-shows. The name of this badly-built contraption which was now grinding to a halt was Parliamentary Democracy, Austrian style.

CHAPTER THREE

The Legacy

THE only way to understand the difficulties Dollfuss faced on his accession to power and the manner he tackled them afterwards is to take another and more searching look at that political merry-go-round which he was called on to operate.

The riders were often restless opportunists, as well as genuinely confused as to where they properly belonged, and a great deal of seat-shifting went on accordingly. But the Austrian, in his politics as in his way of life, is a conservative animal, so that the central pattern of the carrousel stayed un-affected by these motions. Indeed, throughout all the clamour and commotion of the First Republic's life, the same eight basic political groupings can always be identified. Some were, at times, little more than tiny isolated sects. Others were dissident wings of larger parties to which, in a crisis, they invariably adhered. Some were philosophical and racial cults who diffused their influence over several political groups without ever becoming a stable party themselves. Others were really armed bands led by *condottieri* rather than parliamentary factions led by statesmen and, as such, they relied on bullets and not on ballots to help them to power. But, one and all, they clung to a distinctive philosophy or a special approach, and one and all thought that their own wisdom was the only answer to the nation's plight. Taken together, they did indeed produce all of the answers ; but without a single solution.

Looking from left to right consecutively around the circle,

49

there is first, the minute band of Austrian Communists ; second, the radical wing of the Socialists or 'Austro-Marxists' under the leadership of Otto Bauer ; third, the moderate wing of the same party under Karl Renner ; fourth, the 'liberal' section of the Catholic Christian-Socialist party, personified by men like Leopold Kunschak ; fifth, the remaining mass of the Christian-Socials who carried the Republic for most of its twenty years, and from where Dollfuss himself started out ; sixth, the *Heimwehr* movement and its 'Heimatblock' parliamentary front, which together formed an entity in Austrian political life despite their numerous internal rifts and rivalries ; seventh, the pan-Germans, taken here in their broadest sense to range from those with one foot still in Austria to those with nine toes already across the Bavarian border ; and eighth, the Austrian Nazis, who had just begun to be the most vicious bane of the Republic's life a few months before Dollfuss took up office.

In this seating arrangement the radicals, both to left and to right, have been placed as much with regard to their differing loyalty to Austria as with regard to their political philosophy as such. Austrian politics are peculiar in that patriotism, even more than democracy, is their vital touchstone. And here comes the special — and ultimately the lethal — tragedy of the First Republic. The ideological fanatics on both flanks, though poles apart in creed, were united in denying the validity of a separate Austrian state. The Nazis and the Communists actively worked for its destruction. And next to them, respectively, the far bigger camps of the pan-Germans and the radical Austro-Marxists undermined its existence with their ultramontane theories.

It is not uncommon in life to find that 'les extrêmes se touchent'. But here was a case of the extremists, however unwillingly, actually joining forces to drag the rest of the company down. Only at the centre in each arc of this political circle were there moderate elements in the two main parties —

Social Democrats and Christian-Socials — who could have postponed disaster by acting together. And they were kept permanently apart more by the fanatics on their wings than by their own failings. It is thus no wonder that both the historical achievement of Dollfuss and his personal undoing lay in the re-awakening of an Austrian patriotism, for he had to fulfil this mission among a people of whom at least one-third, actively or passively, had written off their own state.

Before going on to this struggle, however, we must examine each of those eight basic groupings among whom Dollfuss was to find all his political allies and foes.

The 'Communist Party of German Austria' had been founded in Vienna in November 1918 — a small but virulent weed which sprouted from the ruins of the Empire. The seed had been sown by Austrian prisoners of war returned from a now Bolshevist Russia, in conjunction with a group of radical students and café intellectuals. There were times in the following chaotic months when the growth looked menacing enough. During the brief Communist *coup d'état* in neighbouring Budapest, for example, the Hungarians sent across the frontier a special Commissar, Ernst Bettelheim, with orders to stage a similar revolt in Vienna. Twice in the first six months of 1919 — on the 18th of April and on the 15th of June — the Austrian Communists, helped by amateur radicals, launched *putsch* attempts, and on both occasions their failure was absolute. This was not simply because the leadership was raw and clumsy, nor just because both the peasantry and the mass of the workers refused to respond. It was also because their own following, by Bolshevik standards, was woefully weak-kneed. One could no more have raised a nation of Communists in Austria than one could have raised a whole nation of Nazis. True, the Austrians produced some choice examples of both in their time. But, as a universal philosophy, both Communism and Nazism demanded too much discipline and too much effort (and also too little humour and too little tolerance) ever to become popular Austrian fare.

After the fiascos of 1919 the Communists sank for nearly fifteen years into oblivion. Only one of their founder-members, the Styrian leader Johann Koplenig, survived the First Republic, and returned from Moscow in 1945 to try and plant the hammer and sickle in the Second. The others, such as Frey, Toman and the Friedlaender couple, had already disappeared from the stage in the 'twenties. Dollfuss himself was probably only conscious of the Austrian Communists as a political force during the last few months of his life, when he had banned the political parties and the Socialist para-military *Schutzbund* army as part of his authoritarian experiment. The Socialists' defeat in the Austrian Civil War of February 1934 had been complete and humiliating ; their radical leaders had promptly sought safety across the Czech border, leaving an embittered rank-and-file on the lost battlefield behind them. The gap on the Left between leadership and the masses, always a wide one, had never been more palpable, and the Austrian Communists managed to stage a brief revival by exploiting the situation. They stepped forward as the 'real revolutionaries' who were alone capable of dealing with the 'Dollfuss-*Heimwehr* dictatorship', and made a small but durable penetration into the Socialist trades unions, women's and youth movements and similar party organizations. They even gained, in these months, an important new political recruit — the writer Ernst Fischer, who stepped one pace across in disgust from the ranks of the extreme Socialist Left. (He was later to become the undisputed intellectual leader of Austria's Communists after 1945.)

But although only that one pace was needed, nobody else of substance in the underground Social Democrat party took it after him. Indeed, one look at the grim fanaticism and the cold remote Moscow control which characterized life in the Communists' ranks was enough to send the average Austrian

Socialist scurrying back to his municipal apartment, and all the Viennese pride of achievement which it represented, like a rabbit to his cosy burrow. Even at this critical junction in the life of Austria, and therefore the career of Dollfuss, the Communists failed to make a real impact on affairs. They did not invade the political field so much as remain a marker on its far left flank, a marker separating the ranks of Austria's 'Marxists in theory' from those of Russia's Marxists in practice. In this position, though they were dedicated to destroy such Austrian state-patriotism as existed, their indirect and unconscious effect may well have been the opposite. At all events, their part in the Austrian story was a minor one.

The picture becomes very different in both respects when we look at the powerful group just next to them — the radical Social Democrats of Otto Bauer. Inasmuch as special blame can be apportioned anywhere, it is these men who share with their *Heimwehr* and pan-German opponents on the Right the basic responsibility for Austria's domestic tragedy. For it was from their fangs that the deadly poison of intolerance, the worship of doctrine above all else, mostly came. Each group directed the jets of venom at its rivals. But inevitably, this venom entered the blood-stream of the sickly nation and everything perished : first the Parliament, then the democracy, and finally the Republic.

Between them, these two factions also largely account for Dollfuss's personal share in this collapse. Whether necessity can be argued in his defence or not, the two heaviest charges against him are that he sustained an alliance with the *Heimwehr* on the Right and failed to make a truce with the Socialists on the Left. Yet he invented neither of these political evils ; he welcomed neither ; and neither corresponded to his innermost self and aims.

Though Otto Bauer himself might have been horrified at the suggestion, it is possible to explain a great deal of his behaviour by that common curse which lay over his whole generation of Austrians : they were all men who grew up as privileged subjects of a great power only to be condemned, after 1918, to live on as citizens of a small, insignificant and struggling Republic. Bauer, the son of middle-class parents, was 33 when the First World War broke out and was approaching the apogee of his considerable mental powers. He belonged to that type of pure Jewish intellectual who is more interested in theories than in either situations or human beings and who regards even politics as a lifetime exercise in dialectics rather than as a public career. The Austria of his youth was not short of theories — above all, theories for welding the thirteen peoples of the Empire into one politically-homogeneous framework which would guarantee both racial liberties at home and the continuance of Austro-Hungary as a great power abroad. And though, by the turn of the century, young Otto Bauer had become an ardent Marxist, it was always on the boards of this great Imperial stage that his outstanding intellect displayed itself. Indeed, much of his early fame as a Left-Wing ideologist rested on his book, *Social Democracy and the Nationalities Question,* which was an attempt to interpret the life-and-death problems of the Empire in terms of his party's creed.

In 1918 Bauer found this resounding Habsburg platform replaced by the busker's booth of the Republic. And, like his equally gifted political rival, the Catholic Chancellor Ignaz Seipel, he found this Vienna of the 'twenties too small a place to be filled by his energies. Unlike Bauer, Seipel was able to prove himself a superb practical statesman in the service of his country, yet both men were constantly seeking wider horizons — the prelate Seipel in the Kingdom of God and the Marxist Bauer in the Socialist International. Indeed, Bauer's brief spell in office as State Secretary for Foreign Affairs in Austria's first and only Socialist Government reflected his party's hope that the new Republic's destiny in 1919 lay with her allies for world revolution.

The hope gradually faded ; but the host of fresh arguments, opportunities and problems which it conjured up so long as it lasted gave Bauer the theoretician that universalist field for which he craved. To him and his colleagues, the first logical step was the extinction of the infant Republic as such, and he accordingly led the fight on the Left for the absorption of 'German-Austria' into the neighbouring Weimar Republic. It was Bauer who, on March 2, 1919, signed in Berlin a formal '*Anschluss*-Protocol' with the then German Foreign Minister Brockdorff-Rantzau. In this remarkable document, the two partners expressed their intention of concluding a state treaty to unite their countries. 'German-Austria' was to join the Weimar Republic as a closed unit, retaining separate rights in the fields of foreign affairs, customs, trade, finance and so on. This was, in fact, simply the familiar vision of Vienna as the 'second German capital', seen through red spectacles.

Bauer was partly driven by that genuine idealism of his which regarded this '*Anschluss* with Socialism' as one stage in a predestined Marxist integration process. But his own subconscious urge to appear as an international, and not just as an Austrian, apostle may well have played a hidden role. His own party colleague, Dr. Adler, wrote Bauer's epitaph when he described him as the 'talented misfortune' of the Austrian Socialists.

In the years which followed, Bauer's dream melted on all horizons, leaving him a frustrated and bitter Demosthenes in the mockingly inadequate setting of Vienna's neo-classical Parliament. This was his party's, and his country's, loss, for Bauer had that commanding type of genius which can be warped by checks and inactivity. His wit turned to sarcasm and his rhetoric to invective ; and thus, with each session of Parliament and every speech outside, he helped to widen that ditch between the 'Austro-Marxists' and the 'Austro-Fascists' which little Dollfuss was eventually called upon to straddle.

Not that Otto Bauer and his mesmerized followers ever preached revolution, for all their revolutionary ardour. Their fierceness consisted in words rather than in deeds, and the further they drifted from power, the more unrealistic their theories became. Here again, the basically Austrian nature of this convinced internationalist is seen, for Bauer suffered all his life from the Austrian's typical and seemingly inescapable terror of action. The intellectual's genuine distaste for violence certainly influenced his attitude and prompted him to plead always for conversions by propaganda or education and never by force. In any case, he knew that the strength of the conservative peasantry and of the Catholic Church in Austria were two massive factors in the path of any *coup d'état*, to say nothing of the dead dynamite of the Austrian proletariat on which the Marxist challenge really rested. But this constant flight from concrete decisions, this tendency to indulge in a hundred discussions rather than take a single practical step, was also something inborn. Like so many of Vienna's politicians, Bauer, for all his undeniable brilliance, really belonged in the coffee-houses of the capital and not in its Parliament ; and indeed he helped to turn the one into the other.

The climax in this headlong flight from action is expressed in the famous 'Linz Programme' which was laid down by Austria's Social Democrats in their party congress of November 1926. The problem before the delegates was the one which, despite all Bauer's dialectical assurances, gnawed like a cancer at the party's flesh : if we continue to call ourselves Marxists of any sort, why do we not take steps, as the book prescribes, to seize power in the state by force ? One group, led by Max Adler, actually advocated this classical 'dictatorship of the proletariat'. But they belonged to that very untypical minority of the Austrian Socialists who were extremist in policy as opposed to extremist in doctrine. With the help of Bauer, they were overcome and yet another theory was produced to salve the party's conscience.

This might be called the thesis of the Reluctant Dragon : the Austro-Marxists declared themselves ready to take over the state by violence, but only if the 'bourgeoisie' compelled them to. In the oft-quoted words of the Linz Programme : 'Should the bourgeoisie, however, resist that process of social transformation which the workers as a state power will set as their task — by systematic suppression of the country's economic life, by forcible resistance or by conspiring with foreign counter-revolutionary forces — then the working classes would be obliged to break such bourgeois resistance with the methods of dictatorship.'[1] This remarkable standpoint reflected theories which Bauer had first enunciated before the World War. He constantly returned to the idea after the October Revolution in Russia, in an attempt to find a half-way house between the brute force of the Bolsheviks and the decadent 'revisionism' of the British Labour Party. But, as pronounced in 1926, it remained in essence just another comfortable excuse for doing nothing.

Ironically enough, it was precisely this fantastic Austro-Marxist prayer of 'Please hit me first' which was answered, and in the very same city where the prayer had been offered up. Eight years later a police search for hidden arms in the Socialists' headquarters at Linz was the random spark which set off the brief Civil War between Right and Left.

What needs to be noted for our present purpose is the formidable psychopathic resistance which Austria's Social Democrats, under such a leadership, were bound to put up to any working truce with the 'bourgeoisie'. (This was no one-sided phenomenon : similar complexes existed, as we shall see, on the Austrian Right Wing.) Precisely because he was so reluctant to fight with sticks and stones, Bauer fought all the more mercilessly with words and programmes. For ten years Chancellor Seipel was the target of all this hate and, after his first bitter clash with the Socialists in Parliament, Chancellor Dollfuss soon inherited it. It needed the lesson of the Civil War to drag the Austrian Social Democrats out of Bauer's cloud-cuckoo-land and bring their practical leaders like Karl Renner back into the fore. But by then the Austrian Right Wing — partly led by Dollfuss, partly dragging him with it — was fast moving off into a special cloud-cuckoo-land of its own.

When we turn to Renner and the pragmatic camp of the Socialists, our feet, like his, are much more on the ground. It is interesting to note that this contrast between Renner and Bauer goes right back to their days as young Socialist thinkers in the age of the Emperor Franz Josef. Renner, the son of a small Moravian farmer, also found himself preoccupied after the turn of the century with the nationalities problem of the old Empire (nobody born in Moravia could fail to be). But what a contrast, both in his approach and in his findings! Whereas Bauer sought theories, Renner sought solutions, and his so-called 'personal nationality' scheme stands as one of the most ingeniously simple blueprints ever drawn up to solve the racial rivalries of the Empire. Like Palacky, Kaucic, Popovic and other fellow-reformers of the day, young Renner advocated in his plan the regrouping of the Habsburg domains into a federation of the main national groups, each with cultural and administrative autonomy. But a completely new element was his proposal that each citizen of the multi-racial Empire, whether living in a compact ethnic bloc or in an isolated pocket of his kinsmen, should be attached to his parent people by enrolment in a national register. By this means Renner sought to achieve the maximum racial harmony with the minimum political upset.

This habit of rebuilding as far as possible on existing foundations and of using serviceable old bricks alongside the new, was to stay with Karl Renner throughout his long and distinguished political life. True to it, he began his career as an efficient servant of the Empire — a library official and later a leading Social Democratic deputy in the old *Reichsrat*

Parliament. (There were those who claimed that, had the
Empire survived, he would have been its first Socialist Prime
Minister.) And, true to character again, he ended that career
as President of the Second Austrian Republic, having served
twice as Chancellor in the crisis periods which followed immediately after both World Wars.

Significantly, in both of his brief spells as Chancellor, it
was a Coalition Government of Socialist partnership with the
Catholic Right Wing which he headed. During the first of
these widely separated spells, which ended in June 1920, he
once described this emergency arrangement between the two
major Austrian parties as being 'like a cloak which two trapped
mountain wanderers throw around themselves to survive the
raging snowstorm'. Within his own party, he fought a
constant struggle against Otto Bauer to try and renew this
partnership and throw the protective cloak around the
Republic's thin shoulders once more. Indeed, for the next
fifteen years, this Renner-Bauer dispute over the Coalition
issue exemplified and perpetuated the doctrinal split in the
Social Democrats' ranks. As we shall see, it was also Renner
who tried the hardest and came the closest to reaching some
working agreement with Dollfuss after Bauer had fled the
country and his uncompromising approach could be disavowed by the predominantly non-Jewish leadership left
behind in Vienna. But, though all possible blends of political
colours were to be tried out in Vienna, the so-called 'Red-
Black' Coalition of 1919–20 was not to be repeated again
until May 1945, when the Soviet occupation authorities called
on Renner to repeat his mixture of the generation before, this
time with an unwelcome dash of Communist crimson added
by themselves.

Inevitably, Renner's constant efforts to come to terms with
reality had unpleasant effects whenever the reality itself was
unpleasant ; the classic case here is his public support for the
Anschluss of March 1938, announced shortly after the Nazi

march-in. The special pleading which his admirers indulged in later on to excuse this only made the target of criticism look larger by hiding it. Apart from the fact that Renner had always shown staunch pan-German sympathies, his opportunism was merely the seamy lining of his pragmatism. But — the 1938 episode apart — there can be no question who served his party and his country the better : Renner, always holding out his long spoon to sup with the Right-Wing devils, or Bauer, trying simply to exorcise them from afar with his magic Marxist formulae. The history of the First Austrian Republic would have been a far happier one, and might well have been a more peaceful one, had Karl Renner and not Otto Bauer won that struggle for the Left-Wing leadership in the 'twenties.

We are now almost half-way round the circle, and have come to the great Christian-Social party itself — the major political pillar of the Austrian Right Wing, and indeed of both the First and Second Austrian Republics. The dominance of the Christian-Socials over Austria's political life between the wars can be judged from the fact that they supplied the country's Chancellors from 1922 right through to 1938, with the sole exception of the 1929/30 pan-German Government of Dr. Schober, for which they provided the Vice-Chancellor. The principal Ministries (Finance, Defence, Trade, Education and Agriculture) were in their hands for most of this period, as were the Governorships of the federal provinces. Excluding Renner, they provided all the leading statesmen of the pre-war Vienna scene — Seipel, Schuschnigg and Dollfuss himself. Finally, during the last decade of the First Republic's life, this powerful party also supplied Austria's Head of State, in the person of Dr. Miklas.

The Christian-Social party developed as a mass movement during the last forty years of the Empire's life, and it grew up as double-headed as the Emperor's eagle. With one face, it was the conservative party of tradition *par excellence*, the political voice of the Church and the landed aristocracy, in so far as these had begun to feel the need for one outside the dynasty. With its other face it was violently reformist, the voice of Vienna's white-collared Catholic proletariat who were clamouring, in true Austrian style, for greater security in the age of 'Manchester Liberalism'. Under Karl Lueger (1844–1910), who led the Christian-Socials to victory in Vienna, the reformist aspect triumphed for a radiant spell. The capital was labouring at that time under the effects of the Bourse collapse of 1873 ; the discontent of the craftsmen, shop-keepers and other *petite bourgeoisie* was at its height ; and Lueger was finally borne up by this wave of economic unrest to the office of Vienna Burgomaster, despite the initial opposition of both the Emperor and the Vatican.

The golden age of Catholic social reform in Austria now began. Lueger and his circle inspired a stream of legislation, all of which was designed in one way or another to protect the economically weak and under-privileged from exploitation. Working hours were revised, health and hospital benefits introduced, new taxation schedules were drawn up, Vienna's municipal services were expanded beyond recognition and, on a broader field, the nationalization of the railways was driven forward. In all this, Lueger was simply putting into practice the theories of Catholic thinkers like Vogelsang, who had called on the Church to lead society out of the moral and economic abyss into which the Industrial Revolution had thrown it. In 1881 both men had the satisfaction of seeing the Papacy swing round in their favour ; the famous Encyclical *Rerum Novarum* which Pope Leo XIII issued in that year threw the Vatican's weight whole-heartedly behind the Christian-Social reform movement and bestowed a special blessing on Lueger as its leader.

Incidentally, social reformism was not the only thing which Vogelsang advocated and Pope Leo blessed : it is here, at the very genesis of the Christian-Social movement, that the doctrine is enunciated of the Catholic corporative state as the sanctified form of political life destined to end all class strife. Lueger had enough on his hands in the 1880's without trying to turn the Habsburg domains into a corporative society. But, fifty years later, the Christian-Social Dollfuss was to make the attempt in that tiny part of the Empire left to him ; and it was back to his own Vienna of Vogelsang and Lueger that he looked in the first place for inspiration, rather than to the Rome of Mussolini.

The triumph of the Christian-Socials in the Town Hall and Parliament carried the seeds of their eclipse. Success brought power ; power brought responsibility ; and responsibility brought with it commitment to the existing order. Thus the other face of the party — its conservative aspect — slowly swung more and more into prominence. By the turn of the century, the Christian-Socials were themselves too much a part of the *status quo* to continue with their transformation work at the old pace ; and in 1907 this development was consummated politically when they merged with the Conservatives proper. Within less than a generation the Christian-Socials had thus changed from the 'party of the little man' to the 'party of state', linked more and more with the peasantry and with the very industrialist interests they had started off by fighting. This robbed them of their impetus and, in 1910, death robbed them of their great leader. Lueger had only been in his grave a year when his party suffered decisive defeat at the polls, and even lost control of the capital to the rising Social Democrats. A Socialist bastion the city has remained ever since ; yet it is ironical to think that this 'Red Vienna', complete with its new gasworks and tramway, was in fact the creation of Catholic reformers, whose radicalism was snuffed out by power.

The Christian-Social party which returned to such a commanding position in the Austria of the 'twenties picked up, as regards conservatism, where Lueger had left off, and very soon went one further. For its new leader, the statesman-priest Ignaz Seipel, made the Catholic faith as such, rather than Catholic reformism, the touchstone of membership and policy ; and the faith, then as always, clamped itself on to the strongest temporal arm available. Yet, though one could never talk of a duality in approach comparable to that which divided the Social Democrats, a restless and sometimes critical radical movement lived on in the Christian-Social party — a nagging souvenir of its old pioneer days as the champion of the under-dog. The spokesman of this group was Leopold Kunschak who, as a young saddler's apprentice, had already founded, back in the 'nineties, a 'Christian-Social Workers' Union for Lower Austria'. Kunschak's Catholic Trade Unionism survived as a political force in the Republic, where it came to represent his party's last surviving link with the urban proletariat.

Thus the party which, in 1932, Dollfuss came to lead in the Government (he never became its Chairman) was itself a coalition from Austria's past. In the first years of the Republic, more even than in the last years of the Empire, it was the 'party of state' *par excellence* : a political alliance between bourgeoisie, peasantry and industry which, for all its faults, managed to preserve for the Austrian people that tradition and way of life which the Socialists were ready to sacrifice. As such, its rank-and-file became the main supporters of all Dollfuss's experiments with state-patriotism, even when he coupled those experiments with ventures into 'Austro-Fascism' and dissolved his own party in the process. But all the time, in the person of Kunschak and his group, this embodiment of Catholic conservatism carried on its shoulders its own uneasy social conscience. And every step which Dollfuss took towards the far Right — whether it was the suspension of Parliament, the banning of parties, or the working alliance with the *Heimwehr* — produced a loud outcry from this conscience. There was no open party split, and Dollfuss had little difficulty in silencing Kunschak's protests in public. Whether he also succeeded in completely stifling their echoes in his own innermost soul is more debatable, for he was himself a man of the people and a social reformer with every fibre of his being.

Like any party representing the Austrian middle-classes of the day, the Christian-Socials had a racial fringe which bordered on pan-Germanism and a political fringe which bordered on Fascism. But it is best, for simplicity's sake, to ignore them. The truest judgement of the party as a whole is that it combined more love for Austria with more respect for Parliament than any other political force in the Republic, and that is why it belongs in the very centre of the arc. To the left of it were those who worshipped parliamentary democracy as an instrument of Socialism but cared little about Austria. To the right of it were many who still loved Austria and some who still respected democracy ; some who did neither ; but none who did both.

The first of these other groups we meet with are Dollfuss's disastrous allies, the paramilitary *Heimwehr*, who might be called the classic case of the patriots who were not democrats. For once, there is no need to dip back into Imperial history. The *Heimwehr* or *Heimatschutz* movement was a direct product of the Republic's first uneasy years ; it was born, flourished, and died never to rise again, all in the space between the two World Wars. As its names suggest (*Heimwehr* = Home Guard, and *Heimatschutz* = Protection of the Homeland) the movement was purely defensive and non-political in origin. It did not, in fact, begin as a movement at all, but rather as an unco-ordinated chain of emergency self-help organizations which sprang up all over Austria in the winter of 1918/19 to keep local law and order and protect the naked frontiers of the new Republic. Most of the bands of foreign marauders or demobilized Austrian *soldateska* it had to deal with were certainly chanting the revolutionary slogans of the hour as a sort of pagan benediction on their plundering. But, in the first year or two, it was their violence rather than their Marxism that these voluntary defence units fought against — as factory guards, railway guards, village police, or as mere gamekeeper patrols armed with shotguns and raised by local landowners. Indeed, in this initial phase, Socialist workers were occasionally to be found in the *Heimwehr's* ranks, while the stocks of ex-army weapons which served as its basic armament were sometimes jointly distributed by representatives of both main parties.

This defensive function was even more plain and even more vital along the borders of Austria : it was *Heimwehr* units under the command of General Ludwig Huelgerth who drove Jugoslav invaders out of Carinthia in 1919 and helped to save this southern province for the Republic. The first solid act of faith in the new Austria was, in fact, a *Heimwehr* one, and this basic patriotism clung to the movement throughout its life, underneath all the dross of demagogy and Fascism. Whatever mistakes and excesses were committed by the leadership, for thousands of its supporters the *Heimwehr* remained the only *active* organization which a good Austrian bourgeois could join — being both anti-Marxist, anti-Nazi and dynamic into the bargain.

The lack of both an adequate federal army and even a strong central civil authority kept these local forces in existence when the first months of crisis had passed. And, as so often, the historic provinces provided the framework which the capital of the Republic lacked. By the early 'twenties, *Heimwehr* organizations raised on a regular provincial basis existed, apart from Carinthia in the Tyrol (commanded by an Innsbruck lawyer Dr. Steidle) ; in Styria (commanded by another local lawyer, this time the notorious Dr. Pfrimer of Judenburg) ; and in Upper Austria (headed by that gifted but feckless playboy of the First Republic, Prince Rudiger Starhemberg).

All these 'private armies' were first in the field as regards regional groups, and all were Right Wing in leadership and flavour. By 1923 they had abandoned their non-political origins and were loosely united as an anti-Marxist force. That same year the Left Wing caught up and went ahead with one bound by converting their local 'workers guards' into the so-called *Schutzbund*, which was the official paramilitary arm of the Social Democrats, trained and organized on a national basis. The name ('Protective League') suggests again the defensive concept. The party sought protection against a Habsburg restoration in Hungary (the Emperor Charles had led two vain attempts in March and in October of 1921) and against the shadows of dictatorship which were lengthening across two other borders (Mussolini's March on Rome and Hitler's Munich *putsch* of November 1923 were even fresher in the memory). And, after 1926, it had to arm itself anyway for that defensive-offensive Marxist Millennium which Otto Bauer was always preaching about, that tremendous day when the Socialists would be driven by the reactionaries into becoming true sons of the revolution. These motives were all doctrinal rather than patriotic (it was significant that the Socialists talked of a 'League' and not of a 'Homeland'), and the last factor particularly injected a permanent element of party strife into the paramilitary struggle. By their own security standards, and by the political standards of the day, the Social Democrats were certainly justified in acting as they did in 1923. But their decision must rank as one of two happenings which made the Civil War ten years later as inevitable as anything can be in the affairs of man.

The second fatal event was the serious rioting in Vienna on the 15th of July, 1927, when a Marxist mob set fire to the Ministry of Justice, cordoned off the blazing building, and turned back even their own beloved Burgomaster Seitz when he appeared mounted on the fire engines to try and put out the flames. It was left to an old servant of the Emperor's, the then Police President Dr. Schober, to clear the streets by force, helped by *Schutzbund* units who turned out to keep their own extremists in check. The cause of the riot was rooted in the paramilitary struggle : anger that a Vienna court had acquitted a group of *Heimwehr* men who had taken two lives in a clash with the *Schutzbund* six months previously. And the effect of the riot was to promote that struggle to the status of an undeclared nation-wide war.

The Socialists, now faced with the bitter truth that even their 'comrades' in the police would fire on them if ordered to, redoubled their drive to equip their *Schutzbund* as a powerful fighting force. On the other side, the Chancellor of the day, Prelate Seipel, took the even graver decision to back and build up the *Heimwehr* as an anti-Marxist counter-army to support the weak regular forces of the Government. The 15th of July, 1927, thus gave birth to the *Heimwehr* as a factor in national politics. It had already dealt mortal wounds to the cause both of justice and of democracy in Austria, for the Vienna court's verdict was as inexcusable as the violence which followed it. Taken together, they formally enthroned party strife over law and order. On that fatal day, which was the beginning of the end of the First Republic, it should be noted that Dollfuss was still far removed from politics. In fact, he had only just been promoted Director of the Lower Austrian Agricultural Chamber and was preparing to get down in earnest to his social reforms among the peasantry.

The *Heimwehr*, which now found itself being commended to the nation by nobody less than the great Seipel ('The yearning for true democracy is one of the strongest driving forces in the *Heimwehr* movement', the prelate had declared in Graz in December 1928), was forced to shake itself out of its purely provincial framework. The search began for national leaders and for a national programme.

Both ended miserably. The provincial basis, which had kept the movement together at the beginning, helped to tear it apart by accentuating personal rivalries at the end. Of these feuds, the most bitter and important was that between Star-hemberg and the leader of the Vienna group, Major Emil Fey, whom we shall eventually meet in the Chancellery building on the day of Dollfuss's murder. This and other quarrels would have sufficed by themselves to condemn the *Heimwehr* to a secondary role in the state's affairs. But an even greater organic weakness was the lack of any unifying philosophy or programme beyond the negative slogans of anti-Marxism which, after 1927, often drowned its patriotic undertones and gave the whole movement a shrill and vicious sound.

Not that the *Heimwehr* can be blamed for this. It had suddenly been transplanted by Seipel's influence from the provinces to the capital, where it found all the standard theories of politics already appropriated by the existing parties. So it was forced to go shopping for something out-of-the-way, like a newcomer to smart female society who looks for an extravagant hat. It soon found what it wanted : the old model of Vogelsang's 'Catholic corporative state', now being fashioned up-to-date by the lectures of Othmar Spann at the Vienna University and the practical example of Mussolini in Rome. '*Faute de mieux*', Spann's theory of the 'vertical grouping' of society according to professions and occupations, instead of the 'horizontal grouping' of the class system, was adopted as the *Heimwehr* credo. As it was something few of the leaders had ever thought about before, and which even fewer of them ever properly digested, the programme always looked somewhat lop-sided. But, for the moment, it suited the *Heimwehr's* need for novelty and for dynamism well enough.

The fact that the *Heimwehr* had been summoned onto the national stage to play the strong-armed hero against Marxism gave it yet another woeful characteristic — the natural leaning to violence as its own justification for existence. And the adoption of the Spann *Ständestaat* doctrine gave this tendency a political content by preaching an alternative to parliamentary democracy as such. As a result of all this, it was little wonder that the lusty captains of the *Heimwehr*, who were mostly of modest intellectual stature, soon began to regard the abolition of Parliament as a sort of sacred duty which God, through the intermediary of the omniscient Prelate Seipel, had thrust upon them. (The fact that Seipel also swung over to corporative doctrines during the last phase of his life made this all the more plausible.)

The *Heimwehr's* defeat in their first and only attempt to achieve power by quasi-constitutional means broke the last barriers on their restraint. In September 1929 — probably the peak period of their influence — they had been largely instrumental in securing the appointment of the pan-Germans' hope, Johannes Schober (the 'hero of 1927'), as Chancellor. Schober took office with the mandate, and with the firm personal intention, of revising the Constitution in order to make it less 'Parliament-heavy'. But the extremists who had hoped that he would introduce an authoritarian Praesidial form of government had misjudged this conscientious, almost pedantic, guardian of law and order. His new constitution removed the Austrian Presidency from being a mere nominee of Parliament and introduced a long overdue centralization of the security forces ; but it strengthened rather than weakened the legal democratic framework of the Republic. The *Heimwehr*, having saddled a fiery horse for Schober, were furious that he refused to gallop, and they now sought other mounts themselves. What resulted was an outright *putsch* philosophy and at least one actual *putsch* attempt.

The philosophy was enunciated by the radicals of the *Heimwehr* leadership in their notorious 'Korneuburg Oath' of May 1930. The 'formal democracy' of Parliament was condemned outright by the oath-takers, who declared their readiness to seize power by force in Austria and turn the country into a *Führerstaat* with a corporative basis. And the *putsch* itself came barely four months later, when the Styrian *Heimwehr* leader Pfrimer suddenly announced to an astonished country that he was the stern Messiah Austria was waiting for, and proceeded to march on Vienna to mount his throne. A few *Heimwehr* units from Upper and Lower Austria took to the road as well, but the revolt soon bogged down in the quicksands of utter popular indifference. Like Bauer in 1934, Pfrimer in 1931 found the Austrians very difficult people to push up on to the barricades. Unhappily, the Government showed itself almost as indifferent as the general public, and what had been a blatant act of revolution was treated as a naughty student prank — yet another sign of the low ebb of the Republic's political conscience.

The reader might well ask, in view of this sorry chronicle of irresponsibility and violence, why the *Heimwehr* have been placed in our circle to the immediate right of the Christian-Socials as regards their 'positive' qualities. The justification is the argument that what the First Austrian Republic needed even more than true democracy (which it never had) was a true sense of its own national identity (which Dollfuss was to give it too late). And, for all its lunatic fringes, for all its philandering with Nazi Germany and Fascist Italy, for all the nonsense talked by its extremist leaders most of the time, and the harm they did nearly all of the time, the *Heimwehr* deep down had an Austrian heart. This often took a lot of finding and gave off confusing sounds but, especially among the rank-and-file, it kept beating somehow. Even that veteran *Anschluss* friend Field-Marshal Bardolff found this essential 'Austrianness' of the *Heimwehr* to his liking. By 1929 he had become one of its leading propagandists and defined its aims in that year as 'the rooting out of Marxism, the sweeping away of the parliamentary party system, the rebuilding of Austria into an authoritarian state corporatively organized, the reorganization of the economy on the principle "common interests before private interests", and finally, the re-establishment of Austria as the Eastern Mark of the German Empire'.²

In a programme like this, there was something for almost everybody, and the *Heimwehr* following was composed accordingly : anti-Semites rubbed shoulders with middle-class Viennese Jews seeking protection in anything which fought both Marxists and Nazis ; social reformers, attracted by its bogus revivalism, jostled with industrialists who saw security in its promises of a 'vertical' state ; Monarchists mingled with Republicans and outright Fascists with disillusioned democrats. The only common planks which this motley company could tread on together were their desire to destroy Social Democracy and a desire to preserve Austria and her way of life in one of various strange settings. The first aspect has been stressed often enough in the writings of Austrian Left-Wing emigrés ; the second has been conveniently ignored. Yet it was Hitler himself who paid the most eloquent tribute to this latter characteristic. Several thousand *Heimwehr* officials in Vienna and the provinces were among the 90,000 Austrians whom, it is estimated, the Nazis arrested between the 12th and 21st of March, 1938 — the first ten days of the seven-year German domination. Even those who, at one time or another, had bargained secretly with the Nazis were not immune, for the bargain they sought had been an Austrian one.

To sum up, the *Heimwehr* had nothing to be ashamed of in their origins and nothing to be ashamed of in their end. Their record in between was a strange blend of the valuable and the vicious. They helped Austrian patriotism into its cradle and Austrian democracy into its grave.

The Austrian pan-Germans we have encountered briefly already in dealing with Bardolffs' circle and the early post-war enthusiasms of Dollfuss himself. They stemmed just as clearly from the old Empire's problems as did the *Heimwehr* from those of the young Republic. In fact, the pan-Germans symbolized that great dilemma which the logic of Bismarck had posed and the cannon of Königgrätz had tried in vain to resolve : how should the two German-speaking powers of Europe, Prussia and Austro-Hungary, live separately once they could no longer live together ?

Seen from the Austrian end, three basic solutions had crystallized during the second half of the 19th century. At one extreme stood those who, like Prince Schwarzenberg, wanted to make Vienna the centre of a revived Holy Roman Empire ; these men were the spiritual fathers of an Austrian patriotism, and were pan-German only in the sense that they regarded the whole racial community of seventy millions, from the Adriatic to the Baltic, as proper subjects for Franz Josef. In the middle were the more classic cases — a large, earnest and confused batch of thinkers who searched for some form of coexistence and partnership between Wilhelmian Germany and Habsburg Austria. This lot were always torn between Vienna as their political capital and Berlin as their spiritual and intellectual centre. In their purest form, they lived on in the Austrian Republic as the advocates of the *Zusammenschluss*, a voluntary merger with Germany which would guarantee some measure of Austrian independence.

At the other extreme in the Empire stood that group, inspired above all by Georg von Schönerer, who wished to dismantle Austro-Hungary altogether and attach its German-speaking provinces to the Prussian crown. These were the purists, the masochists of Austria's pan-German community, seeking salvation in self-injury and, ultimately, in suicide. Their influence under the Habsburg crown they disavowed was small. But their anti-clericalism, their anti-Semitism, their worship of power, their Bismarckian-type personality-cult, and their leaning towards violent and clear-cut solutions were all to find stronger and more sinister echoes in the Austrian Republic among the ranks of the Nazi sympathizers.

The pan-Germans of the middle camp never solved their basic riddle of how much to render unto the Caesar of the

Austrian state and how much to the mystic godhead of the German race. But they muddled and harmed a great many people, apart from themselves, in trying to solve it. Their performance as politicians was similar to their record as philosophers. In the Austrian Republic they never wielded real power ; yet their mere activity was enough to prevent others from doing so.

As a post-war political force, the pan-Germans date from September 1920, when the so-called 'Greater German Peoples Party' was founded in Salzburg out of no fewer than seventeen national and provincial groups. The only pan-German faction, apart from the Austrian Nazis, to maintain its separate existence from now on was the 'German Peasants Party', a forerunner of that strongly anti-clerical *Landbund* which, in the finely-balanced Parliaments of Dollfuss's time, was to have an influence out of all proportion to its handful of seats. This role of makeweight in the parliamentary scales between Christian-Socials and Social Democrats stayed with the pan-Germans from first to last. It gave them what substance they possessed, yet robbed them at the same time of any profile. As their following was exclusively anti-Marxist (civil servants, conservative intellectuals, plus a section of the peasantry), their only chance of office lay in co-operation with the Christian-Socials.

The so-called 'Bourgeois Bloc' which resulted did, in fact, rule Austria with fair stability from 1922 onwards. But this very co-operation led the 'Greater German Peoples Party' to betray the one clear-cut policy it ever stood for — *Anschluss* with Germany. As part of his coalition pact, Chancellor Seipel allowed the pan-Germans complete freedom to propagate their ideas, but no freedom at all to put them into practice. In other words, though they could wag their tongues, they were not allowed even to twiddle their fingers. They were thus obliged by the Christian-Socials to vote for the so-called Geneva Protocols of 1922, despite the fact that, in these financial agreements, the Allies specifically extended their *Anschluss* ban for a further twenty years. Here was the classical pan-German dilemma in action : loyalty to their Austrian state meaning treachery to their Germanic race and vice versa. Ten years later, when asked to repeat exactly the same doctrinal betrayal to secure another badly-needed League of Nations loan for Austria, they jibbed, putting race before state and opportunism before either. The 'Bourgeois Bloc', which had shored up the Republic for a decade, collapsed accordingly and, within a few months, Dollfuss was summoned to clear up the ruins.

The pan-German camp which he found on his accession to power was in a sorry way. It had always been a philosophy rather than a party, and those ten years during which it had been forced to stand on its own head in the Bourgeois Bloc had addled its political senses still further. The end product was an amorphous movement with no practical programme to tempt the electorate and no ideas beyond the escapist philosophy of the German *Volksgemeinschaft* to offer its own followers. Apart from Schober it was not linked with a single national personality ; and he — a typical touch — was a bureaucrat rather than a politician. Even before Hitler seized power in Germany, the Austrian pan-Germans were therefore a drifting and disorganized body. The leaders sought refuge in intellectual theories of no popular appeal, and the estranged rank-and-file (especially the youth) found the racial dynamism they needed in Alpine Clubs and Gymnastic Societies rather than in party meetings. Both trends, though unconnected, led naturally to fanaticism, and Hitler's arrival on the scene merely completed a disintegration process already far advanced.

For years Austrian domestic politics had muddled through on the uneasy consciences of the pan-Germans, and now Hitler forced these unfortunates to do the one thing they dreaded most — to make up their minds. After 1933 they were obliged either to work for the *Anschluss* actively or foreswear it altogether, to choose in fact between their race and their state. Thousands did the latter, and moved over either to the *Heimwehr* or to that wider patriotic movement launched by Dollfuss himself. Another group, led by men like Langoth and Foppa, teamed up with the Nazis to try and push Austria into Hitler's arms. These were the true grandsons of Schönerer ; and the idol they worshipped across the border, if not so acceptable as his, was at least more willing to co-operate in murder than Bismarck had been.

All that is needed now to complete our survey of Austria's political carrousel is a glance at the Austrian Nazis. The glance at this stage can be a brief one for, until Hitler's rise to power in Germany, Austria's Nazis were a negligible factor in the life of the Republic. After 1933 their image grew steadily more powerful and sinister until it dominated the whole domestic scene. At this stage, however, it becomes simply a reflection in the German mirror, without an independent gesture of its own, and is therefore best studied separately within the context of Austro-German relations.

Like much of Austria's pan-Germanism and some of her Socialism, the Nazi movement also had its roots in that classic struggle of the Empire between Czechs and Austrians in Bohemia. The old 'German Workers Party' (renamed 'German National Socialist Workers Party' in 1918) preached watered-down Marxism with a strong racial flavouring, and its prime purpose had been the suppression of Czech influence in the Sudetenland. This aim, at least, Adolf Hitler was to fulfil in drastic form a generation later ; but in the years between, the Austrian Nazi movement was true neither to its origins nor to its destiny. The collapse of the Empire divided the party into an Austrian and a Bohemian branch, and all the efforts of the Austrian leader, Walter Riehl, to build up an integrated National Socialist organization 'for the whole of Greater Germany' petered out in the first post-war years.

(These efforts, incidentally, brought Riehl into close contact with Hitler, who made several trips to Vienna during this experimental period to address joint meetings.) Soon, however, Hitler started striking out for a Greater Germany of his own, and the Austrian Nazis, without a leader of his dynamism and without their old Imperial rallying cry of the Czech issue, sank for nearly a decade into oblivion, their Socialism out-trumped by the Austro-Marxists and their racial nationalism outdone by the pan-Germans. The career of Riehl himself symbolizes these years in the wilderness : he crops up successively as an ally of the pan-German bloc, as a candidate for Seipel's 'Unity List', as a tamed rebel returning to Hitler's fold, and finally, as a relapsed convert in disgrace again for his opposition to the extremist policies ordered by Berlin after 1933.

Hitler's triumph in Germany dragged the Austrian Nazi Party abruptly onto its feet again, and indeed made the puppet look a great deal bigger than it was, with disastrous consequences for Austria. The National Socialists' successes in the Austrian provincial elections of 1932 were mistaken by the Vienna psephologists of the day as heralding a political landslide, when in fact their main feature was merely an internal shift of loyalty within the pan-German camp as such. This miscalculation contributed powerfully to that dread which made Dollfuss — and Schuschnigg after him — shrink back before the challenge of new parliamentary elections in Austria. The challenge became greater the longer it was evaded. The extremists of both Right and Left flourished all the more in illegality, while the youth of Austria were forced to seek their slogans and their salvation outside the democratic party framework.

Thus the only significant electoral influence which the Austrian Nazis exerted in the Republic was both unintentional and undeserved. Their influence across the frontier was smaller still. They were never a brake and seldom an accelerator of

Hitler's policy ; as we shall see, he was reluctant to allow them to become even its passive transmitting link. Yet this forlorn band of Austrian racial warriors have entered into history surely enough, by simply walking backwards in such unforgettable company. After all, they provided German Nazism with its leader (Hitler was born just inside the Austrian border) ; with its official party title ; with its racial demonism ; and even with its swastika (first chosen by Riehl for his Vienna followers in February 1920). Name, mission and badge : all those were stolen from the Austrian movement and fashioned into the symbols of history's greatest tyranny. To such effect that, today, the original is only remembered through the plagiarism.

*   *   *

Such was the roundabout which the young agrarian reformer Engelbert Dollfuss was called on to operate in May 1932. Its bewildering variety reflected not, as in France, the individuality of the electorate, but rather their perplexity. The Austrian admittedly has a congenital reluctance to make up his mind and, for this reason, has always been a better administrator than statesman. Yet it would be uncharitable to blame him entirely for his evasiveness during those twenty years between 1918 and 1938. For the eight basic groups described above represented only some of the many so-called truths which the First Republic had to choose from, the rival Pole Stars hung all over its political firmament. The nation was as confused as its leaders, caught between an Imperial past it could not put behind it and a Republican future it could not face up to. The people were mortally sick, as well as the parties, and it is this national ailment we must now examine in conclusion, before passing on to the radical surgery which Dollfuss tried.

Few countries have been called on to face a new destiny with such feeble resources — both spiritual and material — as were those $6\frac{1}{2}$ million Austro-Germans in November 1918.

As we have seen, the Empire's collapse had robbed them of all notions of identity or mission they had ever possessed, and therefore of all notions of loyalty. The great withered hand of the past, which the Marxists tried in vain to shake off their shoulder, also paralysed the young Republic in another sense. For the age which saw both nationalism and formal democracy triumph simultaneously all along the Danube Basin found the Austrian totally unprepared for either. He had had no training as a patriot and precious little as a parliamentarian ; as a result, he found himself having to learn to love his new state and to respect its institutions almost as though he had lived until then on another planet. And, for that matter, the Austro-Hungarian Empire — universalist, feudal, disenchanted and mystical — *had* belonged to a different world from that bevy of ambitious and bustling nation-states which suddenly replaced it, all of them so much broader in their social base and so much narrower in their political horizons.

For six and a half centuries the Austrians had served that vanished Habsburg system as a caste of supra-national bureaucrats, the stewards of a vast landed estate which time and marriage had pressed into an Empire. The privilege was great, but so was the price demanded : loyalty to the dynasty above any other sentiment, and especially above nationalist sentiment, which was eating away like acid at the frayed bonds of Empire. Thus, until 1918, 'patriotism' to the Austrian meant simply serving his Emperor (who was also King of Bohemia and Apostolic Majesty of Hungary) and resisting the attempts of any other racial group to supplant him in this service. As far as the ordinary Austro-German officer or bureaucrat was concerned, even the great nationalist struggle was a personal rather than a political affair. He was less concerned with how many votes the Czech subjects of the Emperor obtained than with how many Army Corps commands or station-masters' posts they were given. And, for all the fine talk they gave President Wilson, the Czech subjects

Socialist dogmatist — the brilliant but un-
:tical extremist Austro-Marxist leader, Otto
Bauer

The Socialist pragmatist — the moderate and
statesmanlike Karl Renner, later Chancellor
and President

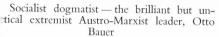

A meeting of the 'Austro-Fascist' *Heimwehr* movement in Vienna. In the
centre, Major Emil Fey, the 'mystery man' of the July 1934 *putsch*

The first Austrian 'patriot' : Dollfuss in First World War uniform addresses a Vienna meeting of his 'Fatherland Front'

The statues to the three Socialist founders of the 1918 Republic, shrouded in Dollfuss symbols after the 'suicide

of the Emperor were mainly preoccupied with the same ideas, until the collapse of 1917–18 offered them better pickings.

Inevitably, this struggle for posts and privilege centred itself around the historic conflict between Slav and German in the Danube Basin, with further dire consequences for the Austrian. For such group-consciousness as he developed in the 19th century became a purely racial one — as a member of that German-speaking élite which in Vienna, as in Agram or in Pardubitz, administered the Emperor's writ among the lesser peoples of his crown. (The Hungarians alone, after 1867, stood on virtually the same footing as the Austro-Germans.) And so the paradox arose that whereas all these other 'non-historic' peoples had some concrete political or territorial concept to build on in 1918, all the aims, in fact, for which they had fought the crown, the Austrian was left stranded with his old-fashioned slogans of dynasty and race. He stood like the butler in a deserted castle, with the family estate parcelled up all around him.

But though the dynasty was gone, the racial refuge remained. In the post-war years the Socialist and pan-German leaders wanted a union with the Weimar Republic to serve their own doctrinal aims. But, as a mass movement, the *Anschluss* drive in those days was primarily the longing to get back some of that security, protection and status which merely speaking the German tongue had conferred on the Austrians for so many centuries. Needless to say, this longing never furthered the Austrian's allegiance to his own infant Republic, and often diametrically opposed it. It was left to Hitler to quell this racial yearning by the simple, brutal process of fulfilling it. Dollfuss, in trying to forestall him with a purely domestic solution, had to fight against both the Imperial universalism and the Germanic racialism which his country-men had inherited. That he succeeded in creating an Austrian patriotism of sorts between these two poles remains one of the political wonders of the 20th century.

The fact that, in 1918, the Austrian was almost as unused to Parliaments as to patriotism was also a product of his immediate past. Universal suffrage had not been introduced anywhere in the Empire until the last ten years of its life, while the institution of Parliament itself dated in Vienna only from the 1860's. Even that so-called 'Imperial Council' of Schmerling's bore little resemblance to a proper legislature responsible to an electorate. With its intricate system of checks and balances, it was primarily just another device to reconcile the fourteen historic provinces and the twelve peoples of the Empire with their ruler and with each other. Centralism and federalism, liberalism and autocracy, Dualism and Trialism had all been debated or tried out by the Habsburgs before. The dynasty now imported Parliamentarism, which seemed to be working wonders with ailing monarchies elsewhere on the continent, in the hope of curing its own endemic racial strife.

The Socialist founders of the Republic made things worse, for they went much further than the Emperor in treating Parliament as a vade-mecum for all political complaints. As it was the only instrument which they thought it safe to manipulate, they turned Austria into an upside-down democracy in which Parliament ran both the Government and the nation, and exercised most of the functions of Head of State into the bargain. During the immediate post-war months, the country was ruled by a Council of State consisting of all three Presidents of the National Assembly and twenty deputies, picked proportionate to party strength. Even when this emergency arrangement was modified, both the Federal President and the Cabinet continued for ten years to be nominated by Parliament and to have little or no independent life outside it.

This was not rule by Parliament but dictatorship by Parliament. It prevented the politicians as well as the private citizens, both total strangers to responsible government in 1918, from understanding and respecting the problems of power. By the time Schober introduced his constitutional reforms in 1929 — creating an independent, popularly elected Head of State with powers to summon and dissolve Parliament — the damage had been done. For a critical decade, Parliament had pressed so close on to the nation that it had had no room to put down roots. When Dollfuss arrived on the scene, it was still an inorganic institution, unsanctified by either history or public opinion. What he crushed in 1933 was the half-empty shell of democracy, not its living yolk.

Apart from these moral handicaps, the new state was born with a more tangible ball and chain tied around its foot in the shape of its economic burden. The monarchy of over fifty millions had shrunk to a Republic of less than seven millions. The Hungarian larder of the Empire had gone, and so had its Bohemian workshop. Even in those Austrian lands which remained to supply Vienna, food production in 1918 had dropped by more than half compared to pre-war level, and industrial output in the non-military sectors by over 60 per cent. Inflation and unemployment raged, and the Budget deficit (five milliard crowns by July 1919) could only be filled by further wads of worthless notes from the printing press. Foreign loans, hard work and the patient retrenchment policy of the first Seipel administration steadied the country as early as 1923 ; and, during the following fifteen years, the Austrian Republic was to confound the experts by showing her potentialities as a highly viable independent Alpine state.

But potentialities they remained until Hitler pounced on them to strengthen the sinews of his Third Reich. All the way from 1918 to 1938 the Austrian economy was in a state of frail convalescence, and any heavy shock from within or without brought on an immediate recurrence of the illness— as in 1924 after the collapse of the Paris Bourse, or in 1930–31 after the failure of the Bodencreditanstalt Bank in Vienna. These repeated bouts of inflation and unemployment (in 1933, 406,000 Austrians, or one out of seventeen in the whole country, were actually registered as out of work) sapped public and private morale. A mood of disgust and desperation grew up which was only heightened by the constant corruption scandals of the time.

Dollfuss took over at the height of Austria's second economic relapse and, however gallantly he fought it back, its shadow hung over his whole Chancellorship. Yet, grave though these material problems were, it still remains true to say that the Republic's fundamental weakness was of the spirit and not of the body. Its economy he could feed with loans and shelter with protective tariffs, relying on the country's natural riches to do the rest in time. But what similar medicine could be found for the body politic? The Austrians of his day simply did not know what they were living for. Imperial nostalgia and pan-German racialism had prevented a plain love of fatherland from breaking through all along the line, even on the traditionalist Right Wing. The new substitute love of democracy preached by the Left Wing had been discredited by its very symbol, the Vienna Parliament.

We must now resume our narrative and see how Dollfuss established the first love, at the expense of the second.

CHAPTER FOUR

The Search for Stability

THE nomination of Dollfuss as Chancellor on the 10th of May, 1932, took the general public somewhat by surprise, for the young Minister of Agriculture was not yet a national figure, despite the energetic mark he had made on the capital. But that jealous little world of Ministers, ex-Ministers, deputies, churchmen, intellectuals, industrialists and bureaucrats which misruled Austria at the time understood well enough the reasons behind President Miklas's choice.

To begin with, by the fleeting standards of the day, Dollfuss was no newcomer to power ; Government changes and re-shuffles had been so frequent since the final retirement of Seipel and the collapse of the Bourgeois Bloc three years before that Dollfuss found himself one of the senior members of the out-going Buresch Cabinet. Furthermore, he was a Minister who had never been a member of Parliament ; and it spoke volumes for the disrepute into which that body had already sunk by 1932 that this could be considered a political virtue in itself. After less than fifteen years of life, the Republic had already got round to the bad habits of the Habsburgs, and was seeking its salvation in periodic bouts of 'rule by experts'.

The weight of support which the new Chancellor-designate could hope to command was, moreover, both large and varied. He was sure of the solid backing of the peasantry and above all of the Lower Austrian peasantry who, in his time even more than today, were the squat pillar of state. Just as the peasants revered him as their image and their benefactor, so the Catholic Church blessed him as one of her most ardent sons. Indeed, for the Vatican, Dollfuss's appearance on the Vienna scene might almost have been providential. It was almost exactly a year after Pope Pius XI had produced his famous encyclical, 'Quadragesimo Anno'; and now, in one Catholic country of Europe at least, a vigorous and devout social reformer had come to power who was to try and turn those ideas into reality.

A new political papal legate was needed in Austria, for the great Monsignor Seipel had at last burnt out his feverish reserves of strength. Dollfuss had entered politics too late to have had much substantial contact with that formidable Christian gladiator. But, though they were total contrasts in social background, upbringing and temperament, there was much that linked the young agrarian with the old ascetic. Both were driven by the same religious inspiration which made them see everything as *sub auspicibus aeternitatis*; both had the same simple tastes and relentlessly high standards of personal integrity; both had the same deep love of their Austrian fatherland and the same struggle to reconcile this with their loyalties to the German race; above all, in the previous decade, both had gone through the same transformation in their political thinking — that silent, almost unconscious swing from Left to Right, from radicalism to authoritarianism, which characterized so many Austrian Catholic intellectuals of the period. Whatever conflicting points can be traced in their development arise mainly from the fact that the pace of this change was different in the two men. The direction remained the same, and both arrived inexorably at the same destination : the ideal of the Christian corporative state which was supposed to solve both the external dilemma of Austrian nation versus German race and the internal riddle of preserving democracy without parliamentarianism. It was their faith in this ideal, and the belief that they were destined as Catholic statesmen to achieve it, which gave both men their strength — Seipel the cold immovability of a marble statue, and Dollfuss the instinctive sure-footedness of a sleep-walker.

Seipel was a mortally sick man when his successor came

to power. But, after a long bedside talk with Dollfuss a few days before the end, he died happy in the conviction that the Kingdom of God, as Pius XI had seen it, would now be established in Austria. 'Sister, the world is getting healthy again', the dying statesman called out to his nurse after Dollfuss had visited him to report on his success over the Lausanne loan and discuss his plans for the future.

So Dollfuss inherited Seipel's blessing and was widely regarded as his successor, almost in the same flesh — a sort of rustic Emperor Bonaparte emerging out of the prelate's First Consul. This was no small advantage, for the *mystique* of Seipel was great. Of equal importance was the very tangible support which the new Chancellor got, at his nomination and throughout his brief career, from the 'Cartellverband', the Catholic students' association, a branch of which he had joined in his university days.

The power of the 'C.V.' in pre-war Austria was something unique : a combination of a Hindu caste, a medieval gild, an American freemasons' order and the British school-tie clique. The 'C.V.' had sprung up soon after the 1848 revolution as an association of the Catholic élite designed to combat liberalism and nationalism (the two arch-enemies of the 19th-century conservative) throughout the German lands. It was ultramontane in origin ; the movement started in Munich in 1854 and the first Vienna branch — the 'Austria' — was founded in 1859, seven years before Bismarck flung the Habsburg Empire out of the German Confederation. In the 1930's, its Austrian members did not number more than a few thousand. But, between them, they counted most of the best brains and stoutest anti-Marxist hearts to be found anywhere on the Catholic Right Wing. Unlike their brothers in Germany, who could vote Centre or even Left if they chose, the 'C.V.' in Austria were forced by party strife into an uncompromising Conservative stand and thus, incidentally, forced into politics : support for the Austro-Marxists or the

Jewish liberals was automatically ruled out, while the Austrian extreme pan-Germans, though socially acceptable, had heinous anti-Roman leanings.

What emerged was a tightly-knit Catholic social and intellectual clan whose political inflexibility was both its strength and its weakness. Every recruit had sworn on joining to be 'a true friend and brother' to his comrades, and the effects of this oath were to be seen in the unfailing support which 'C.V.' members afforded each other throughout their lives in every public and private endeavour. The influence of this organization on Dollfuss was enormous, with corresponding benefits and handicaps. For him, the 'C.V.' was not only a constant source of personal comfort and spiritual strength ; it was also a physical Praetorian Guard. Wherever and whenever he was not absolutely forced to accept a *Heimwehr* nominee for a key post he put in a 'C.V.' colleague : Schuschnigg, Ender, Stepan, Schmitz, Gleissner, Kemptner and E. K. Winter are a few of the many examples we shall meet with later on. It is worth noting here that, despite differences of opinion, none of these betrayed his personal trust. Especially when compared with the woeful standards of the time, the best of Dollfuss's 'C.V.' following were outstanding for their loyalty and integrity.

But even if Church, 'C.V.' and peasantry stood solidly behind Dollfuss in 1932, it must not be assumed that he was the nominee of a closed ultra-conservative group. The unique strength of the new Chancellor was that, while enjoying all this traditional support, he could also look hopefully across to rival camps. His pioneering social reform work in Lower Austria made him one of the very few Catholic leaders acceptable to the Left Wing. In these days, he had good personal relations with both Bauer and Deutsch, while his record showed, plainly and almost embarrassingly, that Dollfuss entered office as good a *practical* Socialist, if not better, than either of these Austro-Marxist radicals. Moreover, his old pan-German enthusiasms and his strong peasant ties suggested that he might be able to lead back both the Greater Germans and the agrarian *Landbund* into the Right-Wing Coalition.

These were all vital factors in the complicated political arithmetics of the day. At Dollfuss's accession, Parliament consisted of 66 Christian-Socialists, 10 members of Schober's Greater German group, 9 representatives of the liberal *Landbund*, eight *Heimwehr* deputies and 72 Social Democrats. The true balance between Right and Left was even slimmer. The month before, on the 24th of April, 1932, municipal elections had been held in Vienna, Lower Austria, Styria, Salzburg and Carinthia, whose outcome indicated that this distribution of seats no longer reflected the electorate's mood. For the first time, the Nazis had competed at the polls, leaping through a costly propaganda paper hoop into the Austrian political arena. They achieved spectacular successes, mopping up large slices of the Greater German, *Landbund* and *Heimwehr* vote and even, in Vienna, making inroads into the Christian-Social camp. Only the Socialists held their ground and could now claim, with every justice, to be the biggest single party in the land. Not unnaturally, therefore, they headed the clamour for new general elections.

The Christian-Social leadership panicked. They failed to realize that the whole pan-German following in Austria, though regrouping noisily under the swastika, was still heavily outnumbered by the two main democratic parties. Instead, frightened by the rather improbable bogy of a Marxist-Nazi majority partnership, they contrived to postpone new elections, first for six months and then for a further year. Those elections were never held ; for when, in March 1933, this unworkable, unrepresentative Parliament obligingly committed suicide, Dollfuss promptly nailed down its coffin and sat himself on the lid. Thus, when the moral challenge of the *Anschluss* finally came in 1938, Austria's leaders had been tapping in the dark for nearly six years as to the nation's true political loyalties. This was a costly error of the whole Catholic Right Wing, for which the hapless Schuschnigg was called on to atone.

In the spring of 1932, however, the sky over Vienna was too full of local squalls for the gathering German tempest to be seen. There had already been a handful of stop-gap administrations since the great Bourgeois Bloc partnership had broken down (the Christian-Socials Streeruwitz, Vaugoin, Ender and Buresch as well as the Greater German leader Schober had all tried their hand) ; and the only concern of the day was the typically Viennese one of 'muddling on'. So Dollfuss was picked to try his skill at the old game of constructing a Right-Wing majority out of the awkward out-of-date parliamentary fragments available.

It took him till May 20, and it is not too much to say that, in those ten days and nights of search for a mandate, Austria's domestic future, as well as his own political destiny, were sealed. His first proposal to his party colleagues—a little-known fact— was for a working agreement with the Socialists. Something might conceivably have come of this, in view of his personal standing with the Left Wing at the time, had it not been for those April municipal elections. But the Socialist now wanted a new ballot, not a new Coalition, so the idea was dropped.

Even more fateful was the refusal of the Greater German Party, who were trying to maintain their political profile by staying in opposition, to throw in their lot with Dollfuss. For though, as had been hoped, he won over the *Landbund*, their 9 seats added to his own party's 66 still only gave him 75 seats in the Parliament of 165. There remained, as the solitary alternative, the eight *Heimwehr* deputies, with whom he had little contact and less sympathy, but without whom he could not even start. His friends testify to the reluctance with which he approached them to join his Coalition, and President Miklas himself is said to have hesitated loudly before agreeing ; but if a Government was to be formed by Dollfuss, there was no other way. The misgivings of both Chancellor and President were amply fulfilled. The *Heimwehr* clambered into power on Dollfuss's shoulders and they hung on there to the tragic end, like a tiger at the kill.

With their pledge, Dollfuss now had a majority of exactly one vote : the 83 of his assorted Right-Wing camp against the 82 of the Socialist and Greater German opposition combined. The first Cabinet he presented showed the price at which this slender lead had been bought. He retained for himself the portfolios of Foreign Affairs and Agriculture and, of his own circle, Schuschnigg and Vaugoin were reappointed Ministers of Justice and War respectively. The *Landbund* leader Winkler was paid for his support by the post of Vice-Chancellor. The *Heimwehr* presented, and were paid, the highest bill for the smallest yet most indispensable service. Their nominee, Guido Jakoncig, became Minister of Trade and two other men with strong *Heimwehr* sympathies, Hermann Ach and the notorious Rintelen, were appointed to the Ministries of Interior and Education. Dollfuss's Cabinet thus started off '*Heimwehr*-heavy', and the weight only seemed to grow heavier with time.

Once a majority of sorts had been achieved, however, the immediate problems to be tackled were not political but economic. Indeed, quite apart from tactical party considerations, it was also the wave of economic misery surging in Austria which had borne Dollfuss into office. The 'little miracle' of stabilization he had achieved the previous year with the Federal Railways was still green in the memory, and it was hoped he could now perform the greater miracle of steadying the economy as a whole. His first governmental programme, produced on the 27th of May, reflected these hopes. Its ideological aspects had to be rewritten two or three times to meet the demands of his *Heimwehr* and *Landbund* allies — an ominous portent of things to come. But the national message was clear enough : the priority of economic requirements over party politics and a call for a concerted effort to overcome the emergency.

Austria's plight at the time was enough to daunt the bravest heart. The collapse of the Creditanstalt bank twelve months before had thrown not only the little Republic but great countries and continents abroad into confusion. At Chequers, country seat of the British Prime Minister, the Governor of the Bank of England broke into a conference between Ramsay MacDonald and the visiting German Chancellor Brüning with the dramatic cry : 'South-East Europe is in flames. The Creditanstalt in Vienna has closed its counters.' And, in faraway Uganda, the same news, received over the tom-toms a few days later, was said to have promptly decreased the number of bullocks being offered for a comely wife. The Creditanstalt was the last of the great old Austro-Hungarian banks still operating in the Austrian capital, and it still carried the magic nimbus of the vanished Empire. It was as though the outside world, despite the reparations burdens which it had piled on Vienna, simply could not believe that this particular piece of history could collapse.

But collapse it did, with a current deficit of 140 million schillings, which leapt up by another 71 million dollars or 500 million schillings after the claims of foreign creditors had poured in. Nearly all of this gigantic sum had to be under-written by the Government, and years of sacrifice and tortuous negotiations were to follow before the debt could be finally settled. What Dollfuss inherited were the short-term repercussions : at home, a shattering blow at the country's finances and with it, another blow at the nation's sorely-tried faith in its rulers ; abroad, the delivering-up of Austria, trussed like a diplomatic turkey, to the Western Powers, who would produce financial aid only on their terms.

Despite the problem, and despite the issues involved in solving it, Dollfuss did, in fact, achieve that greater miracle of rescuing the nation's economy. Whatever else he failed in, or left half-completed at his death, he succeeded within two years in changing Austria's bankruptcy into near-stability and her despair into hope. This achievement, so often blotted out by the political storms which surround his memory, deserves recording briefly here. When he took over power the Austrian Budget was over 300 million schillings in the red, not counting the then incalculable burden of the Credit-anstalt affair ; the number of registered unemployed stood at 329,627 and was soon to rise to a new record of nearly 377,000 ; in less than a year, the savings banks' deposits had dropped by 20 per cent, the gold and foreign currency reserves by 25 per cent, while the amount of currency in circulation had risen by over 10 per cent. The excess of imports over exports equalled a quarter of the country's total trade and the musty smell of inflation was in the air. By the time Nazi bullets removed Dollfuss from the scene he had presented a com-pletely balanced Budget for 1934 ; the figures of registered unemployed had been reduced by 54,000 ; the savings banks' deposits were once more above their pre-crisis level of 2000 million schillings ; the tills of the National Bank were filling up fast, and note circulation had been cut back by almost 30 per cent. The currency had become healthy enough to with-stand the effects of all the Western devaluation measures of 1933, and the nation's adverse trade balance had been reduced from 25 to 19 per cent of the total. Economically at least, the dying Seipel's prophecy had come true.

It is true that all Dollfuss's economic thinking and reform work stood in the shadow of his peasant origin and that he tended to look at the whole economic picture through a farmer's spectacles. This was social, as much as anything else. As he declared in Budapest shortly before his death : 'The days when the poets had to warn that the peasant was no toy are long passed. Today we all know that the peasant is the foundation of a healthy people from the national as well as the economic point of view.' He believed passionately that 'any nation which fails to secure its own bread supply within its own borders gives up a good portion of its political freedom' (Graz, November 6, 1932). And he was greatly impressed by the argument that 'the first crisis of the world-wide depression was the agrarian crisis' (Innsbruck, April 22, 1933).

Yet though he drove up agricultural production with every means at his disposal, fostering Austria's peasants with his 'neighbour-state preference treaties', he never lost sight of those broader perspectives with which he was less familiar ; to have done so, indeed, would have betrayed the whole corporative ideal to which he had become committed. Economically speaking, it is not so much narrow vision he might be reproached with as a view taken habitually from the same standpoint. This he expressed perfectly himself : 'There can be no Austrian economy if the peasant is ruined ; but the peasant cannot exist by himself unless industry and commerce also flourish' (Salzburg, May 10, 1934). In fact, some of the most spectacular strides which the Austrian economy made during his two years of Chancellorship were in the industrial field. The overall index of industrial output jumped from 78 to 88 in the one twelve-month period between October 1932 and October 1933. All branches shared in this expansion, with textiles, timber, cellulose and steel well to the fore. Dollfuss may not have grasped the full significance and speed of the new industrial revolution, but he did not fail to promote it.

The entrance ticket which he had had to pay for his Chancellorship was the alliance with the *Heimwehr* ; and, just as inevitably, the initial price for all these economic reforms was the Western loan. In the summer of 1932 Austria's only road to stability lay through Lausanne. This brings us, as it brought Dollfuss, abruptly back to the domestic political scene.

*   *   *

The name of Engelbert Dollfuss as Austria's leading agrarian reformer, as her economic saviour, as the first and foremost patriot of the young Republic, and as the first challenger of Hitler anywhere on the European continent, is secure. So secure that, despite the bitter and biased controversies of the day, even his Austro-Marxist opponents have endorsed all of these achievements, or at least have left them unchallenged. The central charge levelled by all of his enemies and some of his admirers both in Austria and abroad, is that he was personally responsible for the failure of the Catholic Right Wing to reach an emergency working agreement with the Socialist Left. A corollary to this charge is that the tragedy which resulted, the brief but bloody Civil War of February 1934, was either provoked by him, suppressed by him with unnecessary harshness, or both.

No political study of Dollfuss would be complete which did not attempt to examine this charge as objectively as the old polemical material of the time permits, while drawing on as much new material as the survivors of that period can provide. It is, in fact, the essence of the period, as well as the essence of the man. For to trace the story of his relations with the Socialists is also to trace Austria's *via dolorosa* into domestic ruin. (His parallel problem of how to bridle the Nazis belongs essentially in the field of foreign affairs, and is dealt with separately under that heading.)

Dollfuss's relations with the Austro-Marxists during his two years of power can be divided into three phases : first, between his accession in May 1932 and the disappearance of Parliament in March 1933 ; second, the eleven-month period between the suicide of Parliament and the explosion of February 1934 ; and third, between the Civil War itself and its aftermath and the death of Dollfuss five months later. They might be called the 'pre-March', 'pre-February', and 'pre-July' phases respectively.

It must again be recalled that, when Dollfuss came to power, his personal standing with the Socialists as a practical social worker and a 'progressive Catholic' was high ; on his part, as we have seen, his first thought had been of co-operation with them. Of the gentleness and generosity of his own nature, we have had sufficient evidence already. Either therefore his whole being was transformed by the sheer exercise of power during the next eighteen months from an enlightened reformer into an 'unbridled Fascist dictator'; or he was driven into a form of despotism by events, and mistakes, all around him.

In the first pre-March phase, two events can be singled out as widening that critically mobile gap between Dollfuss and the Austro-Marxists. One does little credit to the fanatics of the Left and the other equally little credit to the fanatics of the Right. It was, unquestionably, the Socialists who started to widen the gap with their stubborn opposition to the life-bringing Lausanne loan. The Government was already committed to emergency Western help in one form or another, for one of the last acts of the previous Buresch Cabinet had been to appeal formally to France, England, Italy and Germany to provide Austria with a new economic basis of existence. This was linked with, but separate from, the international financial discussions over the Creditanstalt disaster. The crisis here had been tempered by a short-term British loan of 150 million schillings, but was still far from resolved; indeed, by the time Dollfuss arrived on the scene, Austria's foreign currency reserves had shrunk to such a pittance that the country could no longer buy the basic raw materials needed for its industries, or even guarantee its Civil Servants' salaries, let alone think about paying off its debts.

The new Chancellor's first journey was therefore to meet the bankers and politicians of the great powers in Switzerland. After some very anxious days of bargaining (the French, in particular, were reluctant to put Austria's special needs before their own integrated 'Tardieu Plan' for the whole Danube Basin), Dollfuss got the agreement in his pocket on the 15th of July. The financial aid was fixed at 300 million schillings,

von Schuschnigg, Dollfuss's closest colleague
and successor as Chancellor

Prince Ernst Rüdiger Starhemberg, a leader of
the extreme Right-Wing Heimwehr movement

The end of Austria's pre-war Parliament. Austrian police occupy and close
down the building on March 4, 1933

Dollfuss leaves London after his one visit in May 1933, a visit which won him a host of British friends and admirers of his struggle against Hitler. Next to him (with top hat) is the late Baron Franckenstein, then Austrian Minister in London. Standing right is Prince Johannes Schwarzenberg, then a junior Austrian diplomat, now Austrian Ambassador in London

Dollfuss among colleagues and rivals — the little Chancellor in his *Kaiserschuetzen* uniform reviews an Austrian Army parade on the Vienna 'Heldenplatz'. Walking in front, the Federal President Miklas. On Dollfuss's left (saluting) Major Emil Fey, the enigmatic Austrian *Heimwehr* leader

loaned for twenty years ; the political price was an extension
of the 1922 '*Anschluss* ban' between Austria and Germany for
a further ten years. The aid meant everything ; the price,
by 1932, meant almost nothing, least of all to the Germany
of the day, who still had a few months of democracy left in
front of her, and was anyway sick to death of Vienna's half-
hearted courtship.

Yet, having fought for the pact at Lausanne, Dollfuss got
home to find he would have to fight for it all over again in his
own Parliament. Socialists and Greater Germans combined
to try and block the passage of the bill. Their arguments
were that the extended *Anschluss* ban was unacceptable and that,
economically, Austria could outride the storm without foreign
help. To what extent they believed in either argument in the
Vienna of 1932 is questionable. Their real aim was tactical :
to break the struggling Dollfuss Government at all costs and
clear the way for new elections.

A nerve-wrecking battle now began which was not cal-
culated to endear the Chancellor either to the opposition or
to the current Parliament itself. He carried the first challenge
by default on the 3rd of August with an 81 : 81 vote, a respite
obtained only because a substitute voter for Dr. Seipel, who
had died the day before, was produced at lightning speed. A
fortnight later he squeezed through by the razor-edge majority
of 81 : 80, thanks to the providential absence of an opposition deputy. The Socialists in the Federal Council promptly
passed a suspensive veto, but on August 30 Dollfuss was
finally able to confirm the bill with an 82 : 80 majority.
Again, the death of an ex-Chancellor, this time the veteran
pan-German leader Schober, came to his aid ; and again, a
lucky defection occurred in his opponents' ranks.

These bitter weeks taught Dollfuss two things. The first
was that Austria's Socialists had as yet no national foreign
policy and, on their radical wing, were just not capable of
thinking as Austrians *tout court*. They knew loyalty to a

H

party narrower than their state and to an ideology broader than their state ; but the one was too little and the other too much for the country's needs. The second was that, as regards the Parliament of the day, the country's fate hinged either on the undertaker or on one single Left-Wing deputy missing his early morning tram or one single Right-Wing member going off to shoot roebuck for the week-end. It is possible to blame him, later on, for not facing the challenge of forming a new Parliament. But he can hardly be reproached in those first months of office for getting heartily fed up with the existing one.

The heated debates over the Lausanne loan had already caused epithets like 'Traitor' and 'Bolshevik' to fly between Dollfuss and Bauer. The gap between the Chancellor and the rest of his parliamentary opposition widened out more in the autumn, when the Greater Germans rejected a direct and secret appeal which Dollfuss sent them to save him from increasing concessions to the *Heimwehr*. These worthies were now demanding, in addition to their existing posts, the nomination of their Vienna leader Major Emil Fey as State Secretary for Security, and had threatened to walk out of the Government Coalition unless the demand were met. Through his Vice-Chancellor Winkler, Dollfuss explained his dilemma to the Greater Germans and implored them once again to join forces, thus enabling him to shed the *Heimwehr* burden. They refused ; Major Fey was appointed ; and with him, the first shadows, both of February 1934 and July 1934, fell across the Vienna scene.

As regards the Socialist sector of the opposition, the Chancellor's second decisive breach was produced by the so-called 'Hirtenberg Arms affair', which broke out in January 1933. Socialist railway workers at the Carinthian rail junction of Villach discovered large consignments of rifles and machine-guns in the sidings which were being transported, under falsified consignment notes, from Italy to Hungary. The

Austrian arms magnate Mandl, an intimate member of the *Heimwehr* circle grouped around Prince Starhemberg, was involved in the operation, which appears to have been inspired by Rome. The Socialists could scarcely be blamed for making the most of their discovery, and banner publicity followed in the party organ *Arbeiter Zeitung*. But though it was a party advantage they sought, what followed was a national embarrassment. Protest notes rained in on Vienna from the Western Powers and the Little Entente against this illegal strengthening of 'revanchist Hungary'. It was only after much prevarication, coupled with alleged attempts to push through the deal by bribery, that the offending arms were requisitioned, and were eventually used to re-equip the Austrian Army.

Hitler's arrival to power in Germany soon gave the Cabinets of Europe more substantial food for thought, and the Hirtenberg affair, judged as a diplomatic incident, subsided almost as rapidly as it had arisen. But Dollfuss, somewhat unreasonably mistaking outcome for intention, accused the Socialists of deliberately trying to discredit the Republic before the world. In fact, the whole affair, which had an unsavoury flavour of Fascist intrigue and private arms-running, must be booked to the debit account of his own Right-Wing coalition, or rather, to those dubious *Heimwehr* allies it reluctantly nourished in its midst.

Dollfuss's initial honeymoon with the Socialists was therefore already over and done with, and his patience with Parliament sorely tried, when that quarrelsome body climaxed its rather clownish career with a public and accidental suicide. The details of the tragi-comedy of the 4th of March, 1933, need only be briefly recounted here. Parliament was debating disciplinary action against striking railway workers (what with his term as Board President, and the munitions train of the Hirtenberg affair, railways seem to have haunted Dollfuss's career). The vital vote to carry an opposition motion of censure had somehow got mixed up in the urns. The Socialist First President of the Assembly, Dr. Renner, laid down his office in order to be able to cast his ballot from the floor in a new division. The Second President, the Christian-Socialist Ramek, followed suit after a confused interval, partly in order to safeguard the Government's majority. There was still a Third President left (the Parliament was as strong on Presidents as the state was weak). But this last bastion of the Assembly, the Greater German Dr. Straffner, acted on a dumb reflex like Pavlov's famous dog. For no apparent reason other than that resignations were in the air that day, he also laid down his office and even forgot, in the general clamour, to declare this monstrous session closed.

No Right-Wing deputy on that fateful afternoon had dreamed of murdering the Assembly as a constitutional body ; and no one of the Left Wing was even aware that, politically speaking, they were taking their own lives. This very self-centred witlessness summed up, better than any words, the deficiencies of Austria's Parliament, which perhaps needs a brief epitaph here. As we have seen, it had been called into life fifteen years before to replace overnight in the Republic all that massive authority that the dynasty had represented for six centuries in the Empire. Even more was expected of those neo-classical caryatids. For if Franz Josef was a 'latent despot', Parliament in the early 'twenties was an active despot, appointing and controlling both the Head of State and the Federal Government ; the *vox populi* gone somewhat hoarse and berserk. Every party bore with this system ; but basically, it was the Socialists' creation, for their only hope of burying all Austrian history before November 1918 was to erect a huge parliamentary structure over its open grave.

Though unchallenged until the Right Wing constitutional reforms of 1929, Parliament had, however, never become respected, let alone revered, by the nation at large. And, for their part, the denizens of Parliament went on behaving, even after 1929, as though that Assembly were Austria itself, and therefore answerable to nobody.   Not a single warning voice seems to have broken through the tumult on the 4th of March, 1933, pointing to the likely effects on the nation of Parliament's behaviour.   Everyone thought of their party, and nobody of their country.   And when the first anxious afterthoughts came, it was too late.   The link between nation and Parliament, always tenuous, had been snapped by Dollfuss. He now took the one in his arms and kicked the other aside.

On the 7th of March the Viennese awoke to find a Government proclamation posted up under the black single-headed eagle all over the capital.   It referred briefly to the paralysis which Parliament had just inflicted on itself and continued : 'However, the leadership of a country does not rest only with the legislature, but equally with the Head of State and the Government.   The legal Government appointed by the Federal President is still in office.   It is not affected by the parliamentary crisis, for which it was in no way responsible. There is therefore no state crisis.'   The proclamation went on to appeal for unity and stressed the Government's resolve to 'secure law and order in these troubled times'.   As an earnest of this resolve, all public meetings and processions were banned and a press censorship was introduced.

This placard was the birth-certificate of 'Austro-Fascism'. But, as yet, Dollfuss had no clear idea that a new child was born, much less how it was to grow up.   Indeed, the sentence he put at the top of the proclamation declaring that 'the Government does not wish to see the country permanently deprived of an effective Parliament serving the common good', probably represented a genuine intention of his, which dwindled into a desperate, ever-receding hope in the violent months ahead.   All that Dollfuss seemed resolved upon immediately was a strengthening of the Government's power at the expense of the hitherto dominant Parliament.   In this, the Second Austrian Republic was to follow his example, twelve years later, with the enthusiastic support of the Socialists as lucrative partners in the Coalition's benevolent despotism.

The police measures which Dollfuss announced went, of course, beyond such a mere shift-of-power emphasis. Austria never became anything resembling an all-out dictatorship. 'Austro-Fascism', as applied to the police state, was just as much a watered-down version of the original elixir as Austro-Marxism. But the road which Dollfuss now started out on led inevitably to the 'Detention Camps' of Wöllersdorf and the like, and to the persecution of Austrians, whether Nazi or Socialist, for their political beliefs. This was a melancholy innovation in the history of the First Republic ; its sole justification, for both Dollfuss and Schuschnigg, was that the country was virtually in a state of war.

And, quite apart from the utter confusion reigning within Austria at the time, these initial measures seemed called for by events outside her borders. On the 5th of March, the day after the collapse of the Vienna Parliament, Hitler had swept to power in the German elections — quite openly and legally, with the Centre Party and, to a lesser degree, the Social Democrats going down like ninepins before him at the polls. This was a far more solid threat than those Nazi gains in Austria's own municipal elections which had panicked the Right Wing a year before, for it was now clear that the Nazi puppet party inside Austria would henceforth have powerful and ruthless foreign arms to guide it. Furthermore, the failure of the Socialists to save the day in Germany seemed to show just as clearly that their Austro-Marxist colleagues could provide no safe electoral dam once the brown flood started to rise in Austria. The lesson of the Catholic Right-Wing collapse before Hitler had been even more melancholy. Indeed, it was beginning to look questionable whether any single party, recruited and organized on traditional parliamentary lines, could withstand the new demonic techniques of the Nazis. In short, these first steps which Dollfuss took towards authoritarian rule were prompted by a desire to save the state, not by any wish to destroy democracy itself. The contrast is worth noting since, to him, it eventually became a question of choosing between the two.

That 7th of March proclamation contained some other interesting points. There is, for example, the statement that a parliamentary crisis and a government crisis are two different things. The assumption could not even have been put forward in a properly functioning democracy and this again shows how far Parliament had moved from the life of the nation. Equally eloquent of the current state of Austrian politics was the fact that, to justify his radical intervention, Dollfuss had to go back to 1917 and cite the so-called Economic Empowering Law which the old Empire had passed in that year to see it through the last phase of the war. That Dollfuss went on to make this law turn violent constitutional somersaults for which it was never intended is a matter that few objective experts would nowadays dispute. But the really significant thing has been forgotten in the legal discussions about its 'validity': the mere fact that this obscure decree of a vanished Empire had to be used at all. For the Austrian Right Wing at least, the seal of authority in a national emergency was still the Habsburg crown — the last symbol in Vienna that had stood above party strife. The Socialists' failure in 1919 to provide their country with a legal and emotional substitute for the Emperor in the shape of a worthy President recoiled, under Dollfuss, on their own heads.

On the 15th of March the Third President, Dr. Straffner, tried to call the Assembly together again (making a virtue out of his folly by pointing out that the previous fatal session had never been closed). Though the Government despatched two hundred policemen to prevent the meeting, an opposition Rump Parliament did manage to convene for ten minutes in a last gesture of protest. In this, their first life-or-death crisis, the Socialists clung to formalities and shrank back from action.

They made no serious attempts to flout the ban on demonstrations ; there was no call for a general strike. The Parliament — Adler's Holy of Holies — had been defiled by policemen's boots, yet the party leadership merely shouted itself hoarse and kept its hands folded. The same docile passivity followed when Dollfuss went on in the next few weeks to ban their traditional May Day procession ; and even when he declared the Socialist paramilitary *Schutzbund* illegal. Considering the hot passions of the day, it was almost like enticement to rape.

Throughout the month of March, however, Dollfuss's mind about the future of Parliament was not finally made up. What seems to have decided him was an unrehearsed incident which happened at Villach on April 2, when he was speaking at a mass peasants' meeting. Like nearly all his speeches, it was a spontaneous affair, with only a few catchwords scribbled on an envelope to prompt him, and on the train journey down to Carinthia he had racked his brains in vain to find the right formula for the current crisis. The words came quickly enough when he stood up in front of thousands of those expectant peasant faces he knew and loved so well. He ran briefly over the events of the previous weeks and then heard himself saying : 'And so Austria's Parliament has destroyed itself ; and nobody can say when it will be allowed to take up its dubious activities again.' The sentence was barely out of his mouth when a roar of applause broke from his audience which took minutes to subside.

Dollfuss later told both his friends and his opponents that it was this sudden tumult of approval, and the emotions it released inside him, which decided his course. Had the reaction come from one of those easily moved city audiences with whom he was seldom completely *en rapport*, the effect might not have been profound. But, springing from a stolid mass of Austrian peasantry in which Dollfuss heard his own heart beat and saw his own soul reflected, this totally unexpected wave of enthusiasm seemed to him like a divine blessing. As he told the rising young Socialist leader Oskar Helmer, whom he met on the train travelling back to Vienna : 'In that moment, I felt the finger of God.'

With anyone who did not have Dollfuss's profound and simple piety, this would have been blasphemy or affectation. But, for the little Chancellor, it expressed a perfectly genuine impulse — a sense of mission to save his country from herself and her enemies, whatever happened to her institutions in the process.

The concept of the corporative state, as finally launched thirteen months later, was still embryonic. Dollfuss's immediate concern after that 'moment of truth' in Villach was what to do with the political parties if Parliament itself were to remain suspended. In the logic of things, they had to go too, for Parliament had been their be- and end-all. An even sterner logic was the emergency created by Hitler's arrival to power. Austria had immediately felt the newly confident Nazi grip tighten around her windpipe. Less than three months after his triumph at the German polls, Hitler had issued a declaration of guerrilla warfare on his old homeland — the famous 'Thousand Mark Blockade' which was designed to cut off the very important flow of German tourist traffic into Austria by making the issue of travel permits prohibitively expensive.

Hitler's dynamism could only be checked by echoing it. A national movement was needed to match the national crisis and this Dollfuss tried to provide with his 'Fatherland Front', which took shape in May 1933. A few weeks before, during an Easter visit to Rome, Dollfuss had received for his project the enthusiastic blessing of Mussolini, who saw in a revitalized Austria his best bulwark against the raw and rampageous dictator in the north. But the founding of the Fatherland Front was neither an Italian command, nor did it follow any Italian blueprint. The beginnings of 'Austro-Fascism' were not rooted in ideology but in desperate patriotism.

The plain fact which lay behind the launching of the new movement was that, in 1933, it was the political parties which divided Austria, bitterly and irreconcilably, whereas the nation's only hope was in unity. The claims later made by Left-Wing propagandists that a Coalition could have achieved this unity are contradicted by the melancholy record of Austrian politics from 1920 onwards. Something new had to be tried in the place of the merry-go-round, and Dollfuss tried the revolutionary idea of patriotism. As he said on a highly successful trip to London a month after the creation of the Fatherland Front, it was there 'for all who dedicated themselves to a free and independent Austria as the home for themselves and their children'.

Coming from a nation known hitherto in the West mainly for its pernicious bankruptcy and its latent pan-Germanism, this sort of talk was electrifying. The British were as enthusiastic as Mussolini had been ; Dollfuss was fêted in England as a lone David arming himself against the Nazi Goliath. He returned to Vienna with redoubled faith and energy.

This was reflected in the speeches he made the length and breadth of Austria during the following summer months. His new slogan 'Austria awake !' reverberated round the country like a battle-cry and the Austrians found themselves both startled by its strangeness and warmed by the vaguely comforting historical echoes it set up in their breasts. Indeed, it had last been heard in this particular setting in 1866. In Dollfuss, the Republic had refound its Imperial soul.

It also found, in the wiry little peasant leader, a sense of confidence and resolution which was just as unfamiliar. Despite the formidable odds, Dollfuss hit back at Hitler from the very start. At the end of June he went down to Innsbruck, which had suffered more than any other Austrian town under the German visa blockade, and put the issue of comfort versus conscience squarely to a mass open-air meeting. 'Are

we going to sell our freedom for a couple of tourist seasons ?'
he demanded. The roar of 'No' which came back at him
from forty thousand Tyrolean throats might have been
produced in the same town square by the peasants of
Andreas Hofer, brandishing their billhooks and scythes against
Napoleon.

During the spring and summer of 1933 Dollfuss thus succeeded in lighting the fire of patriotism among his countrymen, or rather, in rekindling the old flames of Austrian pride
in the new Republican vessel. It was one thing to start the
blaze, however, and quite another to keep it going in the
right direction. The Fatherland Front, which was intended
to rise above party strife, found itself, in turn, a victim of the
political and personal intrigues of the day. It bridged, with
difficulty, some of the gaps on the Right ; yet never succeeded
in spanning the more fundamental gulf between Right and
Left. It gave to the whole people — even those who remained outside its ranks — a new sense of purpose ; but the
organized national unity without which that sense of purpose
could never be put to work eluded its grasp. The Fatherland
Front came nearer than anything else in the First Republic
to being the voice of the country ; yet, in terms of membership,
it remained basically the old Christian-Socialist camp dressed
up in a new ornately-patriotic garb.

To some extent, this was its own fault. Though Dollfuss
had given the Front a flying start as a propaganda movement,
its origins as a political organization were pitiful. For weeks
after the Chancellor had issued his first nation-wide appeals
for membership no adequate apparatus existed to deal with
the response. It was like a publisher advertising a book which
he has neither had printed nor bound. Pledges of support
poured in from clubs, committees and individuals all over
Austria, most of them addressed to Dollfuss personally.
There was nothing for it but to let them accumulate in re-
proachful bundles at his office or his home, and the dust which

settled on them slowly snuffed out the enthusiasm of many of their authors.

Dollfuss's first choice as a Federal Leader for the Front, a journalist named Pankraz Krukenhauser, also proved unfortunate in the extreme. Krukenhauser soon revealed himself as a near-Nazi in ideology and as a dilettante at organization. A Vienna Headquarters of sorts was established, staffed with an odd mixture of radical pan-Germans and Jews. But the provinces were left to their own devices ; this meant in practice that they either marked time or, as with Rintelen in Styria, worked all out to torpedo the scheme. Matters improved somewhat when the Chancellor appointed his own personal secretary Kemptner in Krukenhauser's place ; but it was not until the Styrian leader Karl Maria Stepan was persuaded to take the reins of the Fatherland Front, nine weary months after its creation, that Dollfuss's enthusiasm at the top began to be matched by the same drive and dedication below.

Progress was slow and painful, and Stepan's setbacks reflected the calamitous divisions of the nation.[1] Most of the key figures whose support he sought apparently saw nothing illogical in acclaiming Dollfuss's rescue operation for the nation while opposing it in their own private domains. A vital question which now arose, for example, was the absorption of the *Heimwehr's* powerful paramilitary units into the new Front. The Austrian Regular Army of the day, still trimmed to meet the provisions of the St. Germain Treaty, was incapable, by itself, of dealing with any nation-wide security emergency. This had made Dollfuss dependent from his first weeks of office on the support of the Right-Wing private armies as a counterweight to the Socialist *Schutzbund*, which remained just as active when driven underground.

After the summer of 1933 a new element of violence appeared on the scene in the shape of Nazi bomb and sabotage outrages, to the mounting clamour of which the Austrian state finally subsided five years later. Thus, though the suicide of Parliament had rid Dollfuss of his reliance on the *Heimwehr* as a voting bloc, the deterioration of his domestic situation brought about immediately afterwards by the rise of the Nazis promptly drove him back into their arms as a security prop. He had gone some way towards breaking their dominance by creating the so-called 'Chancellor's Units', a loose union, perhaps 200,000 strong, of patriotic forces grouped around the Catholic youth organization of Schuschnigg. But the formidable ramshackle armed might of the *Heimwehr* remained, and both Fey and Starhemberg were well aware that these ragged and quarrelsome legions constituted their only passport to power in a non-parliamentary age. The latter received Stepan with appropriate princely politeness when he produced his proposals for a working union. But a first re-draft was called for, then a second, a third and a fourth, until the whole negotiations were overtaken by outside events ; at the pace at which those events were moving, this was not difficult.

Stepan even met with difficulties where they were least expected — in the peasant communities which looked on Dollfuss as their own. He succeeded in signing agreements between the Fatherland Front and the Agrarian Unions of Styria and Carinthia only to run up against the jealous obstruction of Reither, Dollfuss's one-time chief and protector, before co-operation on a nation-wide basis could be established. The Church, in this respect, was less helpful still : an attempt to found a unified national youth movement within the framework of the Front was blocked by persistent stonewalling from the Austrian bishops, who were reluctant to relinquish any of their paramount influence over the country's education.

These checks were aggravating enough in themselves ; but the crux of the new movement's future lay in the degree to which it could absorb the rank-and-file of the political parties. And here, as we have said, though the Fatherland Front commanded the support, or at least overcame the scruples, of most of the Right Wing, it never conquered the suspicions of the Left. To the Austro-Marxists, it remained essentially Clerico-Fascism dressed up in Red-White-Red camouflage instead of the conventional Black.

Even the Right Wing, represented basically by the Christian-Socials, only came over with certain mutterings and reservations. For some weeks after the creation of the Front, the Christian-Socials cherished the hope that they could somehow remain the 'party of state' in the strange new Austria which was emerging. Indeed, it was taking shape so haphazardly — out of chance conversations, casual inspirations or notes jotted on slips of paper in conferences and stuffed into the Chancellor's pocket — that the miracle seemed just possible. But, at their party conference held in Salzburg on May 5 and 6, 1933, the Christian-Socials — addicted to self-injury like all Austrian political groups — dealt their own fading prospects a heavy blow. Though he had never played an active role in the party's life, Dollfuss had been a member for many years, and there is good evidence that he now expected to be offered the Chairmanship, on the precedent of his great predecessor Seipel. Dollfuss was not the first and not the last to learn however that, in politics, it is one thing to rule the country and quite another to rule one's own party. The Christian-Social leadership, their consciences lightened by the fact that the Chancellor had not actually canvassed for the nomination, reappointed the veteran Vaugoin as Chairman.

It would be too much to say that this tactless decision settled by itself the future of the Christian-Socials ; in the long run, no parliamentary party could have hoped to survive as such in the new system. But if it did not determine their fate, it sealed it. For though tolerant and easy-going to a fault in his private life, Dollfuss the statesman had already developed an armour of fierce pride — pride in what he represented for Austria, not pride in what he was as a man. And, if this symbolic dignity was punctured, he could prove quick to take offence and slow to forgive. So it was now with his own party. After their May Conference, the Christian-Social leaders found themselves completely by-passed by Dollfuss and began to lose influence accordingly. Within six months he had succeeded in replacing Vaugoin as Chairman by his own nominee, the former Minister of Education, Czermak ; it was tantamount to appointing a public liquidator, for Czermak, not being a deputy, was anyway unable to initiate any parliamentary activity.

Shortly afterwards the party that had carried the Austrian Republic almost since its birth obligingly wound itself up in order that the new Constitution of May 1934 could be proclaimed on a completely party-less horizon. It followed Dollfuss almost to a man in his new course, carrying its resentments with it — the Christian trade union resentment centred around Kunschak and the democratic-parliamentarian resentment centred around men like Vaugoin and Ender. It was partly because of Dollfuss's overriding personality and partly because of the increasing precariousness of the nation's plight that his authority on basic issues remained unchallenged. Deprived of a party forum, the worried ones among his lieutenants concentrated their efforts in keeping the May Constitution as 'liberal' as possible and saving it from the ultra-Fascist clutches of the extreme *Heimwehr* group. In the last few months, several of Dollfuss's old party and 'C.V.' comrades dragged their feet in the forward march to authoritarianism. But not one of them seems to have dreamed of running behind his back to stab him. The back was too straight and small, and the load it was carrying too heavy.

The creation of the 'Fatherland Front' and the gradual emergence of the corporative state also started a new and decisive chapter in Dollfuss's relations with the Socialists, that 'pre-February' phase between the end of Parliament in March 1933 and the outbreak of the Civil War eleven months later. It was a period during which Dollfuss collected more and more of the trump cards. The run of play was inexorably in his favour, for, deprived of their beloved and familiar parliamentary platform, his Social Democrat opponents were as stranded as a troop of cavalrymen without their horses. And as their morale sank lower and lower their mood became, not militant with desperation, but passive with despair. This new tactical relationship between the Right Wing and the Left Wing after March 1933 must constantly be borne in mind in apportioning any personal guilt for their failure to come together. Dollfuss and Bauer were not merely black and red crusaders fighting for opposed ideologies. They were also politicians engaged, like all politicians, in a struggle for power. The suicide of Parliament had turned the basic conditions of that struggle in the Chancellor's favour : the Socialists could no longer harm him by votes and, despite repeated provocations, they showed themselves unwilling or unable to harm him by using their extra-parliamentary weapons of demonstrations and strikes. It was they, in short, who had slipped from the stirrups and were striving at all costs to regain a foothold ; Dollfuss could afford to look down on their efforts from the saddle with a certain detachment. The Socialists were forced into taking the initiative during these months and it is no reproach to them as politicians to say that it was their own power, as well as Austria's democracy, they were trying to save.

The negotiations which followed were a confusing tangle of contacts private and public, secret and open, serious and frivolous, conducted at all levels. Both sides based what hopes they had less on a formal reconciliation of policies than on informal appeals to the consciences of old friends as, for example, when Dollfuss held fruitless talks with the Socialist agricultural workers' leader, Schneeberger. For the most part, however, both he and Bauer remained in the background, Dollfuss deliberately delegating too little authority and Bauer getting so out-of-date that he eventually had to be by-passed.

Civil War, February 1934 — 'Guns against workers'. Austrian Army howitzers firing on the massive Karl-Marx-Hof tenements in an attempt to cut
short the fighting

Civil War, February 1934 — Austrian troops in action against the Goethehof,
another workers' stronghold in the battle

After the bloodshed — Mass funeral cortège of the Government victims of the February 1934 Ci
War, forming up outside the Vienna Town Hall. To the rear, Vienna's famous 'Burgtheater'

After the bloodshed — Dollfuss at a parade of Austrian Army soldiers wounded in the February 19
Civil War. He is greeting Prince Hartenstein-Schönburg, his Minister of War

The Chancellor's spokesmen in these discussions were men like Strobl, Czermak, Schmitz and Karwinsky, all of them chosen more for the personal trust he had in them than for the posts they held. On the Socialist side, the two most tireless truce-seekers were the moderate leader Karl Renner and a bright young Trade Union functionary from Lower Austria, Oskar Helmer.

As things turned out, they were always a jump behind. For no sooner had they produced proposals designed to fit into the existing political situation than Dollfuss moved further down the authoritarian road and they had to chase after him with new suggestions. Thus, in the early summer of 1933, the Socialists offered to recall Parliament for a single session to give that institution a Christian burial and to make a joint demonstration of solidarity before the surging Nazi menace. Having put the records straight, the Assembly would then dissolve indefinitely ; a 24-man Main Committee would function in its name, in which the Socialists conceded the majority, and which would only be summoned in times of crisis. Given the Socialist voting strength in the last Parliament, it was a magnanimous offer. But, given their bargaining strength at the time the offer was made, it was less impressive. The vision of an Austrian medievalist society purged of Parliaments and parties was already taking shape in Dollfuss's mind ; Mussolini, whom he saw again that August, only spurred him on — more for the purge than for the medievalism.

The outcome was expressed in his famous 'Trabrennplatz Speech' in Vienna on the 11th of September, 1933, in which the new ideology of the 'Fatherland Front' and the outlines of the emergent corporative state were fully set out for the first time. We will return to that speech later, when dealing with Dollfuss's political *credo* as a whole. All that need be recorded here is the public and irrevocable death-blow it dealt at the old-type Parliament, and therefore at all Socialist attempts to revive their own fortunes with that Parliament.

Having referred to the 'godless dictatorship of Marxism' which had threatened Austria in 1918, Dollfuss went on :

'I do not want to list in detail all the sins committed in our Parliament and so-called democracy. Those who regret the turn which events have now taken should examine the faults they have committed and then they will understand the developments of our time. Parliament has cut itself out ; it has gone to ruin on its own demagogy and formalism. And this Parliament — such a representation and such a leadership of the people — will never and ought never to come back again.'

This cast the die for Austria, and for the Socialists. New tactics were needed if they were to make their influence felt again. On the 15th of October they held a party conference to discuss the position. It was the last to be held in Austria and we now know that it was Dollfuss, against the opposition of Fey, who enabled it be to convened. 'Radical' voices were raised who clamoured for a show-down by force. But Otto Bauer, that lion in words and lamb in action, was among those who found yet another compromise. It was decided not to take up the challenge which Dollfuss had just thrown out, but four conditions were laid down which were supposed automatically to drive the Socialists to the barricades in the future. These were the dissolution of the party itself ; the imposition of a new constitution ; the undermining of the independent Socialist-run Trades Unions ; and the destruction of 'Red Vienna' by such measures as appointing a Government Commissar for the capital.

This was the 1927 formula all over again — a flight from action into theories and balm for the revolutionary conscience in the shape of threats for the future. The woeful state of the Socialists' morale can be judged from the fact that every single step listed as a *casus belli* by them in October 1933 was in fact taken by Dollfuss in whole or in part during the next eight months without any 'automatic battle' breaking out. As it happened, the only fighting which did flare up was set off by an accidental spark which the Left-Wing leadership did their best to extinguish.

This record of passivity would be admirable if it reflected the deliberate self-control of strong men, putting the cause of law and order above their righteous wrath. But it is difficult to resist the conclusion that what it really represented was not so much cool heads as cold feet. The most flattering interpretation which can be put on the behaviour of the Socialist leadership when faced with these repeated challenges is that they secretly knew the appeal for mass action would never be followed. Indeed, one of their leaders, Julius Deutsch, has actually stated this in private.[2] But, in that case, the constant talk of strikes and 'strong arm' methods which these leaders indulged in at the time only amounted to a deception of their own followers.

At all events, it is likely that some of the venom injected into the Dollfuss legend came from the bitterness of the losers who knew only too well why they had lost; and some, at least, of the personal hate which the Austro-Marxists cherished for Dollfuss may have derived from the simple fact that he was the one thing most of them longed to be but never could be — a man of action.

By shrinking back from even a token trial of strength in the autumn of 1933 — a one-hour lightning strike, for example, to flex their muscles, tone up their morale and improve their organization — the Socialists reduced their bargaining power still further. This became clear in the tangle of negotiations during the next few months by which the Left Wing sought somehow to achieve an honourable foothold within the new corporative state. After discussions with E. K. Winter and his circle, Renner produced a new compromise plan in which Parliament would formally hand over full powers to the Government for an emergency period of five years; this was debated at length between Renner and President Miklas without any concrete result. A more fruitful co-operation did start up, however, at the practical working level in the Lower Austrian Provincial Assembly, where Helmer and Reither made common cause against the local Nazi deputies.

On the 12th of December, 1933, Dollfuss, who had kept in contact with all these movements, took the initiative himself. He sent Czermak as his secret emissary to Renner, who came out with yet another compromise proposal designed to save both Parliament's face and the Government's power. According to this variant, Austria was to be ruled by a Legislative Council of State in which the Christian-Socials would be assured of a majority by delegations from the Provincial Diets, where their lead had always been secure. Judged by the verdict of the last polls held in Austria, this was another magnanimous offer ; and had the Socialists come out with it nine months before in the early spring, when Dollfuss was still wondering how to rule without Parliament, it might have had a real chance of acceptance. But in December 1933 it no longer reflected the political realities of the time. Dollfuss was already busy creating an Austria without parties and had no longer time for ingenious devices to camouflage old parliamentary balances by turning minorities into majorities. Czermak has described how the little Chancellor remained plunged in thought for a minute or two after Renner's proposals had been brought back to him. Then he declared with a sigh : 'It's just not possible to give Austrian politics that sort of twist any more. It's too late.' [3]

'Too late.' Yet still the feelers went out, partly directed by the troubled leaders themselves, partly inspired by a feverish activity of their own. New Year's Eve, for example, saw an unusual gathering convened in the Ministry for Social Affairs to try and solve the problem of fitting the Trade Unions into the new system. Dollfuss was represented by Schmitz, another of his personal cronies, and the Socialists by a strong team of Trade Union leaders under Böhm. The dis-

cussions stretched on well into the first morning of that
fateful 1934 and, at first, it began to look as though here, as in
the Lower Austrian Diet, a practical agreement free from
party politics could be reached.

The Government offered the Socialist-dominated Trade
Unions one-third of the seats in the new Labour Administration
Commission and the presidency of some of the key Chambers,
including, above all, Vienna. In view of the seepage of
membership from the Left-Wing to the Right-Wing Trades
Unions which had been going on throughout the year, this
arrangement was not unreasonable and the Socialist negotiators
seemed prepared to accept it. But when an agreement was
already in sight, their party leadership, afraid that their colleagues were trading away too much power and principle,
stepped in from outside to veto it. The conference broke up
in a cloud of stale cigar smoke and recrimination and no group
so promising ever met again.

Still the contacts fluttered on. On the 18th of January
Dollfuss abandoned the devious secret channels he had been
following and came out with a public appeal to the 'honest
Socialist leadership' for co-operation. 'The workers must
seriously consider', he said, 'whether it is not also their duty
to co-operate, out of inner conviction, with the new system.
Once this duty is recognized by the masses, then I hope that
the immediate future will bring quite new possibilities of
incorporating even those who have hitherto stood aside within
the great front of the defenders of Austria's independence.'
This appeal was addressed directly to the moderate Socialist
leaders over the heads of those predominantly Jewish radicals
with whom they were now in more or less open conflict.
The Socialist Party executive summoned a meeting to consider
the Chancellor's offer, only to cancel it at the last minute in
protest against a circulation ban which the Government had
imposed on their party organ *Arbeiter Zeitung*. An ill-timed
repressive move on the Right Wing and an equally ill-timed

fit of pique on the Left Wing again conspired to keep the two apart.

It is not too much to speak of a veritable Dollfuss peace offensive on the domestic front in those first few weeks of 1934. One reason was grimly practical. His State Secretary for Public Security, Baron Erwin Karwinsky, had warned him with the utmost emphasis that the meagre military and police forces at the Government's disposal were quite incapable of fighting an internal war on two fronts, against both Nazis and Marxists. A truce had to be made with one opponent, and common sense dictated that this should be with the weaker one, who was already on the defensive.[4] Moreover, Dollfuss did not need his peasant intuition to realize that the Socialist camp was going through a severe crisis ; all the political sparrows of Vienna were chirping it from the housetops. The leadership was divided against itself not only on the issue of integration within the new corporative state but on the whole question of party discipline and policy. The younger generation of Socialist leaders was not taking over smoothly, like Dollfuss and Schuschnigg on the Right Wing, from their forerunners ; and on the Left Wing, the Grand Old Men of the party refused to help matters by dying, like Seipel, at the appropriate moment. To this clash of generations were added regional and racial resentments. A bid had already been made in Carinthia, for example, to launch an 'Alpine Socialist Movement' which would be free from the Jewish cosmopolitan dominance of the Vienna Headquarters. By the autumn of 1933 the tensions had grown so severe that Otto Bauer even began to talk of resigning in favour of the 'pragmatist' Socialist group in Lower Austria. This was headed by Pius Schneeberger, an old comrade of Dollfuss from his agrarian reformer days, and much might have been built on this personal link. But, right down to the Civil War, Bauer hung on ; and his pessimistic genius and his outmoded doctrines hung on with him. Deutsch later explained Bauer's retention at this crucial point with these words : 'There seemed no point in him resigning. What would Dollfuss have given us in return ?' [5]   Party before country once again.

The result of all these doubts and tensions was to increase even further the gap between leadership and following on the Left. The events of February 1933 were to show how far this breach yawned. For Dollfuss at the turn of the year it was elementary party tactics to exploit it. Accordingly, in January, he backed up his public appeal for an armistice by still two more secret feelers, both set in motion on his initiative. In the first place he sent Friedrich Funder, the generally respected Christian Socialist journalist and municipal councillor, to sound out armistice possibilities with the Socialist Mayor of Vienna, Seitz. These contacts lasted until January 25. They got to the stage where the Socialist leadership had actually appointed an official negotiator when the police unearthed a large *Schutzbund* explosives dump in the workers suburb of Simmering, together with plans which suggested that organized violence was in the offing.

This seems to have prompted Dollfuss to break off this particular feeler with the Vienna leadership. But, showing more elasticity than logic, he promptly stretched out another to the moderate Socialist deputies of the Lower Austrian Diet, where a working partnership of sorts already existed. His secret envoy on this occasion was Karwinsky, and the Socialist spokesman was the provincial deputy Schneidmadl. As with the Funder-Seitz talks, this contact was also based on a personal acquaintanceship and mutual respect between the two men concerned. Dollfuss authorized Karwinsky to offer the Socialists a guaranteed independence for their Trades Unions within the 'Fatherland Front' if they would co-operate with the movement and renounce class warfare. However reasonable this sounds today, to the Austro-Marxists of the time it was like asking a bishop to renounce his mitre. Schneidmadl expressed himself personally very willing to discuss the proposal. But, on the last day of January, he brought back to Karwinsky a flat refusal to negotiate from the Vienna leadership.[6] This only strengthened the view, held by Dollfuss and most of his advisers, that the Left Wing, for all its convulsions, was still in the grip of the Radicals ; moreover, the unearthing of new illegal arms dumps near the capital suggested that this Bauer-Deutsch group were now resolved on, or resigned to, an early show-down by force. With what reluctance, genuine but hardly flattering, the Socialist leadership was bracing itself for this test can be judged from what has been said so far. This reluctance was probably strengthened by something else that Karwinsky told Schneidmadl 'for onward transmission' in those last days of January. He warned against any *Schutz-bund* action as had been envisaged by the Socialists under the four emergency points of their October Conference ; any deliberate *putsch* attempt, he declared, would find the Government ready. This warning was to take effect a fortnight later. Ironically enough, the *putsch* was hardly deliberate, while the Government was taken completely by surprise.

Only five days before the Civil War broke like a thunderclap over Austria, this morbid game of truce-making, half pretence and half reality, went on. On February 7, 1934, Oskar Helmer called at the home of Ludwig Strobl, a school comrade and close friend of Dollfuss's, and handed over one of the most detailed and far-reaching Socialist compromise solutions yet devised for transmission to the Chancellor. Like most of the earlier blueprints, this was also largely the work of Renner, who was now struggling on without the approval and partly without the knowledge of Bauer. Unlike the other drafts, this particular document has somehow survived intact from all the house-searches of the Gestapo and the bonfires of the Second World War.[7] Despite its formalism, this 21-page typewritten peace offer, with its last-minute pencilled annotations, breathes the urgency and the agony of the hour.

It sets out the following basic condition for an armistice (the word *Waffenstillstand* is used) : 'The creation of a Christian Social minority Government, to include the *Landbund* but to exclude the *Heimwehr*. The Ministries of War, Interior, Security, and Justice to be placed in reliable democratic hands. This sort of Government, and only this sort, will be tolerated.' Suggestions then follow for protecting Socialist interests in the corporative state by devices such as full and independent Trades Union representation ; and yet another ceremonial rigmarole is proposed whereby Parliament should revive itself for one session in order to kill itself legally.

But quite a new element is the position accorded to the Federal President under the 'State Emergency Law' (*Staatsnotstandsgesetz*) which this may-fly Parliament was to pass. Under Article 2 of the proposed law, Parliament handed over to the President its legislative powers, to be exercised by him jointly with a Council of State, roughly representing the Parliamentary Main Committee. All laws passed during the emergency period were normally to be countersigned by the Government but, in a special emergency within the general emergency, the President could even issue decrees on his own authority, and collect the approval of the Council of State later on. His permanent and undisputed powers were to include the summoning and dissolving of Parliament, the nomination and dismissal of the Chancellor and his Ministers, and the calling of elections. In addition to all this, however, the Socialist draft proposed that the President 'can, at any time, personally assume the chairmanship of the Government' and appoint his own observer with the rank of Minister to attend all sessions of the Cabinet. These very substantial powers were to be handed over to the Head of State for a period of two years, with provision for three-monthly extensions if agreed by a two-thirds majority of the State Council.

The pragmatic Socialist leaders who put forward these

proposals had in fact returned — like Dollfuss with his exploitation of the 1917 decree — to the paternal authority of the Empire. In the case of the Socialists, there was a certain paradox in this, for they were consciously seeking salvation in a tradition they had burned at the Marxist stake. The preamble to their draft law shows them still struggling bravely to reconcile democratic forms with the harsh needs of the time. Indeed, there is scarcely a word in this dignified introduction which men of goodwill on either side could have grumbled at. It accepts the principle that 'in case of internal or external peril, unity and speed are the prime requirements in all decisions and actions of the state' and that therefore powers and duties must be handed over in an emergency to organs 'which will deliberate briefly, decide quickly and act together'. But the proviso is made that such a special transfer of power cannot be allowed 'to eliminate the guarantees of the constitution ; blur the boundaries between legislation and executive, nor lead to the creation of an irresponsible and uncontrolled authority'. Though admirable in theory, this was, of course, somewhat unrealistic in practice. What it amounted to was a last attempt to have your democratic cake and, at the same time, to eat it.

The main interest of this document is the insight it gives into the Socialist thinking of the day. It proves that at least the moderate wing of the party had fully accepted both the framework of Dollfuss's corporative state and the need for a strong centralized authority to see the country through the Nazi crisis. This and earlier proposals of Renner's demonstrate above all that these Left-Wing pragmatists were now under no illusions about the role of the old-style Parliament in this crisis. The emphasis is on the Executive, not on the Legislature ; on discipline, not on liberty ; on acting first and talking afterwards. These are points to bear in mind when considering the abuse which the Left Wing as a whole soon began to pour on Dollfuss's head.

It is unlikely that the proposals of February 7 would have led to very much. On the Left Wing they would have been resisted by the 'dogmatists' grouped around Bauer, Deutsch, Austerlitz, Danneberg and Eisler. On the Right Wing, quite apart from the inevitable *Heimwehr* obstruction, Dollfuss himself would have been reluctant to hand over the control of his authoritarian experiment lock, stock and barrel to President Miklas. As it was, the document never came up for serious discussion ; before it could be seriously discussed, the whole powder-keg of Austrian politics blew up before a startled Europe. At 7 A.M. on the morning of the 12th of February, two policemen of a force detailed to search the Socialist *Schutzbund* headquarters in Linz for hidden arms were shot down by the 'garrison', and Austria's four-day Civil War began.

CHAPTER FIVE

The Reckoning

TO try and place the blame for the brief but bloody tragedy of February 1934 on the shoulders of one single party (let alone one single man) would not only be patently unfair ; it would also be utter historical nonsense. That some of the rival Austrian apologists involved refused to accept this — even in the years of war-time emigration or occupation, and even in one or two crass cases today — is another dreadful testimony to the power which political passions have to distort the human mind.

The plain truth which emerges from all the foregoing is that the great mass of moderate men in both camps genuinely recoiled from the thought of bloodshed and earnestly if in-effectively sought to avoid it. Dollfuss's personal and political record right down to that 12th of February place him clearly in this category. As for the extremists, those on the Left Wing were also afraid of violence, with one famous and fatal local exception in Linz whom we shall meet in a moment. It was only on the Right Wing that radicals like Major Fey were to be found who were capable of welcoming and actually provoking an armed show-down ; not because they were necessarily worse in character than their opposite numbers on the Left but rather because they were different in tempera-ment. Allowing that the hotheads on both sides really believed themselves dedicated to a crusade, the basic difference was of method. The Austro-Marxists clung to words which made violence inevitable. The Austro-Fascists preferred vio-lence which made words unnecessary. Fey was a soldier who had drifted into politics through his own ambition and his almost insane hatred of Marxism ; all in all, a naturally disruptive element. Bauer was once summed up by his great teacher Lenin as 'an educated idiot' — an equally dangerous type to have in politics, if the master's verdict on the pupil were true.

As might be expected from this contradiction between intention and effect, the weeks which preceded the February tragedy slithered by with an odd sense of unreality. The political air was heavy and electrified and, in both camps, there seems to have been an uneasy foreboding of the storm about to break. Shortly before it broke, Karl Renner said to a group of fellow-passengers he had met on a train journey from Belgrade to Vienna : 'We Socialists cannot hold Bauer back and the Right Wing cannot hold Fey back. Mark my words, there will be a blood bath. It just has to happen.'[1] And, within the Social Democrat party, the Carinthian reform group made their last-minute efforts to form a common all-party front against the Nazis (a sort of Dollfuss movement in obverse), while Czech Social Democrats, alarmed by the general deterioration of the position, arrived in Vienna to urge their Austrian colleagues into an armistice.

A similar prophetic nervousness seized the Right Wing. Dollfuss, giving his agreement to one of those last futile truce manœuvres, was prompted, for no particular reason, to add the words : 'Quickly, quickly!' in the margin of the letter. Leopold Kunschak, speaking on the 9th of February in the Vienna Town Council on the Nazi peril, was an even more expressive Cassandra : 'May God grant', he cried 'that the rifts which divide the spirit and the soul of our people and its rulers may soon be removed, before the nation and the country stand before open graves and weep.'

His audience heard these terrible words, moved but somehow immovable. In that, they were a microcosm of all Austria. It was as though the whole nation sat mesmerized before that infernal machine of party strife they had all helped to construct over the past fifteen years, listening to it tick away towards the explosion they could now no longer prevent.

Yet, however inevitable a detonation may be, there is always something or someone who sets it off. In the case of the February fighting, two pairs of hands can be singled out as mainly responsible for lighting the actual fuse. One pair belonged to a radical Austro-Fascist, the Vienna *Heimwehr* leader and Minister for Security, Emil Fey ; the other to an equally fanatical and militant Austro-Marxist, the Commander of the Linz *Schutzbund*, Richard Bernaschek. On February 12 Fey and his group dragged a worried Dollfuss into battle with them, while Bernaschek forced an even more unwilling Bauer to the barricades. The dénouement thus has a certain poetic justice ; retrospectively, it is also comment enough on the attempts of the rival camps to shift the blame entirely onto their opponents' shoulders.

It is interesting to note, by the way, that both these men of violence, themselves came to a violent end. Fey committed suicide in his Vienna flat, his entire family with him, less than a week after the *Anschluss* of 1938. Bernaschek's story was even more melancholy. He first went to Germany, having been successfully, if temporarily, courted by the Nazis — like several of his Austrian Socialist colleagues. From there he went on to Moscow where he tried his hand as a Communist — seeking everywhere, it seems, that dynamism he looked for in vain in Austro-Marxism. He eventually returned to Austria via Czechoslovakia, was imprisoned by the Nazis as a political suspect after the July 1944 revolt, and died of mal-treatment in a concentration camp.

The ominous role which Fey played in the weeks im-mediately before the Civil War was to intensify police pressure against both the Socialist Party organization and the now illegal *Schutzbund* to such a degree that an early show-down became unavoidable. As the Government Minister responsible, his searches for hidden Socialist arms were, of course, technically and politically justified ; the size of the dumps discovered, such as that miniature arsenal unearthed at Schwechat in January proved, moreover, that the ferocious Major was not just chasing will-o'-the-wisps. These activities certainly had the approval and authority of Dollfuss who, from the first, had hoped to use Fey's fists to batter down the paramilitary might of the Socialists. They were also, in a glum sort of way, understandable to the victims, for arms-hunting in Austria had long since become an accepted 'Cowboys and Indians' routine.

But Fey went far beyond his ministerial responsibilities when he also tried, in his capacity as a *Heimwehr* leader, to smash the last legal Socialist strongholds in the Provincial Governments. On the 2nd of February, after staging threatening march-pasts in the streets of Innsbruck, the *Heimwehr* succeeded in frightening the Governor of Tyrol into accepting additional nominees of theirs into the administration. On the 6th and 7th of February the *Heimwehr* tried, though in vain, to repeat their blackmail in the provincial capitals of Linz and Graz, and on the 9th the key province of Lower Austria found itself faced with similar *Heimwehr* demands. This produced further anxious consultations between local Socialists like Helmer and the Provincial Governor Reither, who declared himself unable to help on the grounds that his onetime subordinate Dollfuss was now 'completely in the hands of the Fey-Starhemberg people'. That the Chancellor was following these *Heimwehr* antics in the provinces with helpless concern was likely enough — helpless because he needed the same *Heimwehr* for the anti-*Schutzbund* action, and concern because any political strengthening of the *Heimwehr*'s position only lessened his own chances of shaking them off as allies once they had cleaned up this vital paramilitary front for him. Moreover, even at this stage, he was under no illusions about Fey's ambitions to replace him.

What the Socialists dreaded above all was that the *Heimwehr*, with these provincial skirmishes, were building up for a *coup* against 'Red Vienna' itself — their pride and their citadel. Both Fey and Starhemberg had publicly threatened more than once to 'chase the Marxists out of the Town Hall', and now, via Innsbruck, Linz and Graz, the threat seemed to be racing towards them. Sure enough, on the 10th of February, Fey, this time again in his capacity as Minister, struck his first blow in the capital. On the strength of a special ordinance passed on the 26th of January, the Socialist Burgomaster of Vienna was stripped of all his powers in the field of public security, which were transferred with immediate effect to the Police President. For the Government, this merely represented the extension to the capital of the centralized security system set up all over Austria to meet subversive threats and, above all, the Nazi menace.

But, for the Socialists, any frontal attack on the prerogatives of the Town Hall was tantamount to a declaration of war; indeed, the Government's action on February 10 went part-way towards violating one of those four sacred principles which the party leadership had sworn to defend with their lives only five months earlier. From this moment onwards, therefore, the Austro-Marxists were virtually committed to strike back without compunction, if they wished to honour their own revolutionary promises. Yet, beyond a formal protest by Burgomaster Seitz, the Socialist camp in Vienna seemed prepared to swallow even this affront until, 48 hours later, their colleagues in Linz reminded them of their duty.

Before considering the Civil War itself, it remains to be asked why Fey and the other *Heimwehr* leaders decided on such a drastic and fateful tightening of the screws in the second half of January, and what was the personal role of Dollfuss himself in all this. One reason is almost certainly to be found in the visit which Signor Suvich, the Italian Under-Secretary

Left : The Nazi *putsch* attempt, July 25, 1934 : a wounded Austrian is helped out of a building which was under siege by the rebels

Below : The Nazi *putsch* of July 25, 1934 : the battle for the Vienna RAVAG transmitter : Austrian troops and police prepare to clear the radio building of Nazi rebels

The search for an anchor to help Austria ride out the Nazi storm. Dollfuss, in a rather frayed 'best coat', is met at Rome by a jovial Mussolini when he arrived in March 1934 to conclude an assistance pact

The treaty which three leaders hoped would keep Hitler out of the Danube Basin. Mussolini signing the so-called 'Rome Protocols' of March 17, 1934. Second from right Dollfuss watches him

of State for Foreign Affairs, paid to Vienna between January
18-20. Suvich came as Mussolini's envoy, and the main purpose of his trip was to speed up the creation of that authoritarian non-party regime in Austria which Dollfuss had already
outlined to the Duce the previous year. Both men were clear
that this inevitably involved the disappearance of the Austrian
Socialist Party, as of all other parties ; but the little Austrian
Chancellor and his powerful Italian protector differed funda-
mentally over the means. Dollfuss still hoped to split the
Socialists apart into their radical and moderate components,
to isolate the former and absorb the latter peacefully into his
Fatherland Front. Mussolini pressed for an immediate liquida-
tion by force of the whole Austro-Marxist complex, and in
this he was supported to the hilt by the *Heimwehr*, with
whose leaders he stood in close contact. That the *Heimwehr*
received either active encouragement or direct instructions
from Suvich to provoke the Socialists into revolt and suicide
seemed beyond doubt to most foreign observers at the time.
According to the report on the visit made by the German
Minister in Vienna, Dr. Rieth, to Berlin, for example, Suvich
even appears to have secretly encouraged Fey to regard himself, with Rome's blessing, as the future Chancellor of Austria.[2]

But what seems equally clear is that, despite the pressure
which Suvich exerted on him, Dollfuss still refused to abandon
his hopes and efforts for a peaceful penetration of the Austro-
Marxist camp. Allegations that he personally capitulated to
any Italian ultimatum at the time simply ignore the calendar
as well as his own character. Suvich, as we have seen, was in
the Austrian capital from January 18 to January 20. It was
immediately *after* his arrival that Dollfuss issued his public
appeal to the 'honest workers' for co-operation. It was
several days *after* Suvich's departure that Dollfuss authorized
the last of the Funder-Seitz contacts referred to above, and
initiated the first of the Karwinsky-Schneidmadl talks. Whatever lead from Rome the *Heimwehr* may have followed in

the three weeks which preceded the Austrian Civil War, it is evident that Dollfuss still tried to stick during that same critical period to his old tactics of the multiple approach and the instinctive, unrehearsed decision.

The record of events on that 12th of February is also sufficient, without special pleading, to exonerate Dollfuss from having planned, or even heard about, any critical nation-wide action for the day. When the fighting in Linz broke out, the Chancellor and nearly all the members of his Government were kneeling in St. Stephen's Cathedral in Vienna at a festive service held to commemorate the coronation day of the Pope. Only Karwinsky, who had received the first police reports from Linz, stayed in his office, as State Secretary for Security, to watch a situation which was obviously ugly but which seemed, equally obviously, only local. Not only the Chancellor, but all the other key figures of his Cabinet, such as the War Minister Prince Schönburg-Hartenstein, are known to have had a normal list of engagements for the day,[3] and filed out of the Cathedral fully expecting to fulfil them. It was not until all the lights in their offices failed and all the electric street clocks of Vienna stopped at 11.46 A.M. that even the Government Ministers realized something very strange was afoot and began telephoning each other for explanations. This is not the way men behave who have just launched a desperate action on which their own future as well as the future of their country depends.

There remains — standing, as always, outside the general picture — the enigmatic figure of Fey himself. Only the previous day, in an improvised speech at a monument for the war dead at Langenzersdorf, he had shouted : 'Tomorrow we will get to work and we will make a proper job of it for our Fatherland.' Fey spoke specifically in the name of his own *Heimwehr* to an audience composed mostly of *Heimwehr* followers, to whom he promised the country's 'praise and recognition'. But in one sentence he directly implicated the

Head of Government : 'I can set your minds at rest on one point — the discussions of the past two days have given us the assurance that Chancellor Dr. Dollfuss is our man.'

What precisely Fey meant by that remark still remains a mystery. That the *Heimwehr* sought the mantle of Dollfuss's authority for their blackmail demonstrations in the provinces is likely. That Dollfuss welcomed certain anti-Marxist results from those demonstrations without being happy about the methods employed is equally likely. It has been presumed by those close to him at the time that the Chancellor did not forbid the action (which he was virtually powerless to do) but confined himself to urging on the *Heimwehr* the need to avoid violence.[4] For an orator like Major Fey, whose impromptu week-end speeches were the constant terror of his moderate Cabinet colleagues, this was encouragement enough, especially when speaking in an emotional military setting before his own uniformed comrades. At all events, it has not been possible to trace any actual meeting between Fey and Dollfuss, as Fey hinted, during that last week-end of peace. It is known from the diaries kept by their secretaries that no formal appointment was arranged, and none of Dollfuss's friends or colleagues has any recollection of an informal meeting.

One thing must be noted in the context of Fey's notorious speech : its background was the current *Heimwehr* campaign against the provincial administrations, and the threats for the morrow may well have referred to the extension of this action. That not even Fey was prepared for his 'proper job' to develop into a nation-wide armed *coup* and counter-*coup* is shown by the lack of any adequate preparations ordered by himself, both as leader of the Vienna *Heimwehr* and as head of the Government's security apparatus. Even, for that matter, as a private citizen. Early on the morning of the 12th of February Fey's wife was with Baroness Karwinsky in an outer district of the capital, serving at a soup kitchen for poor people. Fey's first order to his adjutant, Major Wrabel, was to bring the ladies to safety.[5] On the other hand, it can fairly be assumed that, without fixing a date, Fey and most of the radical *Heimwehr* leadership were now resolved to crush the Socialist Party and paramilitary organization piece by piece into the ground in the weeks ahead, and were quite prepared to resort to violence if need be.

We must now turn to the man on the other side whose fanatical courage was to make that violence inevitable. Richard Bernaschek, the Socialist *Schutzbund* commander in Upper Austria, was a militant local leader who had long chafed, like many of his type, under the passivity and doctrinal hair-splitting of the party headquarters in Vienna. He seems to have been a confused, impulsive and rather simple man, not ambitious but passionately idealistic — the soul of Marx's unbending proletariat for whom all compromise was capitulation. He had clearly got wind, a day or two in advance, of Government plans to intensify their security campaign in the Linz area and he had made up his own mind to declare war on them single-handed. On the 11th of February, *before* he had even read about or heard of Fey's threatening speech in Langenzersdorf, Bernaschek sat down and wrote the following letter to Bauer and Deutsch :

'If tomorrow, Monday, arms searches are started in an Upper Austrian town or if party cell leaders or *Schutzbund* officers should be arrested, then resistance will be made by force, and from this resistance we will go over into the attack. This decision, and its implementation, are unalterable.

'We expect that, once our telephone message has been received in Vienna saying that arms searches and arrests have been carried out, you Viennese workers and indeed the whole working population will give the signal to hit out. We shall not go back. I have not told the local party committee here of our decision. If the Vienna workers leave us in the lurch, then scorn and shame upon them.'

A slip allegedly enclosed with the letter contained the still more dramatic and compromising message : 'Provoke arms searches!' But it is only fair to add that the existence of this slip has been denied by Socialist leaders of the time [6] and that its exact significance remains as obscure as some of the remarks Fey was making to the rival camp that same day 100 miles away.

This heroic call to arms was delivered by courier that same night to the leadership in Vienna, whose consternation can be imagined. At last a true son of Marx had appeared, waving his red banner among their coffee tables. Their simple, tough comrade in Linz had confronted this demoralized cosmopolitan leadership with the one thing they secretly dreaded even more than defeat — the need for a decision.

Sure enough, Bernaschek's telephone call came through early the following morning, when the bullets had started to whistle around the Hotel 'Ship'. The first reaction of Bauer at the Vienna Headquarters was to localize the Linz action and to avoid a general trial of strength. A code telegram was accordingly despatched to Bernaschek : 'Anna is ill, don't undertake anything'. But, ill or not, Anna, in the guise of the party leadership, was dragged bodily into the fray by her indomitable Hotspur in the provinces.

Still Bauer and Deutsch tried to hold back the great trial of strength, partly because they hoped for a serious split in Dollfuss's camp over the latest *Heimwehr* action, partly because they feared defeat in any major military clash. However, by mid-morning it was clear that the explosion in Linz could no longer be dampened down. In the mounting crisis, the sense of Socialist solidarity (which many people, Dollfuss included, made the mistake of under-estimating) triumphed over pessimism and caution in the leadership. Bernaschek's biting words had gone home. The call for a general strike was issued, and the long-prepared plans by which, in an emergency, the *Schutzbund* was to depose the 'bourgeois dictatorship' by force were put into action.

That a regular Socialist revolt against what was technically the legal Government of the day was launched shortly before midday on the 12th of February is as plain as the fact that this same revolt had been sorely provoked by the allies and agents of that legal Government. Ever since the contingency of justified violence had been laid down in the famous Linz Programme eight years before, the party had trained and rehearsed its powerful *Schutzbund* for this ultimate task. Its organization and strategy on the fatal day are examined below. What needs to be dismissed here is the fiction that the February fighting consisted simply of brutal soldiery mowing down peaceful workers. The Right Wing provoked violence, but without thinking of Civil War ; the Left reacted reluctantly with their long-prepared *defensive putsch*, and thus made Civil War unavoidable. Seen in historical perspective, the whole tragedy was both the culmination and the cure of Austria's fifteen years of party strife — the short delirious fever by which the patient tries to shake off his long illness.

*　　*　　*

When the trial of strength finally began, the Government of the day could count on a miscellaneous armed force of about 80,000 men. The core of this was the Austrian Regular Army which, during the previous twelve months, had been brought up to the maximum of 30,000 laid down in the St. Germain Peace Treaty. To reinforce this came the lightly armed gendarmerie and police, each about 15,000 strong, giving a total Government force of 60,000. And on top of these security pillars of the 'Exekutive', as it was called, came the heavy and wobbly architrave of the *Heimwehr* and other Right-Wing paramilitary organizations. They numbered, all in all, perhaps 25,000 men at the time ; and of this motley band the most important contingent in the Civil War were the four regiments, totalling some 6000 men, of Fey's Vienna *Heimwehr*. Their numerical significance can be seen from the fact that, though the Vienna military garrison had the greatest concentration of heavy equipment in February 1934 (including 32 artillery pieces and 15 mine-throwers), its strength in officers and men was precisely 4239.

The Left Wing followed Bernaschek into battle out-numbered and out-gunned ; but they were by no means in that position of predetermined hopelessness which their apologists suggested after the defeat. Indeed, many a *coup d'état* has succeeded in history against far heavier odds where the leadership was more resolute and inspired and where the mass support of the civilian population was more enthusiastic. The rout of the Socialist levies in 1934 was caused as much by the indecision and defeatism of their leadership and by the inborn passivity of the Austrian temperament as by those Army howitzers which knocked holes in the workers' settlements. It is perhaps because of this that so much fuss was made about the holes.

The *Schutzbund* still numbered about 60,000 when the Civil War broke out (compared with a peak of 80,000 a few years before). In Vienna alone, their strength was about 17,500 lightly armed men, grouped principally into 45 'infantry' battalions, with cycle, motor-cycle, lorry and Danube shipping units in support. The province of Lower Austria, which surrounds the capital, counted 60 *Schutzbund* battalions with 23,000 men ; Styria, 25 battalions with over 25,000 men, and Upper Austria, 20 battalions with 8000 men.[7]

Nor was this large paramilitary force an undisciplined rabble of *sans-culottes*. Long before the various rival organizations of the Right Wing had grouped themselves, loosely and suspiciously, together, the *Schutzbund* had been raised and trained on an integrated national basis by General von Körner-Sigmaringen (General Körner as he was known after 1918) and other ex-Imperial army officers who switched from the Black-Gold banner to the Red Flag. Indeed, one of the paradoxes of the *Schutzbund* was that it owed its efficiency in part to the very regime it so bitterly disavowed.

Immediately below the Vienna 'Central Direction' came the regiments of 2–3 battalions. These battalions split down, in turn, into a headquarters staff and four companies, of which the first was equipped with field telephone and gas platoons. Each of the other companies was allotted on paper two infantry platoons with six grenade-throwers apiece and a machine-gun platoon with two light machine-guns. It is unlikely that the majority of *Schutzbund* battalions could have shown anything like this full 'war establishment' when fighting broke out, thanks to steady raids on their arsenals. Official figures show that between 1926 and 1933 the Government's arms searches had yielded a total haul of 710 machine-guns and 39,580 rifles from *Schutzbund* secret depots. But deliveries from Czechoslovakia and ingenious improvisations had both helped to make good these predictable losses and, in any case, the large arms hoards uncovered during the Civil War itself showed that the Left Wing was not short of weapons for the lightning stroke that was intended. Finally it should be noted that, whatever ditherings and divisions afflicted the leadership, the general fighting morale among the *Schutzbund* units themselves remained high, even after they had been declared illegal. Unlike their organization, this factor had nothing to do with the Habsburgs. It sprang from plain, unfaltering loyalty to the ideal of a better world for the workers — whatever happened to Austria in the process.

Thus, on the 12th of February, the Left Wing had both the men and the materials to topple the Government — always provided the blow was swift and resolute enough and that the nation as a whole gave at least its passive support. In fact, neither condition was fulfilled and, like all revolts which balance on such a tightrope, this one soon toppled over.

Militarily, the key to victory was the battle for Vienna and the key to this battle was possession of the 'Inner City' —

that crammed circle of the capital bounded by the Ringstrasse and the Danube Canal which contained most of the key ministries and buildings, including the President's Office ; the Archbishop's Residence ; the Chancellor's Office and private apartment ; the War Ministry ; the Police Headquarters ; the main Post Office ; and the Ministry of Interior. This elementary truth had been grasped clearly enough by the ex-Imperial strategists of the *Schutzbund*. One of their long-standing plans of action, devised by the *Schutzbund* Chief of Staff, Major Eifler, therefore aimed at isolating the Inner City by occupying the outer district police offices and blockading the outlying barracks. This manœuvre was to be followed by a surprise attack on the Government buildings, launched by picked 'storm units' between 2000-3000 strong, incongruously mounted, if all else failed, on a fleet of mobile incinerators supplied by the Town Hall.

As it was, this troop of smoking Trojan Horses never descended upon the First District. This was partly because vital hours had been lost in the vain attempt to keep Bernaschek back and partly because, though the weapons were handed out soon after 10 A.M. to the *Schutzbund* units, Eifler's offensive strategy was overruled. The main influence here seems again to have been Bauer who argued that there was in any case no point in the Socialists seizing Vienna with Hitler to the north of them and Mussolini to the south.

But what really crippled any fighting operation was the fact that the sacred weapon of the General Strike, to which the Socialist leadership immediately turned, fell, blunt and ineffective, from their hands. When, at 11.30, the lights of Vienna faded, to brighten and fade three times before finally going out, a pre-arranged signal had been given at which every worker in the capital and throughout the country was supposed to fold his hands — thus paralysing production, transport and communications at one blow. As things turned out, even in the Socialist-dominated sector of the economy, the strike call was not unanimously followed, whereas, in Government concerns and in private industry, it was as good as ignored. Thus, in Vienna, the post, telegraph, telephone and railway facilities were never disrupted ; food supplies functioned normally ; the water was not cut off ; and, in less than 24 hours, even the electricity was turned on and the abandoned trams began to grind again down the hushed streets. The mass of the Austrian workers had no clear lead to follow on the 12th of February ; but it is doubtful whether they would have responded much better to any clarion call Otto Bauer had given forth. His world of epoch-making revolutions and their world of cosy three-roomed apartments had just drifted too far apart, without either side fully realizing or admitting it. The motto which had inspired (and at the same time debilitated) the Austro-Marxists ever since 1918 — 'Alle Räder stehen still, wenn dein starker Arm es will' — turned out to be an empty advertising slogan.

According to Dr. Deutsch today, both he and Bauer realized by the night of the 12th of February that 'the masses had left them in the lurch'. Many of their loyal comrades were seen dutifully mounting the trams to go to work in the morning having fought hard all night. When the leaders saw even the main-line trains running and the Right-Wing papers being set and printed by Left-Wing labour they knew that the end had come — at the very beginning.

On the whole, the nation-wide organization of the *Schutzbund* functioned better than the Trades Unions in the hour of crisis. Linz lived up to Bernaschek's lead and a 24-hour battle raged before his units were dislodged from the railway station and other key points of the town. The industrial area of Steyr, a centre of foment ever since the Counter-Reformation, was even more heavily engaged. The *Schutzbund* occupied the whole Ennsleiten and the position became so critical that Fey's rival, Prince Starhemberg, had to set out from Vienna with a strong motorized *Heimwehr* column to rescue the local government forces. Heavy fighting also broke out in one or two provincial Socialist strongholds such as Kapfenberg in Styria, and St. Pölten in Lower Austria. On the other hand, the response around the capital was provincial to a fault, and the Vienna leadership waited in vain on the 13th for Lower Austrian *Schutzbund* levies to march to their aid.

But, as we have said, the *putsch* was lost almost as soon as it was launched by the failure in Vienna. When the first *Schutzbund* detachments began to approach the Inner City, five or six hours after the Linz fighting had blazed up, they found Army, police and Right-Wing paramilitary forces in firm control. The bridges were occupied, road crossings were blocked with barbed wire and covered by machine-guns, every policeman had exchanged his truncheon for a rifle and, behind this improvised cordon, the Government of the day, headed by the energetic Dollfuss, laboured away, undisturbed and unthreatened, to suppress the uprising. Martial law was declared in Vienna and the provinces affected by the disturbances and, on that same day, a number of leading Socialists, including unfortunate 'moderates' such as Renner, Helmer and Seitz, were arrested.

By that evening it was clear from the calm situation in the heart of the capital that the revolt had failed. Bauer immediately took to his heels and fled across the border into Czechoslovakia, and Deutsch followed three days later. They had preached 'justified revolution' for nearly ten years before the 12th of February ; had tried for a few hours to hold the revolution back on the day of reckoning itself and then, within the space of a few more hours, had bungled it and abandoned it. There is no reason to accuse either Bauer or Deutsch of actual physical cowardice, as some of their enemies did. But a fire-eating leader like Bauer, who deserts a fight before it has even reached its height, cannot expect to be treated too kindly either by his contemporaries or by his chroniclers. To many men on both sides in 1934 he resembled a brilliantly coloured Marxist moth, too fascinated by violence to keep away from the flame but too cautious to get his wings singed, who had flitted off when the candle overturned to leave others to face the blaze.

It was an irony characteristic of the whole Austro-Marxist plight that the brave and fanatical local commanders who had driven the leaders into the battle fought on after those same leaders had fled. Indeed, the heaviest fighting in Vienna did not begin until February 13th, when the workers' district of Floridsdorf joined Döbling, Ottakring and the rest in a desperate 'Maginot Line' defensive action based on the huge workers' settlements. Only when the cause was lost did the losers in Vienna find the resolution which, a day before, might have carried them, at least temporarily, to victory. Now, it merely carried them straight to prison. It was a very Austrian situation.

Dollfuss's decision to order artillery fire against these settlements, in order to cut short the dangers of the crisis and lessen its ultimate blood toll, was both the most agonizing and the most controversial step of his whole career. From a defeated and self-exiled Socialist leadership, who now resumed their fight with words, it promptly earned him the epithet of 'the murderer of defenceless workers'. In the Western world, which was as busy preaching democracy as it was appeasing the dictators, something of this propaganda odium survived his death and clung to the whole four-year Chancellorship of his successor Schuschnigg. Like most of the party slogans of the day, the charge substituted emotions for facts.

To begin with, the character and function of the workers' settlements themselves must be considered. It would be too much to claim, as did the Right-Wing apologists of the day, that they were constructed primarily as armed strongholds. But, on the other hand, it would be naïve to suppose that they did not serve a valuable military and strategic purpose. In the grand revolutionary design of the *Schutzbund*, they figured as local defence bases, arms stores, communications centres and last-ditch fortresses, and the course of the Civil War showed patently enough this design in operation. The headquarters of the whole *putsch* was sited in the workers' settlement of Ahornhof in the 10th District and, after this had been abandoned by Bauer and Deutsch and surrounded by Government forces, the leaderless district commanders based their independent actions, almost without exception, on local settlement buildings. Whether intentional or not, most of these turned out to have a valuable tactical role — controlling with their linked fields of fire either a railway, a Danube bridge or a barracks.

Whatever the truth about their siting, there can be no doubt whatsoever about their predetermined role as *Schutzbund* arsenals. The police records for the February action show that substantial hoards of arms were seized in practically every workers' settlement which was stormed and searched. One small housing block in Favoriten, for example, yielded 9 machine-guns, 122 Mannlicher rifles and 30,000 rounds of ammunition ; four separate arms dumps were discovered in Rudolfsheim, of which the biggest contained 2 heavy machine-guns, 146 Mannlichers, 45 steel helmets, 5 gas masks and other accoutrements ; the workers' settlements of Währing, where hardly a shot was fired, produced 1 machine-gun, 230 rifles and a pile of hand-grenades. The great settlements of Floridsdorf yielded the biggest haul of all : no fewer than 2500 rifles, 250 revolvers, 1500 hand-grenades, enough dynamite to blow every Ministry in the capital to smithereens, and nearly 100,000 rounds of ammunition. These few extracts from the police reports of the time suffice to show that it was not exactly 'defenceless workers' whom Dollfuss turned the howitzers on ; they also expose one of the excuses later put out by the decamped Socialist leaders that their revolt had failed through 'lack of ammunition'.

None the less, in a world still unused to Hitler's 'total

warfare', the bombardment of civilian dwellings which housed women and children as well as a rebel army was an appalling and unique affair. From everything which has been said about Dollfuss's character and record from his earliest childhood on, the *prima facie* assumption can only be that the Chancellor took that decision with a heavy heart and under compelling pressure. This assumption is borne out by four personal accounts which have become available of his behaviour during those days.

The first and most significant is an episode which took place in the modest apartment of the Dollfuss family in the Stallburggasse shortly before midday on that same 12th of February. It was witnessed only by his wife (whose birthday, by a bitter irony, it happened to be) and by an old friend, Irmgard Burjau-Domanig, who had been invited over to eat roast chicken for the occasion.[8] The birthday guest arrived to find that it was Austria instead of the chicken that was cooking in the oven. Dollfuss had come home after attending the cathedral service in order to collect his thoughts on the rapidly mounting crisis. White in the face but outwardly calm, he paced up and down a small room in the flat between the drawing-room and the bedroom, where his only telephone was fixed to the wall.

His one concern was to stop the fighting immediately — not merely to avoid a full-scale civil war but also to avoid giving Hitler a pretext for intervening 'to restore order'. And his first thought was not howitzers but tear-gas. He unhooked the telephone, called up the main military Arsenal, and ordered them to collect all available supplies for immediate use. To his astonishment and anger, the apologetic reply which came back was that the Austrian Army had no tear-gas because all forms of gas warfare had been forbidden her by the Treaty of St. Germain.

With a cry of 'These idiots — that's utterly absurd!' he jammed the receiver back on its hook, began pacing up and down again, and resumed his monologue before the two silent women.

'I can think of another way to bring them to their heels quickly . . . bring up artillery and fire on the houses where they are fighting from. We could save countless lives that way and the houses can easily be rebuilt. I must do it even if I'm condemned for it. Everyone will shout out — also abroad — "artillery against the people" — but it's the only way to get the business over quickly and with little sacrifice. I must take it on my conscience.'

An hour or two later, at an emergency Cabinet meeting summoned in the Ministry of Agriculture nearby, his decision to allow the military to take any steps they thought necessary to bring the fighting to an immediate stop was approved by his colleagues. Agreement was unanimous, though some members of the Government greeted the move with grave concern and others with undisguised glee. Among the latter was Emil Fey who, according to one eye-witness,[9] emerged from the meeting with an air of brisk satisfaction and declared, as he buttoned on his military cape : 'That's that ; and now we will clean their stomachs out for them!'

Late that same night, as a result of the Cabinet's decision, half a battery of light mountain howitzers, commanded by one Captain Schwarz, took up position outside the gigantic 1200 yards long complex of the 'Karl-Marx-Hof' in Heiligenstadt and opened fire against its massive central archway. The next day, other artillery units followed suit, at Floridsdorf and at other centres of the fighting.

Subsequent talk of an 'indiscriminate rain of shells' seems to have been more of that subjective bathos by which the Socialist leadership tried to cover up its own failures. The Austrian Army's factual records for the four days' action show that artillery was only employed when the local commander concerned and the staff had convinced themselves that an infantry attack would have been more costly in life to both sides (one look at a vast concrete rabbit warren like the Karl-Marx-Hof, with its four courtyards, its corner towers up to 18 inches thick, and its iron communicating doors proves the reasonableness of this). Furthermore, the 'bombardment' itself was normally a series of single shots, preceded and usually followed by trumpet calls and appeals to surrender. Finally, in many cases, the shells simply failed to explode, as part of the ammunition issued was First World War material of dubious quality.[10]

All the while, at hourly or half-hourly intervals, Dollfuss's own appeal came over the radio, calling on the workers to cease a senseless revolt now abandoned by its instigators, and promising pardon to all but the ringleaders if arms were laid down by a certain hour. The Karl-Marx-Hof itself was one of the last *Schutzbund* strongholds to yield ; but its surrender on the 15th of February proved the wisdom of the Government's plan. Half an hour before the Chancellor's final ultimatum was due to expire, the white flag was hoisted ; the rebels trooped out, and two battalions of infantry moved in. The fighting was over and the anecdotes began. One that the police gladly noted down was told by an indignant inhabitant of the settlement. He described how, soon after the shooting began, *Schutzbund* men burst into his flat, cracked the wall of his bedroom open with pickaxes and removed, before his astounded eyes, a machine-gun which had been carefully cemented in there when the building was first put up.

Dollfuss's drastic actions during the February tragedy have been described, as he himself reached them, in the perspective of the crisis itself. But there is no doubt that his solution by violence caused him mental anguish right down to the day of his own death in another abortive *putsch* five months later. A second personal glimpse of the Chancellor at this time of stress is given by Dr. Stepan, who had arrived in Vienna from Graz on that 12th of February—unaware that a Civil War was in process until his taxi-driver at the station told him—for talks with Dollfuss. It was not until late that night that a meeting could be arranged, and again the scene was the dining-room of the Chancellor's little flat in the Stallburggasse, now dimly lit by two candles. When the talk turned to the events of the day, Dollfuss's immediate concern was whether he had in fact exhausted every peaceful approach, before resorting to all-out force. Should another armistice time-limit be set, in the hope that reason would prevail over passion? Both his visitors (the Minister of Trade, Fritz Stockinger, was also present) urged against such a step, on the grounds that any fresh mediation offer at this stage would only be interpreted as a sign of weakness and lead to worse bloodshed. But Dollfuss, though standing by the order he had issued to the Army that afternoon, was still restless. Political as well as humanitarian considerations haunted him ; he was worried, for example, about the possible reaction from the Western Powers, and begged his friends to realize what a bad effect on Austria's reputation any unjustified violence was bound to have there. With the country on the brink of chaos and Hitler *ante portas*, it could easily be argued that the justification was there. But, in the early hours of the morning, Stepan left a Dollfuss 'plunged in spiritual torment and in the bitterness of solitary decision'.[11]

Two other brief outbursts, made by Dollfuss himself to close personal friends, show the pressure of emotions inside him. The first came when the coffins of the Civil War dead were lined up in long neat rows before the Town Hall, at a public ceremony of mourning. (The Government forces lost 128 dead, the *Schutzbund* and civilians 193.) Dollfuss turned to an old school-mate [12] from Hollabrunn who was standing beside him and muttered : 'To order that shooting was the most terrible decision of my life, but it was the only way to cut short the fighting'. And, a week or two later, when Austria had returned to a semblance of normality, he exclaimed bitterly to another childhood friend : [13] 'Just imagine, of all people in this world it had to be me who ordered the Army to shoot on workers. But what else could I have done as Chancellor?'

Though there was genuine grief in these outbursts, there seems to have been no sense of remorseful guilt ; and that very last remark of Dollfuss's explains why. That a clash between Austria's private armies had become as good as inevitable by 1934 is admitted by both sides : there were too many itching fingers on too many light triggers for any other outcome. We have seen how the responsibility, both for the gradual build-up of the rival paramilitary forces and for the immediate cause of their joining battle, was a divided one. Yet the responsibility for ending that battle was not a divided one ; it rested squarely on the Government of the day, whatever its political colour. It was not Dollfuss's crime to be Austrian Chancellor on the 12th of February, 1934, but rather his supreme misfortune. What he was called on to put an end to was not so much a rebellion against his own person or policies as a sickening domestic crisis which had been mounting steadily in Austria for the previous fifteen years.

Had Parliament not eliminated itself a year before, had elections been held and a Socialist Cabinet been formed, the same explosion would almost certainly have come, and the same force, applied from above, would have been needed to stop it blowing the country to pieces. The peace-loving pragmatist Karl Renner, to say nothing of the firebrand Otto Bauer, would hardly have acted otherwise had they been in Dollfuss's shoes, faced with a rebellion led by the detested *Heimwehr* instead of a *putsch* led by the equally detested *Schutzbund*. The roles would then have been reversed, but the action would have been essentially the same. Instead of an aristocratic Minister of War, Prince Schönburg-Hartenstein, lobbing shells into the Karl-Marx-Hof, a Marxist Minister of War, Julius Deutsch (also an ex-Imperial officer) would then have been seen drawing up the same Army howitzers before Fey's Vienna *Heimwehr* headquarters, or pounding away at the battlements of Eferding Castle, Starhemberg's main country seat. Whether they could have ended the senseless fratricidal strife in four days, as Dollfuss did, is a moot point. And whether Prince Starhemberg would have taken as prompt political asylum on the Venice Lido as Otto Bauer did in Brno is another moot point.

But, at the end, Austria's position abroad would not have been one whit better. There might have been sympathy in France, as long as the Government of the day lasted, and there would certainly have been applause from the Socialist International, which the Austro-Marxists persisted in mistaking for a political force. But the Conservatives in England, to say nothing of the Fascists in Italy, would not have loved 'Red Vienna' any more as a result. In short, the whole Left-Wing witch hunt started up against Dollfuss because of the Civil War is partly rooted in dishonesty. At the best, one might call it genuine self-deception. For, in 1934, the Austrian Socialists were so far removed from the realities of power that they no longer realized what the responsibilities of Government meant.

That individual excesses took place in the discharging of those responsibilities, both during and after the fighting, was inexcusable, even if it was an evil by-product of the passions of the hour. Among these excesses must be numbered the shooting by Austrian Army units, without trial, of a group of *Schutzbund* captives at Holzleiten and the formal execution of another *Schutzbund* prisoner, Münichreiter, despite his serious wounds. These excesses turned brave men into heroes, heroes into martyrs, and perpetuated the fury of the moment into a bitter legend. (Münichreiter still has a street named after him in the Vienna suburb of Hietzing.) But, from the point of view of the Government of the day — *any* Government of the day — the total of nine death sentences which were subsequently passed for treason was not excessive. Whatever the provocations and however reluctantly, it was, after all, a full-scale revolt which the Left Wing had launched. To complain, after defeat, of the victors' severity is like wanting to cook your revolutionary omelette without being prepared to break any eggs. This, in fact, was precisely what Bauer's brand of Austro-Marxism — radical but cosy — added up to.

The charge sometimes heard that, by 'smashing democracy in Austria' in February 1934, Dollfuss 'paved the way for Hitler four years later' is another of those propaganda glosses which ignore the plain facts. The Socialists — to their great credit — did *not* make common cause with the Nazis after the Civil War, though a few temporary and tactical 'working agreements' sprang up. And to their even greater credit, when the challenge came in 1938, the party leadership which was then, at long last, in the firm hands of the moderates, was prepared to stand by Schuschnigg in his abortive gesture of a national referendum.

As for Dollfuss himself, it was precisely to save Austria from a Nazi intervention that he bore down so heavily to bring the February fighting to an end. It was not the first time, and not the last, that the vision of an Austrian fatherland as he saw it and the vision of international Socialism as the Left Wing saw it clashed head on. But what this particular line of argument against Dollfuss conveniently ignores above all is that, in the Europe of 1934-38, Hitler was not going to be held up by demonstrations of democratic solidarity among 6½ million Austrians (indeed, these would only have strained his famous 'patience' all the more). Nor would such solidarity, even assuming it could ever have been achieved in pre-war Austria, have roused the Western Powers from their appeasement slumbers. What the Rhineland, Abyssinia and Czechoslovakia failed to achieve, the case of Austria, Hitler's own homeland, could never have brought about. It was a show of armed might, and not of fine phrases, which alone could have checked the Nazi advance. And had the Austrians, united in some miraculous emergency Coalition, strewn Hitler's path to Vienna with democratic declarations at every step, he would have trodden them into the ground with his jackboots like Michaelmas daisies. As we shall see later, this harsh truth dominated the whole of Dollfuss's foreign policy like an implacable and relentless shadow.

*   *   *

However, when the brief Civil War was over, Dollfuss's first concern was neither with the Socialists who had been subdued nor with the Nazis who were emerging. The immediate peril, both to his own position and to the stability of the Government, came from Major Fey and his radical faction of the *Heimwehr*. The Right-Wing paramilitary forces had stood in the front line of the fighting and, due to their inexperience as much as to their valour, they had suffered the heaviest losses in the Government camp (52 dead and 103 wounded out of the total of 128 dead and 400 wounded). Their role in Vienna had been particularly prominent and vital ; Fey, who had conducted himself throughout with the bravery expected of an ex-Imperial *Theresienritter*, was the hero of the hour. As Minister for Security, Head of the Vienna *Heimwehr* and Vice-Chancellor, he had not only commanded the police, gendarmerie and paramilitary actions, but had also exercised considerable influence over the Army's operations. (The first wave of arrests was also, incidentally, his doing.)

We now know that, in both Italian and German eyes, Fey was regarded as the first man in Austria and the imminent successor to Dollfuss. Rintelen, who had by this time been 'banished' by Dollfuss to the post of Austrian Minister in Rome, reported in early March to his Nazi friends with approval and relish that, in the Italian view, 'the most powerful influence in the Austrian Government at the moment was Fey ; after him came Starhemberg ; then, for a long interval, no one at all; and then at last, Dollfuss'.[14] Even more significant, the Germans themselves considered Fey's position in March 1934 to be so powerful that suggestions were being seriously considered in Berlin for a personal talk between him and Hitler. The German Foreign Office, in a strictly confidential telegram to their envoy in Vienna, Dr. Rieth, announced the postponement of this project until the struggle for position in Austria was clearly resolved.[15] As late as April 9, the German State Secretary for Foreign Affairs, von Bülow, in a secret memorandum entitled 'Further Handling of the Austrian Question', himself laid down that discussions with the Austrian Government would have to wait until it was clear 'who the person in Vienna is who is in a position to negotiate'.[16]

Emil Fey, himself consumed with a gnawing ambition, was not unaware of these opinions, nor of the possibilities in front of him. As things turned out, he hovered indecisively between half-loyalty and half-treachery — an exact foretaste of his behaviour during the Nazi *coup d'état* in Vienna five months later. But, in his own torn mind, and even more so among his family and his immediate entourage, there were impulses at work urging him to seize the Chancellor's chair. In an open affront to his chief's authority, he supplemented Dollfuss's press conference on the Civil War with another and differently slanted one of his own; flushed by their sudden surge of power and publicity, his lieutenants openly dropped hints to foreign correspondents in Vienna that 'government changes were imminent'.

Dollfuss himself had never trusted nor liked Fey but he had never been afraid of him. ('Emil Fey is an Army Major and that's all he ever will be' was how he had dismissed the matter once to an anxious friend.) After the Civil War, however, he was forced to take the Major seriously, politically and even personally. A special office was set up, responsible only to him, to keep his dangerous Vice-Chancellor under constant surveillance. And it is now known that Dollfuss was even considering sleeping away from his own flat in the Stallburggasse in case Fey's henchmen might resort to some desperate kidnapping operation ; he aired this possibility in private to at least one of his old school friends.[17]

Formally, the main battle was fought out on that key issue already mentioned of how to reconcile the *Heimwehr* with the new Fatherland Front. From Dollfuss's point of view, one of the Front's principal political advantages was that it offered some patriotic face-saving platform by which the *Heimwehr* could be absorbed ; and Fey's public behaviour after the Civil War had only underlined the need for this, for it was arrogant in the extreme. 'How can I reward Fey for what he did during the fighting,' Dollfuss once remarked bitterly to his wife, 'when he insists on putting the laurel wreath himself on his own head ?'

However, Dollfuss was unexpectedly rescued from his plight by a new flare-up in the rivalry between Fey and Starhemberg. That gay and irresponsible prince was also not afraid of Fey (it is doubtful if he ever feared anything except, perhaps, old age). But he was distinctly piqued by seeing his rival steal all the limelight and virtually ignoring the valuable action he had fought down in Steyr. Accordingly, at an elegant press reception in a Vienna palace hired for the occasion, Starhemberg in turn gave his own version of the Civil War, mixing old-world chivalry with present-day politics. He praised the fighting valour of the *Schutzbund* (a gesture almost as revolutionary as Churchill's tribute to Rommel during a somewhat greater conflict eight years later), and he publicly pledged his loyalty to Dollfuss. This was no tactical switch on his part, for Starhemberg as a Minister had always been loyal, if idle ; but the announcement was none the less of decisive tactical importance to the beleaguered Chancellor. Just how decisive can be seen from a crucial gathering of *Heimwehr* and Fatherland Front leaders which convened in the Stallburggasse flat on the 6th of March to hammer out a common plan of action. Of this meeting an eye-witness account has survived.[18]

The *Heimwehr* were represented by Fey, Starhemberg and Neustädter-Stürmer, a man of Italian origin who, appropriately enough, belonged to the most violent Fascist wing in the movement. On the other side, three of Dollfuss's followers in the Government were present — Buresch, Stockinger and Schuschnigg, who were at that time Ministers for Finance, Trade and Education respectively ; in addition, Dollfuss had called in Stepan, the new leader of his Fatherland Front.

Dollfuss began, in the hallowed Austrian tradition, by filling wine glasses all round the table. He then introduced the discussion in a way which left no doubt that it was the state he had been fighting to preserve, not just an ideology. There was no note of triumph, vindictiveness or revenge in his words. The clash of weapons, he said, had brought a purely nominal victory to the Government ; everything now depended on reaching a genuine truce with the workers. The danger from Germany had grown greater than ever before as a result of the Civil War ; while the Western Powers, thanks partly to the wildly tendentious and exaggerated accounts sent home by some of the foreign correspondents, 'now regard us simply as a government of workers' murderers'. At home and abroad the perils were thus greater than ever, and only by uniting forces could they hope to master the situation.

The reply of Fey and Neustädter-Stürmer to this appeal for reason was a long tirade culminating in the accusation that 'when our men returned from the front line it was to find that the gentlemen of the Fatherland Front had divided the spoils of victory between them'. Under these circumstances of a 'planned campaign to suppress the *Heimwehr*' there could be no question of a paramilitary integration. Renewed appeals weakened Fey's resistance but failed to break it, until Starhemberg, who had been sipping his wine till then in complete silence and apparent boredom, delivered the decisive blow. 'There's no argument about it,' he declared, 'the *Heimwehr* is part of the Fatherland Front. Stories that we want to rule the country by ourselves are just nonsense, a nonsense believed in by a few misguided careerists and then spread by stupid or wilful rumour-mongers. In my view, all the fighting forces should be unified and an agreement should be drawn up to this effect.'

As Starhemberg at that time was leader of the *Heimwehr* army, though holding no Government post, his words squashed the immediate hopes of the 'misguided careerists'. Two *Heimwehr* leaders who, pretty plainly, filled this description, were sitting next to him ; yet it would be unjust to explain Starhemberg's behaviour at this critical conference as being purely motivated by spite against Fey and his group. Starhemberg was just not to be had for a *putsch* against Dollfuss, for whom he had a warm personal regard. Indeed, it is doubtful if, for all his occasional wild talk, Prince Ernst Rüdiger was to be had for a *putsch* against any Austrian Government provided it was not outright Austro-Marxist.

Almost alone of all the actors on the Vienna political stage, both on the Right Wing and the Left, Starhemberg did not need power to tickle his ego or to pay his bills. His was the approach of the rich and disenchanted *grand seigneur* who saw in politics basically just another distraction to while away the gap between birth and death. Ambition could never devour him, as it did a Bauer, a Fey or a Rintelen ; nor, on the other hand, could he be licked by the purer but equally powerful flames of a divine mission, as Seipel and Dollfuss were. He treated politics as a sport and he emptied his pockets for it in an age and in a country where politics was filling the pockets of most. He did just the same, with the same object, for beautiful women and for hunting ; and, while in the game, he observed the rules. To have tried putting little Dollfuss in the bag, his friend and his Chancellor, would have been like shooting a baby deer in May. Starhemberg was above the worst temptations of politics simply because he was indifferent to its brightest attractions.

At all events, whatever the motivation, his behaviour at that midnight meeting on the 6th of March, and the rift which widened ever deeper between himself and Fey, rescued Dollfuss from the immediate *Heimwehr* threat. The problem of absorbing the paramilitary forces into the Government was one that Dollfuss never lived to resolve, and it took his successor Schuschnigg the best part of two years to achieve it. During the last four months of Dollfuss's Chancellorship and life, the struggle with the *Heimwehr* moved back again from the military front to the political where, for nearly a year, a battle had been raging over Austria's new authoritarian constitution. That question, and the background of mounting Nazi violence against which it was debated, we shall return to later.

To finish off this survey of domestic developments, we must now summarize the final phase of Dollfuss's relations with his Socialist opponents. On the security side, the threat from the Left Wing after the Civil War was never again overwhelming. The *Schutzbund* had been shattered in its brittle morale by the defeat and broken in its organization by the flight or arrest of its leaders. Many of the rank-and-file members both salved their own consciences and strengthened Dollfuss's position by joining the so-called *Freiheitsbund*, a patriotic though anti-clerical Right-Wing paramilitary movement which formed part of the recently constituted 'Chancellor's units'. The dreaded swing-over of illegal *Schutzbund* warriors into the Nazi camp, which was the Government's security nightmare, never took place ; if anything, it was the *Heimwehr* which gained Nazi recruits in the immediate post-February period.

Dollfuss's last attempts to square the circle by incorporating the Austro-Marxist proletariat into his authoritarian Catholic

New Order could thus proceed free from mob pressure on the Left. It proved, none the less, an almost insuperable task. Until and after Dollfuss's death, no formula could be devised, for example, to integrate the 'free' Socialist Trade Unions into the new corporative labour organization. The compromise concept of the Chancellor's was to set up a nation-wide non-party Trades Union Federation, headed by a respected ex-Christian-Social, Josef Staud, which the Socialists could join on a voluntary basis while retaining wide autonomy.[19] As we have seen, this theme had run through most of the eleventh-hour armistice negotiations between Left and Right. But again, the spectre of the *Heimwehr*, represented in this instance by Neustädter-Stürmer in his capacity as Minister for Social Affairs, intervened to frighten the Socialists away. For him, Trades Union was a phrase which had no place in the Fascist vocabulary, and his influence was so strong and so immediate that the 'free' Trades Unionists had little honourable choice but to boycott the new Federation.

A similar fate — a lack of Left-Wing trust aggravated by Right-Wing extremism — met the so-called 'Winter Action' which Dollfuss launched soon after the Civil War. With the extremist Socialist leaders sitting in bitter, self-imposed exile in Czechoslovakia and their more moderate colleagues either in jail or in despair in Austria, Dollfuss thought the moment had come to consummate the long-standing breach in the Left-Wing leadership, and to step himself into the gap which yawned between the workers and their oracles. He accordingly appointed his old student friend and Cartell-Verband rival Ernst Karl Winter as Third Deputy Mayor of Vienna, with the express task of building up a common Catholic-Socialist mass front against the Nazi menace.

From April till July, Winter laboured away with his characteristic devotion at the task. He has himself admitted that Dollfuss allowed him, as an old sparring partner, complete freedom of criticism as well as of action, and both sides adhered to this strange pact between two *homines politici* of such contrasting natures. Winter, for example, made full use of his privileges by campaigning for a May 1 amnesty of the imprisoned Socialist leaders ; Dollfuss, though irritated and embarrassed by the agitation, did nothing to suppress it. Winter also testifies in his memoirs that, on one or two occasions, Dollfuss gave him 'very effective help' against both the *Heimwehr* and the police in pursuing his truce efforts. But, in the short time that was left to Dollfuss, these efforts led to nothing. The brave illusion of unity among themselves, and the even braver illusion of the international Socialist brotherhood in the dictators' Europe of the 1930's, was all the Austro-Marxists had to cling on to. Even if they could not fulfil their cause, they refused to betray it. The shadow of February was too close. That of the *Anschluss* still seemed too far away, until the murder of Dollfuss himself flashed it, briefly and prophetically, across the Vienna scene.

Looking back over this long, suspicious parley between Left and Right which runs like a twisting thread through Dollfuss's two years of power, one is more conscious of the underlying futility of it all than of any deliberate and conscious guilt. The whole thing was like a broken dialogue in which neither side really listened and neither side really spoke the same language. When one adds that the exchanges were always conducted against the clamour of party passions at home and the conflicting Rome-Berlin pressure abroad, it is not surprising that little sense was made.

But one side cannot be blamed to the exclusion of the other. Neither Left nor Right was completely deaf or completely dumb, but both were, for most of the time, inarticulate or hard of hearing. Dollfuss talked sincerely of the Christian brotherhood of men, but spoke to the workers as a clerical peasant under Fascist patronage. The Austrian Socialists, for their part, learned from him to think about their country as a fatherland, instead of a bastion of Marxism ; but they never really fitted this strange new patriotic concept into their woolly lost horizons of the Third International. In the last analysis, both Dollfuss and his Marxist opponents were defeated by the deficiencies of their countrymen. Or perhaps it would be more charitable, and more truthful, to say that it was the *Zeitgeist*, the spirit of the age, which mocked and destroyed them both.

CHAPTER SIX

The Dream and the Dreamer

IN Vienna on the 1st of May, 1934, the first and almost certainly the last attempt was made in the 20th century to erect the Kingdom of God upon earth. Despite all its deficiencies and absurdities, despite its pathetically artificial birth, its brief four years of painful half-life and its ignominious end, this is how the 'May Constitution' of Dollfuss should be judged ; for this was how he judged it himself. For him, it was not an instrument of secular tyranny but an emergency charter of divine enlightenment. It drew its basic inspiration not (as has so often and so falsely been stated) from the contemporary Fascism of Mussolini but from the ancient vision of St. Augustine's *Civitas Dei*. With it, Dollfuss made a desperate and utterly doomed attempt to cure the ills of Austria and of Europe with the forgotten political physic of the Universal Church, summoning back the medieval order of life from behind the Renaissance to redress the wrongs of his modern age.

The first words of this extraordinary document read : 'In the name of God, the Almighty, from Whom all Justice derives, the Austrian people receive . . . this Constitution'. And the last words of the famous speech in which Dollfuss announced his new project ran : 'We all go away today in the faith that we are fulfilling a higher mission. Just as the crusaders were permeated with this same faith . . . so we also look with firm trust to the future, in the conviction — God wills it!'[1] There were many other ingredients in the experiment, either borrowed direct from Fascist Italy or culled indiscriminately from the political and religious philosophies of the previous fifty years. Most were of Dollfuss's own choosing ; some he was talked into and some he was forced into. The end-product of all this ideological compromise and cross-breeding would scarcely have been recognized by Augustine. Yet that venerable saint would have detected, however submerged and distorted, his own spirit pulsating somewhere beneath its creation.

What sets Dollfuss apart from all the dictators and semidictators of the authoritarian age in which he lived is that it was this Christian ideal which always drove him on, and it was the Christian values and responsibilities by which he always sought to act. This was not a mere cloak of respectability to throw over his ambition, no more than those opening words of the Constitution were intended as a mere gloss over despotism. As far as is possible in politics, the man was the statesman ; and Dollfuss as Chancellor was still, at heart, that pious peasant child who had been struck dumb by the altar-piece at Kirnberg, or that earnest divinity student who had abandoned theology 'because he would rather be a good Christian than a bad priest'.

Before examining the various elements in Dollfuss's reform programme, and the various ends it was designed to fulfil, it is worth glancing at some of the main provisions in the Constitution itself. From the political point of view, the 1934 Constitution was simply an attempt to provide Austria with an alternative to that form of parliamentarianism which had capsized so dramatically in Vienna the year before. The Constitution was thus the legal and logical extension of the Fatherland Front. Like that movement, it also tried to adapt the overwhelmingly authoritarian trends of the day to suit Austria's history and national character and, above all, to give her unity, security and protection against those who tried openly to destroy her. Whatever ancient and divine parentage it could trace in St. Augustine and Pope Leo XIII, the May Constitution was directly descended on the distaff side from

Adolf Hitler. Those same bricks with which Dollfuss hoped eventually to build a new Christian order were also used immediately for a protective wall to keep out the Nazis. He tried to learn from the past to guide the future ; but it was Austria's present he was really trying to save. The whole concept thus inevitably became a hopeless mixture of long-range idealism and short-term improvisations.

This is reflected in the elaborate system of advisory bodies it set up. These were meant to represent the new order of society more democratically than Parliament had ever represented the old, yet without impairing that strong centralized authority on which the country's best hopes of safety were thought to depend. Thus the Dollfuss Constitution provided for no fewer than five legislative bodies to 'advise' the Government. All were interlocked and interconnected and the sum total of their real power was, to begin with, slight. Yet their mere presence reflected the Chancellor's wish to avoid any one-man despotism — a wish he could not have fulfilled in the Austria of his day even had he tried.

The first of these queer components in the new Legislative was the so-called Council of State, a sort of Senate consisting of not less than 40 and not more than 50 persons, appointed and selected by the Federal President from among 'worthy citizens of good character whose behaviour and achievements to date justify the expectation that they will have complete understanding for the needs and tasks of the state'. This prim, almost Cromwellian-sounding body was to sit in permanence, 'renewing itself by the replacement of its individual members', to discuss the Government's draft laws in conjunction with three other organs. Two of these, the so-called Federal Cultural Council and the Federal Economic Council, reflected the corporative-syndicalist structure of the new system. The third, the Provincial Council, embodied the reduced powers and privileges which Austria's ancient provinces were allowed to carry forward into the centralized state.

The Federal Cultural Council consisted of 30-40 representatives drawn from the recognized churches and religious communities, the school and education authorities, and the world of Austrian science and culture. On paper, this looked a reasonably compact and homogeneous organ. But the composition of its sister-body, the Economic Council, showed up the awkward jagged edges of Dollfuss's *Ständestaat* at their worst. This was to be made up of 70-80 delegates from the various professional or occupational groupings (the nearest translation for '*Stand*' in this context) into which the new Austrian society was being reshuffled. These groupings were seven in number — Agriculture and Forestry ; Industry and Mining ; Crafts (*Gewerbe*) ; Trade and Communications ; Banking, Credit and Insurance ; the free professions ; and finally, the Civil Servants.

Even when set down in the bold, fat type and neat sub-paragraphs of the official Constitution text, this looks a strangely inadequate way to try and organize 6½ million Europeans in the 20th century ; and real life was to present difficulties of which even the lawyers had never dreamed. By comparison, the Provincial Council seems natural and straightforward enough. This is no wonder, for the historic provinces of Austria were the real foundations of the state — centuries older and far more firmly rooted in the soil than the Republic itself. Their joint Council in the new legislative system consisted simply of the eight Provincial Governors (plus the Mayor of Vienna), together with their respective financial advisors.

All of these four bodies were consultative only and could merely comment on the laws passed to them by the Government. Together they elected from their own ranks the 59 members of the so-called Federal Diet, which was given the power of accepting or rejecting the measures put before it. As, however, the Government, which was the initiator of all legislation, could determine which laws to send to the Diet, and as that same Government anyway retained emergency powers to legislate by simple Cabinet decree, the Diet's prerogative of rejection did not amount to much.

Other salient points of the Constitution will be dealt with when describing Dollfuss's eleven-month struggle to save his original concept from the clutches of the *Heimwehr*. Only one symbolic feature need be mentioned here — the coat-of-arms which he had designed for the new Austria. That heraldic abortion which the Socialists inflicted on the Republic in 1918 — a single-headed eagle with broken chains dangling from its spurs and a hammer and sickle brandished in its claws, was blown clean off its perch. Dollfuss brought back the familiar double-headed eagle which had flown over the Austrian lands since the 13th century ; he restored it without, of course, the Habsburg insignia, but also without all the Marxist trimmings. This was a deliberate attempt to summon back the old Imperial glamour to flout in the face of the swastika and typified his whole endeavour to reach back into a past of which the Austrians could be proud, in order to give their hesitant new patriotism some emotional ground to stand on. Whatever one may feel of the rest of the 1934 Constitution, it is difficult not to regret that this particular reform was to last less than four years. Hitler brought in his own German eagle in 1938, and when Austria re-emerged again in 1945, the old single-headed eagle of 1918, still clanking its chains and brandishing its political tools of trade, rose up again from the smoking ruins with it, like a tattered and obstinate Phoenix.

The May Constitution was inorganic politically simply because the new social order which it was supposed to embody was itself an unnatural one. For Dollfuss, the idea of the *Stände* had conscious medieval associations ; yet he overlooked the fact that it could only have made real sense in the Middle Ages. In a relatively undeveloped society, whose primitive industries could be confined within the straitjacket of the gild system, a people could be divided into those who fought, those who prayed, those who traded and those who ploughed. But after the Industrial Revolution, the mechanism of human society had become too intricate, and the divisions between classes and occupations too blurred, to organize a whole nation simply according to what its individual citizens did for a living. The idealism of the old crusading age helped to give Dollfuss — and Austria — the spiritual faith they both sought. But when he copied the economics of the Middle Ages, Dollfuss tripped over the very history he was trying to lean upon.

Having once said that, however, a whole series of provisos must be made to modify the generally accepted picture of the 1934 Constitution as a pure 'instrument of Fascism' and of Dollfuss as its cynical creator. And we must begin with a partial contradiction of what has just been stated. For, however impracticable any form of *Ständestaat* might ultimately be in the 20th century, the one people with whom it could conceivably have worked in Europe were, and still are, the Austrians. Whatever nonsense Dollfuss's blueprint may have made economically, it responded socially to many of the natural instincts of his countrymen : above all to their worship of *Stand* in the broader sense of professional or technical *standing*, and all those visible trimmings and attributes which go with it.

Even in his day, this was not just the nostalgia of the Austrian bureaucracy and bourgeoisie for the outward prestige and the inner security of the old Empire (though this played a major role). Both the workers and their leaders, caught up in their own vast ordered hierarchy of party and trade unions, had joined in the search for what are now known as 'status symbols'. Anyone who thinks that, on the social level, Dollfuss was tapping in the dark with his fellow-countrymen need only look at a complete Ball Calendar for the Vienna Carnival season, either of his time or today. For here, quite unconsciously, the whole *Ständestaat* turns out each year in a

spontaneous fancy dress parade. It is not simply the industrialists, the doctors, the lawyers, the journalists, the
scientists, the actors, the civil servants, policemen and firemen
who organize their separate functions. The electricians, the
seamstresses, the butchers, the chimney-sweeps and a score of
other trades join in as well, sometimes representing the whole
capital and sometimes one district, but one and all insisting
that their particular ball is the only worthy social manifestation
of their calling. Indeed, one is tempted to think that if Vienna
really did dance all the year, as the Prince de Ligne once
accused it of doing, Dollfuss might have squeezed through with
his reforms. Were any further evidence on this point needed,
Austria's system of motor-car registration could provide it. If
the Vienna police today could be persuaded to publish the complete list of the owners of car registration numbers from 1 to
2000, together with the reasons, official or unofficial, as to why
those numbers were issued, in separate blocks to separate groups
of claimants, the 1934 Council of State, Cultural Council and
Economic Council would all re-emerge once again, this time
changing gear instead of changing partners.

Near to Dollfuss's own grave in the Vienna suburb of
Hietzing there is a tombstone erected to the memory of a
'Federal Railways Locomotive Driver's Widow'. The good
woman had nothing else to leave on record about herself;
and she needed nothing else. The railways in Austria were
nationalized, and to have been married to a state employee,
however humble, was a good enough recommendation to
posterity. So the title was solemnly chiselled in for her.
That humble tombstone is perhaps the most genuine tribute
the murdered Chancellor could have desired to have near his
last resting-place. The man and the social psychology of his
New Order have their permanent monuments side by side.

A more fundamental and controversial issue is the political
one : to what extent was the May Constitution designed as an
instrument of oppressive state power ? Were liberal and

democratic aspects included somewhere in its rigid super-structure ? If so, were they included deliberately or accidentally ? And, as it is Dollfuss who concerns us, how did he personally try and distribute this emphasis between authority and popular rights ?

It must be noted to begin with that, even in the severe form in which it was finally adopted, the new system was far from being a dictatorship in the sense of the Nazi or Communist tyrannies. It was, indeed, some distance removed from Mussolini's Fascism, which influenced it more powerfully than any other foreign model. Its genuine basis of Christian morality mentioned above was only one of the factors which rescued it historically from this ignominious company. Another equally important distinction was that, unlike his powerful neighbours, Dollfuss never preached nor practised the doctrine of state omnipotence. The Government kept total powers in reserve for an emergency, and the Nazi *putsch* which ended Dollfuss's life showed that this was no idle whim. But there was no attempt made, beyond earnestly preaching patriotism and Catholic reformism, to condition the thinking of the individual citizen or to control every aspect of his private life.

Dollfuss himself opposed all efforts made by his extreme Right-Wing allies to drive him down that path of tyranny which so many countries of contemporary Europe were treading. His own words reveal this opposition; they show, incidentally, that in trying to soften the harsh trend of the age for his own people he was acting as an Austrian as well as a Christian. It was not merely that he morally condemned the excesses of a Hitler. His peasant's instinct told him that, in terms of practical politics, they could never be imposed on the mass of his own countrymen.

Thus, on the theme of state omnipotence he once declared:[2] 'Authority does not mean arbitrary rule or dictatorship, but leadership by men who are aware of their responsibilities and prepared to make sacrifices. The national character of the Austrian people would make a so-called *Gleichschalterei* (political integration) which conceals nothing but a centralized mechanization, quite intolerable. . . . In order that her own spiritual and material resources can be developed, Austria needs a free folk life, one that gives room for the individual personality and his native creative power to grow, all bound together by the duties of neighbourly love, common racial descent and the common enjoyment of a thousand years of historical experience.' This is not just a different language from Mussolini's in the Piazza Venezia ; it is a different philosophy of life. And to have mentioned Dollfuss in the same breath as Hitler would have been as unjust, and as offensive, to both.

The story which has now become available of that bitter behind-the-scenes dispute over the new Constitution between the Chancellor and the radical *Heimwehr* leaders shows, more-over, that Dollfuss tried honestly to live up to his words. We have seen how the suicide of Parliament in March 1933 created a temporary political vacuum and how, after the long period of sterile deadlock, a new approach to the problems and perils of the day was almost invited ; we have also seen how Dollfuss, for four weeks undecided how to proceed, was first launched on his non-party and non-Parliament course by that personal experience in Villach in early April. The non-party aspect of his programme had taken shape already the following May with the hurried creation of the 'Fatherland Front'. But the non-Parliament aspect called just as urgently for a new theory of government, in other words a new Constitution ; and on June 29, 1933, while on a visit to Bregenz, Dollfuss requested his former chief, Dr. Ender, to undertake this task. Ender at first hesitated, smelling trouble for his own conscience as well as for Austria. It was only when Dollfuss assured him that the constitution he had in mind 'must be and will be democratic' that the ex-Chancellor gave his consent. Three weeks later, assisted by a small flock of legal advisers, Ender moved back into the Vienna Ballhausplatz as 'Minister for Constitutional Reform'. The violent struggle within the Austrian Right Wing over the new political order had begun.

This continued throughout that summer, autumn and winter, and it was not until the 2nd of February, 1934, that the Austrian Cabinet first glimpsed a provisional text of the Constitution. The document presented to them then was the product of no fewer than thirteen major re-drafts, whose compromises and internal contradictions reflected all the ideological confusion and the clash of wills which bedevilled Dollfuss at his task. In true Austrian style, what had emerged was not a simple instrument for dictatorship or for anything else, but rather a mixed bag of political tools thrown together in the hope that, even if most of them could not be used at the moment, a use would be found for all of them some time.

This very muddle provided, however, a certain measure of checks and safeguards on that authoritarian government which was installed at the centre. The Federal President was not a powerful figure ; but he was no mere nominated nonentity. The provinces had relinquished much of their prized freedom to the capital, but they still retained their separate personality. The five advisory chambers of the *Stände* had no power to make or break laws, but their mere existence served to clog up the wheels of any state authority, whether Fascist or liberal. And quite apart from the nineteen unexceptionable articles on the Rights of the Citizen, the theory of democracy itself got a somewhat pathetic honourable mention in the introduction. The commentary to the very first article which (quite dishonestly) declares the new Austria to be a Federal State reads : 'How far the democratic principle will be given expression can only be judged after the laws concerning the creation of the Federal Cultural Council etc. are in force'.

In fact, just before Hitler marched in four years later,

negotiations had started up to give the two most important of these advisory bodies, the Council of State and the Federal Diet, the right to initiate laws as well as discuss them. This was not a contradiction of Dollfuss's concept but the expression of his own desperate long-term hope that somehow, sometime, when the Nazi threat had been mastered abroad and the 'honest workers' had been turned into loyal patriots at home, a sort of paternalist democracy would evolve in Austria. It was just as typical a compromise with reality as Austro-Marxism, and just as doomed.

Even the vaguest of these democratic loopholes had to be fought for, however, against the Right-Wing extremists, above all against the *Heimwehr* leaders Fey and Neustädter-Stürmer. The very first concept which Ender worked out had described Austria, for example, as a 'democratic corporative Republic' (his own view, and that of Dollfuss, being that these two attributes could easily be reconciled). And, though the word 'democratic' was later dropped, the word 'Fascist' was never substituted, despite the fact that the *Heimwehr* were busy at the time proclaiming this as the only possible basis for the new order.

Dollfuss's own efforts to give the Constitution as liberal a flavour as possible are best illustrated by the dispute over the election of the Federal President, which held up agreement over the final draft until a few days before its publication. The Right-Wing extremists were determined to have an indirect election — either by the Council of State or by a special Electoral College — in order to emphasize that the President was purely a nominee of the *Stände*. Dollfuss's democratic advisers — above all Ender and the *Landbund* leader Winkler — insisted that the Head of State must be freely elected by the people, even if their choice of candidates were to be restricted. It was Dollfuss himself who found a formula in between, but leaning closer to the democrats than to the *Heimwehr* : the President was to be elected in secret ballot by all the mayors of Austria, choosing between three names selected by the State Council.

A similar conflict raged over the degree of centralization the new system was to possess. Ender urged the retention of wide autonomy for the provinces ; the *Heimwehr* clamoured for a strongly centralist order based on the Fascist pattern. Again, Dollfuss tried to mediate in order to get Cabinet agreement for the text. Again a compromise emerged, though this time it was one which suited the *Heimwehr* better than the Right-Wing democrats. However, even those concessions which the Chancellor made to the *Heimwehr* thesis on these points were directed more against Adolf Hitler than against liberalism.

Dollfuss was too much of an Austrian not to have realized that, in the long run, the provinces would always remain the pillars of the state, and his views on diversity as the essential basis of Austrian life have already been quoted. But, in the immediate future, a higher degree of centralism seemed vital on security grounds, for the provinces were the entrance gates to the capital. This consideration was, for example, decisive in the Chancellor's mind in agreeing to the appointment of a Security Director, nominated by Vienna, to guide each Provincial Governor. His object in trimming such traditional rights of the provinces was not to destroy their existence, but to preserve it. That his Socialist opponents came to agree with him here is shown by the fact that this particular aspect of his centralization programme was retained by the Coalition Government of the Second Republic, to deal with the new emergency of the occupation, and is still in force in the free Austria of today.

Here we come up against the hard rock underlying all the tangle of legal shrubbery with which the Constitution was invested. Despite the idealism which, on Dollfuss's part, inspired it, for the Austria of the day it was a 'Provisorium' designed to meet an emergency rather than to match any one ideology or destroy another. Just as the supreme convenience of the Fatherland Front had been the excuse it provided for dissolving the Nazi Party along with all other parties, so the supreme object of the May Constitution was to ward off a German *Anschluss* by its tightened security at the top and its patriotism at the bottom. That Dollfuss intended to ease off this firm anchor of state control as soon as he thought the ship could ride the Nazi storm has been testified to by all his principal advisers and friends who have survived from those hectic days.

The best known of them, his successor Kurt Schuschnigg, has put it in the following words: [3] 'Dollfuss's ultimate aim was to revive the old Parliament, even if in a modified form, and build the various corporative Councils and Diets of the 1934 Constitution around it. We all knew that the system as it stood was too rigid and inorganic. But none of us saw how any relaxation of the central authority could be permitted as long as the Nazi pressure, inside and outside the country, was so strong. It was a vicious circle. Hitler's threats seemed to justify our adopting even some of the *Heimwehr*'s political demands as a temporary stiffening of the Government's power. Yet the threats and the pressure only went on mounting steadily after May 1934. We were given no peace and no time to make adjustments. However, I am sure of one thing : something new and drastic had to be attempted after 1933 to jolt some sense into the radicals on both sides. Even a Left-Wing dictatorship would have been better than continuing with the suspicious, intolerant deadlock of the old party system.'

This is of course the heartfelt cry of politicians in all ages and all nations : reformers have always pleaded for more time just as generals have always pleaded for more arms. But in the case of a Chancellor who, in the space of two years, tried to rescue his country's economy, recast its whole social and political system, restore its faith and pride in itself, realign its foreign policy and keep the most ruthless tyrant of the 20th century from its throat, the plea, for once, might be considered reasonable.

*   *   *

Having looked at some of the strange blossoms of Dollfuss's New Order, we must now search briefly for its roots. To a far greater extent than is generally realized, these can be found in Dollfuss himself. The version presented by his political opponents — that Dollfuss more or less took down the 1934 Constitution at dictation from Mussolini — is just as bad history as it is good propaganda. We have seen what battles in fact raged over the creation of the new system. Reference has also been made earlier to those corporative theories of government which had been current in Austria since the time of Vogelsang and which, in Dollfuss's day, had been vigorously revived by philosophers such as Othmar Spann. Indeed it can be proved, not only that Dollfuss was familiar with these theories, but that he personally subscribed to them, long before he could ever have dreamed of applying them politically. Dollfuss's law teacher and lifelong friend Dr. Rischanek has described how,[4] in 1920, he entered his Vienna lecture room to hear a lively debate in progress between young Dollfuss and another law student, a woman employee of the Town Hall. Like any true representative of that Socialist stronghold, she was defending the merits of the Trades Union system. Dollfuss, on the other hand, was supporting the thesis that the relationship between the craftsman and his apprentice or between the peasant-farmer and his labourer, which was both paternal and fraternal, made far better social sense. At this time, Mussolini was still an unknown adventurer and the word Fascism had barely been heard north of the Alps.

During the following ten years, when his work as an agrarian reformer absorbed all his interests, Dollfuss's thinking was basically non-political. Yet, if only because the peasantry constituted the *Stand*, the closed interest community *par ex-cellence*, these convictions must have unconsciously ripened. Sure enough, Schuschnigg confirms that when he first met Dollfuss in 1930 — at a time when neither was yet even in the Cabinet — the little peasant leader spoke at length of solving Austria's current difficulties by the corporative approach of the *Stände*, which alone might settle the friction between employer and employed. Typically, it was of practical economic problems which Dollfuss was thinking — to be precise, the difficulties of ensuring stable wheat prices for his farmers. But the philosophy itself seems to have been already fully implanted, and it only needed power, added to opportunity, for him to transpose it into the political field.

It is true that, from the early 1930's onwards, Rome gave a mounting impetus and an increasing authority to these ideas — for Dollfuss as for all of Vogelsang's followers. It is also true that, by the beginning of 1934, the personal pressure of Mussolini in this respect was prodding Dollfuss along and driving his *Heimwehr* allies forward in a headlong rush. But, in that spring of 1933, when Dollfuss took his first decision about the New Order, it was to the Vatican rather than to the Palazzo Chigi whence he looked for inspiration. The initial Italian influence, and a dominating one throughout, was spiritual.

On May 15, 1931, Pope Pius XI issued his famous encyclical on Catholic social reform 'Quadragesimo Anno', thus called because it was published on the fortieth anniversary of Pope Leo XIII's pioneering encyclical on a similar theme, the *Rerum Novarum*. Pope Pius's words gave the devout Dollfuss all the blessing and the backing he needed to turn his back on the wreckage of a self-detonated Austrian Parliament. As he declared himself two years later : 'We want to be the first to turn the words of this noble encyclical into reality'.

It must be made clear that, though 'Quadragesimo Anno' was patently anti-Communist and anti-Socialist, it gave no support to the idea of the authoritarian state as such, let alone to any form of Fascism. Indeed, the political framework in which the Pope's ideas were to be fulfilled was left by him deliberately open with these words : 'The people should have complete liberty to choose any state form they please, provided it meets the needs of justice and of the common good'. But the corporative ideal, with all the negation of normal party and parliamentary systems it implied, was backed up to the hilt.

The encyclical begins by deploring the 'split of society' into two classes brought about by the Industrial Revolution : 'One class, small in number, enjoying almost alone the amenities so richly provided by modern inventions ; the other class, comprising the vast mass of the workers, suffering under the burden of piteous need, and unable, despite their most vigorous efforts, to free themselves from their woeful situation'. Unscrupulous Liberalism had become the doctrine of the possessing class, and equally unscrupulous Marxism the doctrine of the dispossessed. To prevent the Christian values of society being destroyed by the conflict between these two, both the state and the individual, inspired alike by the religious faith of true neighbourly love, must make a completely new approach to the problems of social and economic organization. The aim of this new approach must be to end the conflict between capital and labour, preached by the Marxists, by showing that such a conflict is not only unnecessary but unnatural. Thus : 'Capital can do just as little without labour as labour can without capital . . . it is completely contrary to justice when one side or the other, claiming exclusive rights, tries to appropriate the total gain for itself'. The new approach needed can only offset the 'sweet-tasting poison' of Marxist doctrine by 'de-proletarizing the proletariat' ; and this, in turn, can only be done by enabling the worker to accumulate property and some reserve of capital himself.

Politically, the encyclical continues, these aims can only be achieved by reorganizing human society on a corporative basis : 'The revival of a corporative order is the socio-political aim . . . really effective remedies can hardly be achieved except through creating properly-fashioned limbs of the social organism, in other words *Stände*, which the individual joins not because he belongs to the different labour market camps of employer and employed, but because of his own individual social function'. Once these *Stände* have been organized, they should take over the day-to-day administration of 'less important matters'. Having delegated these responsibilities the state authority 'thus becomes freer, stronger and more effective to discharge those tasks which are its exclusive province — guiding, supervising, emphasizing and chastening according to needs and circumstances'.

And finally, unless any believer should be under the illusion that this could all be brought about through the current Social Democratic doctrines of the day, a six-line paragraph is added with the terse heading : 'A Catholic and a Socialist cannot be reconciled'. Despite some of its positive aspects, the theory of Socialism is declared to be 'in contradiction with the true Christian concept'. Then follows the categorical edict : 'It is impossible to be at the same time a good Catholic and a real Socialist'.

These were the doctrines, not Mussolini's parody of them, which Dollfuss seized upon — doctrines which, as we have seen, already formed the central pole of his simple political philosophy. And it is safe to say that, despite the emergencies of the hour, Dollfuss only let himself be driven down Mussolini's path to the extent to which he thought he could reconcile this with the Vatican's teaching. It was the crossed keys of St. Peter, not the Fascio of the Black Shirts, which he tried to hold before him. Pope Pius's concept of the state as a strong, untrammelled guiding hand ; benevolent, yet severe if need be ; paternal yet brotherly, and firmly marshalling humanity along the road to corporative bliss, was exactly the Dollfuss ideal.

When related to the intricacies of modern society and to the harsh realities of his own dictatorship era it was, of course, hopeless to try and achieve this ideal and naïve even to contemplate it. But what we are concerned to demonstrate here is the sincerity, not the profundity, of Dollfuss's political thinking ; and also its unique Christian inspiration. He read and re-read the 1931 Encyclical a hundred times, and direct echoes of it are always appearing in his speeches. The whole of the historical introduction to his major Trabrennplatz speech of September 11, 1933, is a faithful copy of the Pope's words, even down to the conflict described between those two political 'evils' — Manchester Liberalism and Marxism.

In this way, Pope Pius XI both completed and sanctified the Chancellor's vision 'Austriam Instaurare in Christo'. And this Dollfuss linked, in turn, with his rediscovery of Austria's 'historical mission'. For him, the May Constitution was a 20th-century projection of the Habsburgs' role in the Counter-Reformation or of the part played by Vienna in 1683 in saving the Empire (and Europe) from the Turks. The awful snag was that, instead of Martin Luther or the Sultan Kara Mustafa, it was now, according to Pius XI, the Socialist who was the Infidel. Those fateful six lines in the Encyclical caused Dollfuss — and probably Austria — a lot of trouble.

On the crucial point of authoritarianism, it can be argued that this seemed to some extent 'justified' by the Pope's references to a 'strong state arm' which would chide as well as guide. But it must also be remembered that there was much in Dollfuss's own background and training which made 'healthy discipline' appeal to him. His education at Hollabrunn had been strict and regulated, and his years in the Army had continued the conditioning process. Dollfuss as a young man never showed the slightest tendencies to becoming either a martinet in public life or a bully in private life. Yet, before he entered into politics, he was a man who had learnt to give orders by the simple process of first learning to obey them.

Above all, of course, it was the strong paternal discipline of his stepfather's farm in Kirnberg which remained with him all his life — as a political model as well as a spiritual support. The fact, already noted, that the peasantry of Austria represented the one really natural *Stand* (they and the civil servants were in fact the only groups to get properly organized in the new system) made this model even more compelling. This comes out quite literally in the speech with which he announced the forthcoming reforms. To quote this again : 'In the farmhouse where the peasant sits down at the same table with his labourers after their common work, eating his soup out of the same bowl — there you find a real sense of corporative belonging, a true corporative conception. And their relationship becomes even nobler when they kneel down together to say their prayers.' As one sees, the Pope did not need to add anything to that picture. All he had to do was to bless it.

But however devout a Catholic Dollfuss may have been, he was also Chancellor of Austria, and a fighter. His new order had to fulfil certain practical objectives, which were separate from the religious ideal, even if related in some way to it. The most immediate of these objectives has already been mentioned : to devise a non-party system which could swallow the Austrian Nazis with the maximum of security to the country and the minimum of offence to Hitler.

There were two other aims in Dollfuss's mind — broader, deeper and of longer range. One was to fashion a mass movement which would both reflect and foster the new doctrine of state-patriotism he was preaching *vis-à-vis* Nazi Germany. The second was to devise an ideology which would justify, to himself and to posterity, this opposition to that parent German race whose tongue and culture Austria shared, and in which so many Austrians, Dollfuss included, had sought salvation after the war. He found both. The Fatherland Front and the May Constitution not only matched his spiritual needs. They also solved the problem — as far as it ever was solved, or ever will be — of how to be a good Austrian without being a bad German.

For all these solutions, spiritual or secular, Dollfuss sought the blessing of history. Indeed, the revolutionary thing about his unashamed patriotism (and it *was* revolutionary in the Vienna of 1934 to cover the capital with placards proclaiming 'Österreich über alles!') was that — deliberately and publicly — he tried to link the country's troubled present with her resplendent past. He was the first to nail down that lie implicit in the whole Austro-Marxist approach to life, the lie that the Austrians only began existing in November 1918. All those centuries which the fanatics of the Left Wing tried to ignore he brought back to their rightful place in the affections of his people.

In all this, even his bitterest enemies could never accuse him of trying to put the clock back by restoring the Imperialist order in the Danube Basin. In his upbringing, Dollfuss had been Republican rather than Monarchist (as his student conflict with E. K. Winter showed) ; and as Chancellor he never lent his influence to any Restoration schemes, if only because he considered them totally impracticable. Talking to that same E. K. Winter on the eve of his own murder he remarked : 'The House of Austria, with its ancient roots, must anyway be able to wait if it ever hopes to come to power again'. Here was the realism of a Republican Chancellor, combined with the respect of a former Imperial Army lieutenant.

But if he did not fight for the return of the Empire he fought for its memory. What else indeed — except the fatalistic cosmopolitan pipe-dreams of the Austro-Marxists — *did* the Austrians have to help them look Nazi Germany squarely in the face ? Their present was altogether too 'nasty, brutish and short'.

Accordingly, when Dollfuss announced his new pro-gramme to the nation, on a date deliberately picked because it was the 250th anniversary of the defeat of the Turks before

Vienna, this was the note he struck with his opening words :

'St. Stephen's Cathedral and the memory of the Turkish siege recall for us the great history of our homeland. Two hundred and fifty years ago the Viennese held out, loyal and brave, under Starhemberg, the commander of the defence. We rejoice that the name of Starhemberg has been preserved in our homeland and that one of the descendants of that Rüdiger Starhemberg of old is among those who are rebuilding Austria today.'

After a few words of praise for Prince Eugene, whose relief army raised the great siege, Dollfuss went back lovingly to the Middle Ages, 'that period in which the people were organized and formed up according to their calling or occupation ; when the worker was not incited against his master ; when the economy and social order were both based on the grouping together of all those who earned their bread by the same form of work'.

Then came the attacks, already referred to, on 19th-century Liberalism ; on Marxism, its equally evil rival ; and on Austria's post-war parliamentarianism, in which this barren conflict of ideologies had continued until its own self-destruction as an institution the year before. All this led up to the central pledge which was as resonant as it was confusing : 'The age of the capitalist system and of the capitalist-liberalist economic order is past ; the days of materialistic Marxist betrayal are also finished. The rule of parties is over and done with. We reject terror and *Gleichschalterei*. What we want is the social, Christian, German state of Austria, built on a corporative basis and under firm authoritarian leadership.'

Everything is in this pledge, including the acknowledgement of Austria's German character. This led Dollfuss on to his second theme — the resolving of the state versus nation antithesis within the new order. In words directed at Adolf Hitler as well as at that split personality which hovered like an ectoplasm over his audience, he continued :

'We are German, so obviously German that it seems to us superfluous to stress the fact. And we declare here that it is our aim to serve this German people, in loyalty and honour. What we seek to do is to preserve the good qualities of the German race . . . and we refuse to be talked out of this even if attempts are made to deny our essentially genuine German character. We believe that it is our duty to preserve the true German culture in these Christian lands of Central Europe . . . to fashion this culture into an Austrian mould. We leave it to future generations to judge who in this question is serving the German cause the best.'

A few months later, he developed this theme in that same Christmas address in which he had rejected the Nazi-type tyranny and state omnipotence as a model for Austria. 'Our guiding principle in our relations with other people is universalist', he said, 'and in this we have preserved an important and characteristic element in the German way of life. . . . It is thus unfair to reproach us Austrians for standing apart from and even opposing the German nation. It is precisely in our Austrian way that we feel ourselves to be a genuine component of the German whole . . . and it is our duty as individuals and as a people not only to safeguard this Austrian way of life but to get it realized in the life of the whole German people and of Europe.'

In other words, Austria could be proud of her new patriotism directed at Nazi Germany because what this essentially sought to do was to rescue the old German values, prostituted by Hitler, for future happier generations which would be unplagued by dictatorships. It was, in particular, the universalist concept of the old Holy Roman Empire which Hitler (and the Prussian nationalists before him) had betrayed : both at home, by seeking to bend all cultures and all opinions to one mould, and abroad, by trying to impose the swastika on the whole of a diversified continent. Austria's task was to preserve this ancient German universalism, with all the tolerance which the concept implied, from the clutches of Goebbels and Rosenberg ; to blend and combine, as Barbarossa had once done ; to re-create, on the quaking political battle-field of the present, her own cultural miracle of the Baroque ; to preserve, in a sort of Danubian Shangri-La, the essence of German civilization for a calmer future to enjoy.

The fact that it was a David and Goliath proposition only lent the struggle a Biblical radiance. 'Nolite timere, pusillus grex.' 'Fear not, little flock.' And when one thinks of the odds, the surprising thing is not that Dollfuss failed in his task, but that he, or any other Austrian of his time, should ever have tackled it.

*   *   *

Before passing on to Goliath's bloody triumph we must try and fix a closer personal picture of his little challenger. The only similarity between the two unequal protagonists, apart from the fact that both were born on Austrian soil, was the magnetism they exerted on their fellow-men. Yet even this common factor pointed the contrast rather than the likeness. The force of Hitler's personality was demonic and therefore impersonal : it was the complexes, expressed in passions, which compelled, and not the human being. Dollfuss, with his huge mild eyes of a quite startling blue, his infectious smile, and his almost childish simplicity of manner, drew others in his wake primarily as a warm and likeable person. His political passions, such as they were, sprang from his own nature and were filtered through it into action.

This essential humanity shone through all the trials and temptations of power. For the statesman, as for the student, family and friends remained an indispensable part of his life, and he never sought to replant his own personal roots in the artificial soil of politics. The company of others was always a mental as well as a social necessity. He was incapable of brooding, and Hitler's concept of the politician as a solitary superman dwelling on Olympian heights always struck him as faintly comic, as well as distinctly vulgar and 'un-Austrian'. He was a debater rather than an orator and loved to listen as much as to talk. He thus sought the truth by allowing ideas to interplay rather than by imposing them ; so much so that most of his major speeches as Chancellor were the product of informal round-table discussions deliberately convened beforehand, with Dollfuss jotting down on the back of a match-box salient catchwords from the conversation. All this gave to his words in sincerity and spontaneity what they lacked in elegance or brilliance. He was the improvisor *par excellence*, and never the premeditated intellectual.

As a man, he was remarkably free from personal inhibitions, those deadly cancers of the man in power. One must write 'remarkably' because, after all, he was born a bastard and only grew to be five foot high. Socially, he was without embarrassment simply because he was without ambition. He made no attempt to cover up his obscure and humble origins, and this very lack of affectation enabled him to move with the same natural assurance under the crystal chandeliers of Vienna as under the oil lamps of his native Kirnberg parlour. He was always at ease because he never pretended ; and, since such simplicity of manner is most often found among the very highest or the very lowest born, Dollfuss could move in any society without either snobbery or shame. The best example of this is the human contact he found with Prince Starhemberg, despite the vast disparities, physical as well as social, which separated that tall and indolent descendant of the hero of 1683 from the tiny, hard-working peasant's son. For him, Starhemberg was always 'Ernstl', never 'the Prince', and the two men used the familiar 'Du' to each other without a shred of awkwardness.

Indeed, Dollfuss was not even put out of countenance on those occasions when the two men were forcibly reminded of their difference in origin. A friend has described how the

Chancellor, about to go to Rome, started discussing with Starhemberg the unofficial political possibilities of the trip. A Congress of the Knights of Malta was due to meet in the Italian capital at the same time, and Dollfuss felt this might give him a useful chance of tackling other visitors, like the German statesman von Papen, informally. 'After all,' he said, 'I can easily turn up at one of their functions.' The handsome princely brows knitted. 'But,' exclaimed Starhemberg, 'that's only for the aristocracy.' 'Oh, get away with you,' was Dollfuss's immediate reply, 'I have a decoration from the Vatican that makes me technically a Duke of Rome — surely to goodness *that* would be enough for all your precious Maltese Knights ?' Produced with his disarming grin and utter lack of pompousness, remarks like this penetrated the stiffest armour of protocol.

A question less easy to determine is how far Dollfuss suffered inwardly from his small stature and to what extent his political career, the authoritarianism included, represented a conscious or subconscious attempt to compensate for this. At first sight, the opinions and anecdotes collected on this point from thirty or forty of his surviving admirers and opponents seem to form a complete and baffling contrast. On the one hand we hear, time and time again, that he relished the famous 'Dollfuss jokes', even collecting them on his travels and telling them against himself; yet many who worked close to him claim that, on the contrary, he secretly detested all this ridicule, however fondly it was meant.

But the contradiction is perhaps resolved when we discover that nearly all of those who have pleaded his indifference belonged to his intimate circle of family and friends, whereas those who have pleaded his sensitivity belonged more to his official life. Dollfuss was, in all personal matters, tolerant to a fault. Yet, whether as an officer, a bureaucrat or a Minister, he had a high sense of the duty and the inherent dignity of office. This may be the clue to the riddle. In his home at

the Stallburggasse, or at a game of 'Taroque' in the local
Café 'Korb', anything was allowed that was not vicious or
in doubtful moral taste. (He had no love for the dirty joke,
whether it concerned him or not.) Such was Dollfuss the
man. But in public life, where the man was also the statesman, the same liberty was not permitted. Thus he never
resigned himself to the mocking soubriquet of 'Millimetter-
nich': partly because it had been coined by the Nazis, partly
because it concerned his official self and was therefore aimed
against Austria as well as against his person. This sensitivity
to the dignity of his office was always near the surface, and it
was no respecter of persons.

Early in 1934, for example, one of his closest supporters
reproached him privately in the Chancellery for his excessive
patience under the constant provocation of Austrian Nazis (it
was shortly after an evening when the entire audience at the
Graz Opera, borne aloft on waves of Teutonic music, had
risen from their seats and given the Hitler salute). 'The Nazis
are just laughing at an Austrian Chancellor and at an Austrian
Government which can be insulted with such impunity,' the
friend urged, and went on : 'What do you suppose would
have happened had the same sort of provocation taken place
in Germany?' For the first and last time in this particular
colleague's presence, Dollfuss exploded with rage. The anger
subsided almost as quickly as it had risen, but his final words,
spoken quietly from the great window recess of his office, were
significant : 'You may be right in what you say and I know
you meant it for the best. But remember one thing. You
just cannot talk in that way to the Chancellor of Austria.' It
was not Engelbert Dollfuss, but the leader of his country, on
whose corns the friend had trodden.[5]

It is an irony that the man who was so often portrayed
by his political opponents as a ruthless tyrant should be remembered by all those who came into personal contact with
him as the kindest and gentlest of mortals. The evidence here

is overwhelming : even from the camp of his enemies, not a single anecdote has survived which points to viciousness or brutality in his private character. And those who knew and loved Dollfuss remember him, quite simply, as the best of men.

His selfless generosity and constant concern for the lame dogs of this world is his most obviously endearing feature. We have seen examples of this in Dollfuss the soldier and Dollfuss the peasants' friend. The statesman, judged as a human being, was no different. To him, money was something to give, not to spend. He possessed not a penny in the world beyond his Chancellor's salary, yet, soon after taking office, he set up a purely private charity, financed with 1000 schillings from his monthly earnings, for distribution to deserving cases. A flat immediately under his own, occupied by the police for security reasons, served as the headquarters for this personal activity. The secretary [6] who administered the fund for him has testified that politics did not enter into the distribution. Need, not ideology, was the only yardstick Dollfuss prescribed, and he furthermore gave orders that the whole operation should be kept secret so that it could never be exploited for party or personal propaganda. Month in and month out, an average of thirty requests came in every day, from cranks, spongers and job-seekers as well as the genuinely destitute. All were heard with patience and as many as possible were helped.

Not satisfied with this, Dollfuss became a walking charity himself. His hand was always in his pocket for any 'poor devil' who approached him or whom he had simply glimpsed on the street, and it was small wonder that the pockets rapidly emptied. His widow remembers many a month when the family of the Austrian Federal Chancellor had no housekeeping money left after the twentieth ; and his secretary, Dr. Krisch, grew cheerfully resigned to lending his chief a few hundred schillings as the thirtieth approached, and he had nothing left to give an old *Kaiserschuetzen* comrade who had turned up at the Ballhausplatz to 'pump' him. This was the real charity which sought neither thanks nor advertisement nor reward, and the deep kindness of the man is shown by his concern even to avoid causing pain by his giving.

Once, for example, he sighted in his ante-room an old friend who had fallen on bad days — down-at-heel, bedraggled and perched like a scruffy hen on one of the little gilt chairs outside the Chancellor's office. It was obvious that a request for help was coming and equally obvious that the friend would be acutely embarrassed to be received in this desolate state. So Dollfuss, without giving a sign of recognition as he walked past, summoned a senior official and ordered him to approach the abject figure on any wild pretext he could think up, inviting him for a brief stay at a 'state rest home'. This was simply an inn, picked at random on the outskirts of Vienna, where the bewildered tramp was lodged for a fortnight at Dollfuss's expense, fattened up with good food and made generally presentable. Soon after the end of this 'convalescence' he reappeared in the Chancellor's waiting-room, was received by Dollfuss with a show of delighted astonishment, and duly provided with a job and a new start in life.[7]

Dollfuss could never have given at this rate had his own tastes not been frugal in the extreme. Cigarettes, of which he often smoked forty a day, were, in fact, his only indulgence. He was a moderate drinker. Cards, a game of skittles or a horse ride in the Prater Fun Fair satisfied what little need he felt for distraction outside his work and family. Wine he enjoyed, but in moderation, and, to the end of his days, his favourite meal was the 'Stohsuppe' of the Lower Austrian peasant — a bowl of thick sour milk soup, eaten with slices of that cheap Vienna 'Salafadi' sausage which, in the Emperor Franz Josef's day, had been the cabman's dinner at five kreutzer a time.

His flat as Chancellor was the same that he had occupied

as an agrarian official and, despite the momentous gatherings which convened there, it still breathed the modest rustic spirit of those days. The dining-room was so narrow that the maid had trouble squeezing between the table and the back wall when guests were present; the sitting-room was plainly furnished with chairs and a sofa of dark leather, and a book-case filled with agrarian handbooks, economic treatises and theological works. The ornaments were few, but they included another relic of the old days whose history is again typical of the occupant. This was a bronze bust of one Zwetzbacher, a well-known and well-loved Lower Austrian peasant leader of the Empire who had fallen into disgrace and oblivion in the post-war years through some personal scandal. The bust, which had once proudly graced the Conference Room of the Agricultural Chamber, had accordingly been banished to a dusty cupboard. There it languished until Dollfuss, at that time Director of the same Chamber which Zwetzbacher had helped to build up, discovered it and declared he would take it home with him. When asked by a surprised friend what the controversial figure was doing in the drawing-room of the Chancellor, Dollfuss replied with a shrug: 'I brought it here because I simply can't bear to see a man like that being thrown aside like a dirty rag'.

The remark was typical of that loyalty which Dollfuss showed to all who had ever enjoyed his love or friendship. He rose to the top without a trace of 'side', and the humblest of his former comrades from the Kirnberg fields, the Hollabrunn school-rooms or the Isonzo trenches was always welcome. Indeed, his staff learned to greet the appearance of any of these old-time friends with a philosophic groan, for, even if Austria and the rest of the world seemed on fire, Dollfuss would push aside his mound of papers and find an hour for a gossip.

Anyone from his lowly past who tried to avoid the Chancellor just to save him embarrassment got short shrift. One modest village priest [8] who had sat with Dollfuss in the same class for eight years at Hollabrunn, has described how he turned up at the Catholic Congress in Vienna in 1933, to hear his famous friend make a major speech. The Chancellor was seated at the front, flanked by the Papal Legate, the Cardinal-Archbishop and other high dignitaries of Church and State. The village priest, who had rarely seen such an assembly of purple at close quarters, hid himself shyly many rows behind. But the moment Dollfuss spotted him among the sea of heads, his well-meant concealment was over and done with. The Chancellor left his guests, pushed his way back to greet his school comrade, and then insisted on bringing him down to be introduced to all the resplendent figures on the rostrum. This was no electioneering trick, for Austria anyway had passed beyond elections. Dollfuss had found an old friend, and was doing on a public platform what he would have done at home.

His devotion to the old Kirnberg farmhouse and everyone inside it has been mentioned already. One of his greatest joys, in those two terrible years of power, was to be driven home for a day along the dusty, scented side-roads of Lower Austria and there, for a few hours, to feel again the roots of his being. On these visits, politics were forgotten, and the ageless gossip of the peasant took their place : local weddings and scandals, the buying and selling of land, the state of the crops, the health of the cattle, the price of wheat and the ravages of the hail-storm. And though Dollfuss was firmly established as one of the leading agrarian experts of Europe, he listened to his stepfather Leopold Schmutz talking about winter seed or the cattle plague with the same deference he had always shown him. Incidentally, no member of the entire family either asked for or was given a single favour at the hands of their famous son. Nepotism, like materialism, was not in the Dollfuss blood.

As the agony of Austria grew and the work piled up, these visits became steadily rarer. Often, the best Dollfuss could do was to fly over Sattlehen Number Four on his way to or from some foreign capital and wave down at the black and white dots assembled on the meadow before the house. They seem never to have been far from his thoughts. On one of his visits to the Vatican, for example, he asked the Pope if he would bless a crucifix specially for his family. Pius XI gladly consented ; but, as Dollfuss was needed with great urgency back in Vienna, the problem was how to deliver the sacred image. The Chancellor decided he would pass over Kirnberg on the return flight and drop the crucifix quite literally from the skies.

One who flew back with him has described the scene : 'Almost before the small two-engined plane had droned over the familiar village church, Dollfuss had picked out his farmhouse and the Schmutz family — who had been alerted — assembled in front of it. He leant out of the cabin window, his hair streaming in the wind, and ordered his long-suffering personal pilot to circle lower and lower. With complete disregard of the pilot's protests, of air safety regulations and of our own skins, he forced the plane down and down until we were banking barely one hundred feet above the farmhouse roof. Then, at the last minute, he dropped the precious relic over the heads of his excited family. He misjudged the distance a little so that the Pope's crucifix fell, safely and softly, right on top of a dung-hill. With a wave of his hand we were up and away to Vienna, the pilot muttering softly and wiping his brow and the Chancellor beaming and chuckling all the way.' 9

This peasant background was sometimes dominant, but sometimes curiously absent, in Dollfuss's character and behaviour as a politician. His mental agility and adaptability, the speed with which he could reach decisions, his sensitivity and, above all, his easy charm of manner — all these belonged more to a cosmopolitan Viennese banker rather than to a heavy slow-thinking farmer. Yet the Lower Austrian peasant stock came out strongly enough in his sheer tenacity and physical toughness, his ability to out-sit and out-talk both colleagues and critics at all-night sessions in smoky rooms ; it came out in the moral unshakeability of a man who could never be bribed or bullied out of a course he felt to be right ; in his habit of reaching decisions by instinct rather than by logic and sticking to them through thick and thin once they were reached ; it came out in his frugality and in his piety.

Inevitably, some of these qualities got bent out of shape by the pressures of power. The mental nimbleness, for example, led him to pursue a dozen possible solutions to a problem at once, like a conjurer spinning his coloured balls in the air ; and though Dollfuss's own dexterity rarely failed him, he often succeeded in confusing his colleagues as well as his opponents with his juggling. Politically speaking, his piety was also a double-edged weapon. It robbed him of that minimum of mistrust in his fellows which is useful to any statesman and, towards the end, it took on an irrational crusading tinge. This gave him strength but exposed him to the dangers of political intolerance. He seems to have grown fully convinced of this 'divine mission' of his after escaping with slight injuries from an attack by a political crank in 1933. At all events, it was shortly afterwards that he told a circle of close friends : 'As I recovered from those wounds I became convinced that I had been given a task to follow, irrespective of whether I should succeed or not. We are all God's messengers and each of us has a message to pass on. Once I wanted to be a priest. But it seems I was intended for the world after all. Only Christ can save men's souls and only He can help society. I feel I must now try and lead this society to Him. That is my mission.' [10]

This, and other utterances like it were, however, made without any show of 'hybris'. For though his sense of mission had to be identified with his high office, the latter always seems to have been subordinated to it in his mind. He certainly remained under no illusions about the way in which power could eat like a slow acid into men's hearts. Shortly before he was murdered he exclaimed to an old friend who had always kept himself out of public office : 'One of the reasons why I always enjoy coming to talk with you is that I get an honest opinion, whether it contradicts my own or not. The big trouble which I'm always trying to guard myself against is that, as Chancellor, one is surrounded by "Yes-men" and, before you know where you are, there is a terrible danger of thinking yourself infallible.' [11]

And the same spoken reverie in which Dollfuss first mentioned his 'mission' was ended by him with these words : 'Politics ! What on earth do I really care about them ? I can't go on anyway for much longer as my hearing is slowly going,[12] and in a way I'm glad. When the new Constitution is properly launched, and when the situation abroad has calmed down a bit, then I want to quit and do the thing I've always wanted to do — write books. I don't want to hang on until I'm of no use any more. In the middle of one's work — it's anyway never finished — that's how I'd like to go!' This wish, at any rate, was to be granted.

The reader may well be beginning to ask himself with a rather weary curiosity : had this little paragon then no failings ? In truth, he seems to have been without a serious moral vice ; so much so that, after his death, a sincere agitation could be launched to have him pronounced a blessed martyr by the Church. Of his ordinary human weaknesses, most were of the type that are endearing in a private person and damaging only in a statesman. He was, for example, uncertain in his judgement of men, mainly because of his naïve and almost boundless faith in the fundamental goodness of his fellows. This led him, on at least one occasion, to appoint to public office a friend whose hands were certainly not as clean as his own. More dangerous, it sometimes meant that men were kept too long at their posts who were loyal but ineffective, as was Kemptner, Secretary of the Fatherland Front, or Seydel, Director of the Vienna Police ; or who were even openly intriguing against him, like his own Minister for Security, Emil Fey. In the last critical months of his Chancellorship, this particular exhibition of tolerance could only be called hair-raising ; yet, whenever he was reproached in private about his attitude to Fey, Dollfuss would reply : 'I can prove nothing against him and, until I have the proof, he is innocent as far as I'm concerned'.

This trustfulness, verging at times on gullibility, certainly weakened his administration. And, as far as party politics went, he suffered just as plainly from being excessively susceptible. He was quick to feel and slow to forgive any affront to his public dignity and, on occasions, could behave churlishly to the offenders. An example already mentioned is his treatment of Vaugoin, whose election as Chairman of the Christian-Social Party seemed to rouse a personal resentment in Dollfuss's mind. A lesser-known case was that of a certain Baron Beck, a worthy ex-Imperial official, whose career in the Republic was said to have been blighted from the moment he inadvertently announced someone ahead of Dollfuss at the top of a list of platform speakers. This same acute sensitivity came automatically into play whenever the Chancellor was attacked *ad personam* by his Socialist opponents. After each attack, the piers of that never-to-be-built golden bridge between Left and Right were weakened accordingly.

Yet, right to the end, Dollfuss remained in his private life kindly, tolerant and relaxed — without a sign of that pettiness or touchiness which he was capable of displaying in office. The explanation we have already suggested for this paradox was that, in his eyes, the man counted for nothing and the Chancellor for everything ; an insult to his office was an insult to his country and all that he was striving to make out of it. Such ambivalence is not unique in politics.

Indeed, in his mysticism, his pride, his fanatical patriotism, his sense of mission to revive all that was splendid and noble in his nation's past, Dollfuss felt for Austria exactly as, twenty-five years later, Charles de Gaulle was to feel for France. Fittingly enough, both were brave soldiers and devout Catholics ; both had the same simplicity of tastes and the same relentless standards of personal conduct ; both were given power in a domestic and external emergency ; both summoned back history to prop up a tottering present ; both feared and despised parliamentary formalism as the canker in the nation's soul ; both introduced a new constitution which replaced democracy with authoritarianism in an attempt to save the day ; both saw themselves as the innermost conscience and image of their countrymen and were widely acclaimed as such. Also, fittingly, Dollfuss was a tiny Chancellor for a small country, and de Gaulle a towering President for a great power.

CHAPTER SEVEN

The Search for Security

I T was typical of Dollfuss's dilemma, and just as typical of
his countrymen, that he should have been reproached even
for doing the inevitable. This irony came out most strongly
with his foreign policy which was dominated, from his first to his
last day of office, by the ugly brown shadow of Nazi aggression.

There were only three ways to meet this threat, and all of
them had to be tried simultaneously, constantly and with
every ounce of resource and energy at the Government's
command, if the little Republic was to have any chance of
surviving. These three parallel courses were the creation of
an Austrian patriotism strong enough not to be washed away
by all the emotional tides of racial sentiment ; the quest for
some form of 'peace with honour' to be concluded directly
with the big German neighbour and brother ; and, on the
growing assumption that such a truce would either never be
reached or not be respected, the search for a foreign protector
who was both willing and able to shield Austria from Hitler's
blows.

The last requirement gradually became the most urgent of
the three, and in the Europe of 1933/34, Vienna could only
fulfil it by looking across the Alps to Rome. This was not a
question of ideology but of downright necessity ; had Austria
been ruled at the time by a realistic Socialist of Karl Renner's
stamp, he would most probably have swallowed his anti-
Fascist pride and sought some form of guarantees from the
same direction. A drowning man is in no position to grumble
at the colour of the life-belt.

Where else, indeed, could any Austrian Chancellor of the day have looked for effective, as opposed to nominal, support? Russia and America were both still on the moon as regards the worries of the smaller nations of Europe. Britain's only concern at the time was to avoid any rumpus on the continent in the hope that the dictators might leave something of the Versailles crockery intact. France, to whom Austria's Socialists often gazed in their hopeful despair, headed the opposite diplomatic camp : she was the patron of the Little Entente which was designed to keep Austria and Hungary, the *ci-devants* of the old Danubian order, in perpetual check, and whose members (Czechoslovakia, Rumania and Jugoslavia) looked upon Vienna with undisguised suspicion.

It is true that their common fear of a German invasion did help to bring Austria and Czechoslovakia closer together and that, especially under Dollfuss, the economic links between the two countries were strengthened. But the old enmities smouldered on underneath this thin blanket of expediency. Even economically, anything approaching a real integration would have foundered on the high tariff walls set up to protect Czech industry. Politically, like all the succession states, Czechoslovakia mistrusted any ambitious plan for a Danube Federation fearing that, one day, a Habsburg solution might emerge from it. On top of everything came territorial issues inseparable from all Danubian combinations. Prague never abandoned her dream of an 'Austrian corridor' to the sea and, in secret military talks with their Jugoslav and Rumanian allies, the Czechs continued to plan the joint invasion and dismemberment of Austria and Hungary at the slightest 'revanchist provocation'. As for leaning on the old 'sister-nation' of Hungary herself, any isolated move which Vienna might have made towards a pact with Budapest would only have stirred this anti-Habsburg coalition into action, to say nothing of the fact that Horthy's Hungary was anyway flirting too intensively with Hitler to be a reliable ally against him.

Historically and politically, the Vienna-Budapest alignment was, of course, the logical one : it was both the traditional front of the past and the revisionist front of the present.
But diplomatically, it could only come into being in the form
it actually took — a new Central European grouping under
Italian patronage, inserted as a wedge between the rival French
and German ambitions in the Danube Basin. The simple
truth, which overrode all other considerations in 1933–34,
was that Italy, alone of all the Great Powers, had both the
military ability and the political determination to stop German
expansion south-eastwards. At this time Mussolini was an
established European leader whose glittering uniforms reflected
armed might as well as personal vanity ; Hitler was a raw
newcomer to power whose greasy raincoat seemed to sym-
bolize the fact that he was still only one jump away from the
Munich beer-cellars.

By the end of 1932 Mussolini had none the less recognized
the danger from the north. His own long-range plan (to be
completed at leisure after he had founded his African Empire)
was to establish Italian supremacy not only all round the
Adriatic but also deep in the Danubian hinterland beyond —
using Albania, Jugoslavia and Hungary as successive spring-
boards. Hitler's noisily-proclaimed ambitions to take over
Austria did more than just threaten this dream ; they menaced
the security of the Italian fatherland itself. The Italians were
not just using dramatic phrases when they assured Colonel
Liebitzky,[1] the Austrian Military Attaché in Rome : 'We can
never accept a common frontier with Hitler. If the Germans
have breakfast in Innsbruck, they will want to eat their dinner
in Milan.' In short, the alliance between Vienna and Rome
was based on that oldest and strongest principle of politics, a
principle that will always cut across the boundaries of ideology
when the need calls loudly enough : 'The enemies of my
enemies are my friends'.

Only one combination might have been even better, from

Austria's point of view and from Europe's — a united Franco-Italian initiative in the Danube Basin which would have enabled the Little Entente to join up with Vienna and Budapest under a common umbrella of power politics. This idea Dollfuss actually raised in the summer of 1933. But it was only after his murder and partly under the impact of his murder that it was ever seriously discussed between Laval and Mussolini, to be blocked by Hungarian and German opposition, and finally buried under the sands of Mussolini's Abyssinian adventure.

*   *   *

The Nazis began to show their claws in Austria in the summer of 1932, only a few months after they had settled themselves on their perch in Germany. On June 30th of that year, a group of Austrian 'S.A.' rowdies attacked the club-house of the Country Club at Lainz, on the outskirts of Vienna, severely injuring several of the astonished members. It was the first of that long series of outrages — by bomb, bullet or knuckle-duster, by sabotage, blackmail or propaganda insults — which was to continue right up to the final *Anschluss* of March 1938 ; a constant background of violence, broken only by tactical pauses ordered from Munich or Berlin, against which the Austria of Dollfuss and Schuschnigg had to live.

One such comparative lull set in after that initial escapade in the Lainz Tiergarten. For nine months the Nazis just kept in training with an occasional attack on a Jewish shop, but contented themselves mainly with strong-arm tactics at party meetings and street marches, and with building up their secret stocks of arms and explosives. The suicide of Austria's Parliament in March 1933 set them, like the Austrian *Heimwehr*, on a new course. It was now clear to both these rival groups that violence was the only road to power, and the Nazis accordingly launched a nation-wide offensive. This cul-

minated, between the 12th and 19th of June, in a bloody week
of dynamite and hand-grenade outrages perpetrated throughout the country at the cost of several innocent Austrian lives.

Dollfuss had been itching for action for months and was
not reluctant to have his hand forced. He now retorted with
an immediate and total ban on all the activities of the NSDAP
and its paramilitary forces ; 1142 Nazi officials were arrested,
including 387 civil servants and 81 mayors ; but many more
went underground, while the majority of the top-rank
leaders managed to flee across the border to Munich. Here
they were welcomed by Theo Habicht, a German citizen and
Reichstag deputy whom Hitler had already officially appointed
as Nazi 'Inspector-General for Austria' and whom Dollfuss
had expelled from Austria at the beginning of the month.

With this drastic step, Dollfuss thus flung down the
challenge which ended with his own murder the following
summer ; and it was during those intervening thirteen months
that his struggle for protection was fought out. It was characterized on the one hand by a complex tangle of secret 'peace
negotiations' with the Nazis at all levels, conducted through
many channels and sometimes in several widely separated
cities of Europe at once ; and, on the other, by a gradual
strengthening of the Italian alliance, which soon emerged as
the only concrete safeguard against Hitler's cynical evasiveness.

Both sides entered this central phase of the conflict with
the ground well prepared. In Berlin, the professional diplomats already had their kid-glove methods worked out for
'solving the Austrian problem', while the Nazi Party leadership were evolving different and somewhat rougher plans of
their own. (This deliberately unco-ordinated approach was
to persist up to Dollfuss's murder and beyond.)

A useful insight into the German Foreign Office tactics
towards Austria, in the new situation created by the disappearance of Parliament, is given in a long and strictly confidential memorandum sent on March 22, 1933, to the German

Minister in Vienna, Dr. Rieth, for his guidance.[2] This document amounts to a directive for peaceful penetration by quasi-legal means. Rieth is warned against even 'broaching the *Anschluss* question prematurely'. The Austrian Nazis are advised to consider forming a 'black-brown Coalition' with the Dollfuss group. The principle of non-intervention is acknowledged, and it is laid down that 'all influence from the Reich must be limited exclusively to the channels opened up by the ideological and organizational bonds between the National Socialist movements in the Reich and in Austria'.

The very next day, however, Hitler was bluntly informing Cerruti, the Italian Ambassador in Berlin, that 'he would not support the Dollfuss Cabinet under any circumstances'.[3] And it was already obvious what a wide interpretation Hitler placed on those 'ideological and organizational bonds'. The current *Dienstbuch* which Habicht had issued for the NSDAP in Austria made it clear that the Nazi Party was, in essence, the state, and that it was purely a question of time before it replaced the Austrian constitution *de jure*. (The German *Dienstbuch* issued a year later in fact showed Austria as the 34th Gau of the Third Reich.) This approach, from which Habicht, on Hitler's orders, never budged, really doomed all Dollfuss's peace-feelers in advance ; for the movement which he was seeking to absorb as a party regarded itself from the outset as a rival state-system in the making. By the summer of 1933 Habicht had gone one further, and had formed in Bavaria his own 'army in exile'. This so-called 'Austrian Legion', composed principally of Austrian Nazis who had fled across the border, reached an estimated strength of nearly 15,000 well-equipped and well-trained men. Though it never, in fact, marched, the Legion's presence left little doubt that it was 'liberation' rather than non-intervention that was uppermost in Hitler's mind.

For his part, Dollfuss had already sounded out the ground in Rome before the decisive Nazi challenge was launched. He paid his first visits to the Italian capital over Easter and Whitsun of 1933, nominally to discuss an Austrian Concordat with the Vatican but, in reality, to seek the Duce's support and to gain the private ear of Goering and von Papen, who were also in Rome to conclude the German Concordat. Dollfuss did not get far with his approaches to Hitler's emissaries. But with Mussolini he immediately established a warm personal contact and, on the muddy banks of the Tiber, he found the sheet-anchor he was looking for. On the second day of the Easter visit, Mussolini had set the diplomatic tone by drinking to the 'future of the Austrian Republic' at a banquet in the Austrian Chancellor's honour. By the end of Dollfuss's Whitsun trip, public reference was already being made to the possibility of a triple association between Italy, Austria and Hungary, while, in secret, Mussolini was even giving certain military assurances to his guest.

Dollfuss's success in these initial soundings can be measured by the consternation of his enemies. Hassell, the German Ambassador in Rome, reported back to Hitler : 'It is most certain that the [Austrian] Chancellor departed with the impression that Italy regards the preservation of an independent Austria as one of the cardinal points of her European policy. There can be no doubt that this impression is correct. . . . I am forced to draw the conclusion that Italy still maintains her opposition to the *Anschluss*. A particularly outspoken advocate of this policy is Under-State Secretary Suvich, a former subject of the old Austria from Trieste. But I do not think that Mussolini, either, is open to argument on this point, at the present time at least.' 4 The worried envoy went on to recommend to his Führer that the best way to meet this situation would be to work for 'the widest possible meshing of German and Italian interests in the Danube Basin'. This would preclude 'the forging of an Italo-Austro-Hungarian bloc' and gradually establish a 'relationship of mutual trust between Italy and Germany that would facilitate attacking the issue of the political relationship to Austria which cannot be yet directly approached today'.

But events moved too fast for this advice to be followed, even if it was heard in Berlin. On May 14 the German Minister of Justice, Dr. Frank, on a 'private visit' to Austria, publicly appealed to a meeting of the Styrian NSDAP to resist the Government in Vienna. A fortnight later the famous 'Thousand Mark blockade' was launched against Austria's important trade with German tourists ; and a fortnight after that the series of bomb outrages began which forced Dollfuss to ban the Nazi Party in Austria altogether. The cards were now on the table, and they included the Ace of Spades.

This first ugly crisis in Austro-German relations sent Dollfuss scampering off in all directions to try and instil some sense or moderation into Hitler. Already in May he had authorized Buresch, Schuschnigg and Rintelen to approach the Führer through the Nazi pro-Consul in Munich, Herr Habicht, for a *modus vivendi* within the existing governmental framework. But the price Habicht demanded was too high for safety, including, as it did, the appointment of a Nazi nominee to the key Ministry of Security, the 'neutralization' of the Defence Ministry and the expulsion of the *Heimwehr* leaders from the Cabinet. These negotiations culminated in a meeting between Habicht, Rintelen, Schuschnigg and Buresch in Vienna ; not surprisingly, they came to nothing.

At the beginning of July, Dollfuss tried again himself, through the hardly less slippery channels of formal diplomacy. He summoned the German Minister in Vienna to his office for a ninety-minute talk and delivered a firm and dignified plea for an understanding between the two German-speaking countries.

Reporting to State Secretary Bülow on this meeting, Dr. Rieth commented : 'Herr Dollfuss is not yet ready for an understanding with the National Socialists here, to say nothing of yielding to their demands. On the other hand, he would obviously very much like to restore peace with the German Reich. I believe, however, that after our conversation it has become clearer to him that the one would hardly be possible without the other.' Rieth went on to say that he considered time was working for Germany's interests in Austria but added : 'However, a considerable effort will still be required to dissuade Herr Dollfuss from the illusion he cherishes that he will be able, on the one hand and with the help of the *Heimwehr*, to suppress National Socialism forcefully and, on the other hand, to put through a constitutional reform together with the Social Democrats by parliamentary methods . . . which would in practice eliminate the Parliament'. This was not a bad description of Dollfuss's fond if fading hopes on the domestic front at the time. Neither aspect of the programme suited Berlin ; so much so that the reader of Rieth's despatch in the Wilhelmstrasse covered the text at this point with exclamation marks and scribbled in the margin : 'These plans are really sheer lunacy!' [5]

In the last week of July, however, the Western Powers made one of their rare combined efforts to relieve the German pressure upon Austria ; even rarer, it was Britain who on this occasion took the initiative. The personal impression which Dollfuss had left behind him after his visit to London the previous month to attend the World Economic Conference had been a splendid one and Whitehall's sporting conscience seems to have been momentarily stirred into trying to help the little Chancellor in his unequal struggle. The result was a British note delivered in Paris and Rome suggesting that a joint Italo-Franco-British intervention be made in Berlin requesting the German Government 'to refrain in the future from all subversive actions with respect to Austria'.[6]

The intervention was duly made. The British *démarche* was categoric, listing all the Austrian complaints at interference and declaring Britain's 'serious concern about the conduct of the German Government'. The French followed suit but

Mussolini, who seems to have been annoyed at anyone else taking a hand in 'his' Austrian affairs, played a double game. He associated himself orally with the Western protest, but assured Berlin of the 'friendly and personal' nature of his step. However, despite their less formal approach, the Italians pressed just as strongly as the other Western Powers for safeguards on Dollfuss's behalf. The whole operation threw the German Foreign Office into some confusion, particularly as von Neurath, the Foreign Minister, was away on leave. Hitler was consulted. He reacted by rejecting any 'outside interference in Austro-German relations'; but he did go so far as to order a temporary halt to such flagrant breaches of international law as the air leaflet raids over Austrian soil.[7]

Apart from one joint declaration of support in February 1934, this was virtually the sole tripartite Western action in Dollfuss's time. Even this move may not have been a genuine top-level initiative : the Germans, for example, were convinced that the whole affair was the work of the pro-Austrian British permanent Under-Secretary Sir Robert Vansittart, acting while both his Prime Minister and his Foreign Minister were absent. Yet it showed what a single twinge of conscience, when jointly felt and expressed, could achieve.

For his more immediate and solid backing, Dollfuss was thrown back by the June crisis onto Mussolini, who had anyway tried to function as the broker in the British action. A significant private exchange of letters now takes place between the two statesmen, of which the originals have survived. In them, the Italian dictator displays his enthusiastic admiration for the new spirit of self-reliance and patriotism which Dollfuss has managed to instil into his countrymen, and urges the Austrian Chancellor to crown his dynamic reforms by an immediate blow at the 'Austro-Marxists' and the creation of an outright Fascist state. Dollfuss, on his part, leaves no doubt of his determination to go on rallying Austria against the German menace until his last breath ; but, in domestic affairs, he studiously avoids all mention of the word 'Fascist' and gives no pledge as to exactly how or when he will deal with the Social Democrat opposition.

Thus Mussolini praises the 'genuine re-awakening of Austrian patriotic feeling, polarized around the ideas of the independence of the state and of the historic mission of German Austria'.[8] In a tacit admission that Dollfuss was, in fact, treading his own path, he goes on : 'I consider the concept of creating the Fatherland Front to be a very good one and I believe that the more the various parties which stand for Austria's national interest can be fused together, the greater will be the success of the movement'. Mussolini even praises his friend for his energetic police action against the 'criminal attacks' of the Nazis and recommends 'internal reforms of a decisively Fascist character' precisely in order that these security measures can be the more effectively applied. Urging the dissolution of the Austrian Social Democratic Party in this connection, Mussolini again comes back to the threat of Hitler. He points out that, if the Socialist opposition is more mildly dealt with than the Nazis, the latter 'would have the weapon of anti-Marxism put into their hands and would be able to parade themselves, at a given moment, as the saviours of the situation'. The 'given moment' was to come with the sudden outbreak of civil war the following winter, and one cannot help wondering whether, on that agonizing morning of the 12th of February, Dollfuss also thought of Mussolini's words when he ordered first tear-gas and then artillery to stop the fighting with all possible speed.

Dollfuss replied three weeks later, on the 22nd of July, 1933. The letter has all the ornate politeness of diplomatic jargon with an extra dash of Viennese flattery, floating like whipped cream on the top. But there is no servility and no suggestion of following Mussolini's words as divine wisdom, a sort of Fascist Sermon on the Mount. It is the letter of an independent statesman, not a satellite, as one would expect from a man who was as proud to be Chancellor of Austria as Mussolini was of being the Duce of Italy. He pointedly refers to his own internal reforms as a 'corporative and authoritarian constitution', and tells Mussolini little more about the Social Democrats than he was telling all Austria in his own speeches : 'The government holds unshakeably to the course it has laid down, of overcoming the Marxist mentality and the Marxist organizations, replacing them with a state patriotism which stands above the classes . . .'

In his letter Mussolini, probably acting on a plea from Starhemberg, had commended the *Heimwehr* to Dollfuss as loyal allies for his task. Dollfuss replied to this rather double-edged recommendation by acknowledging the help which the *Heimwehr* and its leaders were giving towards 'strengthening the nation's loyalty to its homeland'. And he expressed his basic security dilemma when he added : 'Particularly praiseworthy is their firm standpoint and energetic activity against the National Socialists'. This particular exchange of pleasantries is of domestic interest. A subsidiary reason behind Dollfuss's journeys to Rome — however much overshadowed by the supreme issue of the search for protection — was to try and take into his own hands as Chancellor the fine threads of intrigue which the *Heimwehr* leaders had begun to spin themselves in the Italian capital. (These contacts, as Starhemberg himself admitted in his memoirs, soon culminated in the regular and virtually 'official' receipt of large money grants from Mussolini.)

Dollfuss ended his long epistle with words whose bravery and sincerity ring out through the formal text which encloses them : 'Austria naturally has the greatest interest in a friendly relationship with Germany, but always providing that the principle of maintaining the full independence of Austria is both guaranteed and recognized by the German Government and its organs without any reservation whatsoever. Before we can begin to unravel the situation, this aspect must first

of all be put into practice in that the German Government —
or the Nazi leadership which is synonymous with it — must
at last recognize, and completely establish the fact that the
NSDAP in Austria is an *Austrian* movement . . . and must
refrain finally and absolutely from all meddling in our internal
affairs.' In the Europe of the Big Dictators, this was resonant
talk, especially as Dollfuss's Austria had only just found the
patriotic tongue to speak it with.

As will be seen, the only thing Mussolini and Dollfuss were
in complete agreement over was the need to bar Hitler's
threatened march south to the Brenner and south-eastwards
into the Danube Basin. Here, in diplomacy, they saw eye to
eye. In ideology, they looked over each other's shoulders.
The Italian aimed at an extremist goal which the Austrian,
eternal child of compromise, distrusted and shunned ; for the
same reasons of temperament, the gallop at which Rome
wanted to proceed did not match the leisurely canter of
Vienna.

This disparity of aim and approach came out clearly at the
third and most important meeting between the two men —
the 'bathing costume conference' at Riccione on the 19th and
20th of August, 1933. An invaluable eye-witness account of
these talks has survived, to which we shall return in a moment.
But even the two written records which are available — a
prologue and an epilogue — enable us to reconstruct with
fair accuracy what happened on that hot Adriatic beach.
The prologue is a draft plan, possibly written by Mussolini
himself, of what he wanted the meeting to achieve. The
epilogue is an *aide-mémoire* by an Austrian official as to how,
in fact, the meeting went off. The Italian prologue is im-
perious, urgent and drastic. The Austrian epilogue is evasive,
elastic and reserved.

Thus, on Mussolini's side, the 'Considerations to be put
before Dollfuss' [9] set out a number of sweeping reforms which
the Austrian Chancellor was supposed to put into practice ;

action on all these points was to be immediate, in order to underline the 'sudden and dramatic' nature of the Riccione meeting. Generalities apart, these suggested measures included the admission of two additional *Heimwehr* leaders, Steidle and Starhemberg, into the Cabinet ; the destruction of Socialist predominance in the Austrian capital by the appointment of a 'Government Commissar for Vienna' ; and the formal launching of the new system, 'on a Fascist basis', with a major speech to be made by Dollfuss during the following month of September.

The first requirement almost certainly reflected the influence of Starhemberg, who was sunning himself at the time on the Venice Lido only a hundred miles away, and it was resisted by Dollfuss. Under the sub-title 'Domestic Policy' the Austrian memorandum comments retrospectively on this : 'Mussolini sought to exert pressure on the Chancellor to bring out a stronger participation of the *Heimwehr*, but the Chancellor successfully evaded these attempts'.

The second concrete requirement, the immediate nomination of a 'Commissar for Vienna', Dollfuss put off for over six months. He resorted to it only in the emergency of February 1934 and then appointed his own moderate candidate and not the *Heimwehr's* nominee. The third requirement — a programmatic speech on the theme 'Austria's external independence and internal rebirth' — Dollfuss was happy to fulfil, for it anyway corresponded with his own intentions. The address at the Vienna Trabrennplatz meeting on September 11 was the result. This marked the irretrievable public abandonment of that post-1918 Viennese parliamentary system which Dollfuss had already written off in his heart ; but, as we have seen, the new Austria it proclaimed was Christian and authoritarian rather than Fascist and dictatorial.

It is unlikely that this last aspect worried the Duce as much as has been supposed. Indeed, Dr. Hornbostel,[10] who was present at all these talks as Dollfuss's diplomatic adviser and interpreter, has stated that, contrary to popular belief, Mussolini never urged the adoption of Italian Fascism *tel quel* in Austria. He declared more than once : 'Il fascismo non è adatto per l' esportazione ; è italiano'. What he really tried to talk Dollfuss into at Riccione was not theoretical but highly concrete : the legalization of an immediate *coup à la Heimwehr*. And this the Austrian Chancellor declined to do, still hoping for the miracle of a peaceful disintegration and patriotic conversion within the Austro-Marxist camp.

On the whole question of Austria's domestic policy, Dollfuss stood his ground. He repeatedly pointed out to Mussolini the vast differences in their respective political landscapes, stressing that the power of the Trades Union movement in Austria, as well as the Austrian national mentality, made any radical and total suppression of the Socialist opposition in Vienna an impossibility. According to Dr. Hornbostel's account, Mussolini did not challenge this argument and never tried to convert any of his 'suggestions' into conditions for short- or long-term help. It was Dollfuss who seems to have been the suspicious partner, both towards the Duce in Riccione and, later, towards Gömbös in Rome.

On foreign affairs there was complete accord. In view of the forthcoming disarmament negotiations, Mussolini was anxious to mend the breach between Germany and the Western Powers which had arisen three weeks before out of the British-inspired *démarche* over Austria. He therefore proposed the formula : 'Declaration of Austrian friendship towards all neighbours, and therefore also towards Germany, but resting on the historic and irreplaceable functions of an independent Austria'. This was mild but firm, and the closing words showed that there was no question of Mussolini going back on his earlier pledges to Dollfuss. According to the Austrian Foreign Office memorandum, the Duce became quite explicit on this point at Riccione. Under the heading 'Foreign Policy' this Austrian account of the talks reads :

'Mussolini was concerned about developments in Germany and especially over the emergence of Prussianism. He stated that if, contrary to his expectations, there should be an invasion launched from Bavaria, Italy would react militarily.'

A fortnight later, both Herr Habicht in Munich and the German Military Attaché in Vienna, General Muff, were reporting to Berlin that a military convention was about to be concluded between Austria and Italy.[11] By this pact, both sources alleged, Mussolini had undertaken 'in the event of an invasion of Austrian territory by regular or irregular troops or organizations from the Reich, to occupy the Innsbruck-Salzburg line at once'. We now know that these fears were premature. The only concrete military aid to come soon after the Riccione meeting was the return, free of charge, of Austrian artillery and ammunition captured by the Italians in 1918. (As the Austrian Army of the day only had 90 guns, this was a most welcome reinforcement.) It was not until the following year that supplies of Italian aircraft also began to reach Austria and that exchanges of intelligence and talks on common defence plans were started up between Generals Jansa and Roatta, the two Chiefs of Staff.

But, though no formal pact was concluded, either at Riccione or later, Dollfuss got the firm promise of protection which he sought, and Mussolini underlined his intentions by strengthening the Italian Army forces on the Brenner. Equally important for Dollfuss was the fact that he had succeeded in worrying Berlin with a host of rumours on the subject. The gains far outweighed the concessions. Those who interpret his trip to Riccione as a meek pilgrimage to receive orders not only ignore the character of the Austrian Chancellor; they also forget that, in a freely-entered-into alliance between a large power and a small and vulnerable one, it is often the latter which sets the pace.

Immediately after the Adriatic meeting, however, Starhemberg stirred himself into one of his periodic bouts of political activity and succeeded in modifying at least one aspect of Dollfuss's delaying tactics. As always, the gallant prince paid due regard to his personal priorities. He dallied in pleasant company on the Lido until the fashionable season was over. Punctually on September 1, when the better bathing-tents of Venice were emptying, he travelled down to Rome. He had learned from Dollfuss, who had called on him on his way back to Vienna, that neither the wishes of the *Heimwehr* in general nor the personal wishes of Prince Starhemberg in particular had been met at Riccione. Clearly, the massive influence of Mussolini had to be harnessed once again, and even more violently, to drag a stubborn Dollfuss along the desired path. Starhemberg spent eight days of mixed pleasure and business in the Italian capital. He was received in audience by the Pope, and had two long meetings with the Duce at which he urged a new and more forceful intervention in Vienna.

The result was another letter to Dollfuss in which Mussolini, though friendlier than ever before ('Dear Chancellor' instead of 'Your Excellency') was also much more plain-spoken. Referring openly to his talks with Starhemberg, the Duce expressed his concern lest Dollfuss's 'praiseworthy endeavours and great devotion towards the regeneration of the Austrian state' might be neutralized by the presence in the Cabinet of men 'who will never be able honestly to share such ideas'. To leave no doubts on the matter, Mussolini named the *Landbund* leaders Winkler and Schumy as examples of Ministers who were reluctant to drag Austria out of the *morta gora* of liberalism. Starhemberg's claims to high office were not directly mentioned, but the prince went home convinced that both he and the *Heimwehr* would now ride into power on the wave of Mussolini's persuasion. His first public words on his return to Vienna, which spoke of 'putting into practice the Fascist totality', expressed this mood of exultation.

Dollfuss accordingly moved a pace back ; or rather, a

pace back and sideways, for the Cabinet reshuffle he announced on September 21 was a mixture of what he wanted to do and what he was being pressed to do. Winkler and Schumy were duly dropped from the Government. Both men were anyway in open opposition to Dollfuss's 'new course', but his dismissal of them a few days after receiving Mussolini's letter appeared like a clear concession to Italian pressure. On the other hand, the Chancellor astutely used the changes urged by Mussolini to strengthen his own position, rather than that of the restless *Heimwehr*. Fey, who was never a friend of the Italian alliance, was made Vice-Chancellor instead of the suddenly dangerous Starhemberg. Dollfuss took into his own hands the portfolios of Security and Defence (in addition to Foreign Affairs and Agriculture) so that, for the time being, the *Heimwehr* found itself excluded from all the key centres of government power.

Finally, Dollfuss took the opportunity to carry out a plan he had decided on long ago : the establishment of a 'non-party' administration which matched, at Cabinet level, the aims which the Fatherland Front was struggling to achieve with the nation. His own Christian-Socials were excluded as a party from the Government just like the liberal *Landbund*, and Vaugoin disappeared from office together with Winkler. By the autumn of 1933, in fact, Dollfuss looked to be more firmly in the saddle than ever before, however much the *Heimwehr* were pulling at the bridle, and however loudly Mussolini was shouting advice from behind.

A lull of nearly four months now intervenes in the Austro-Italian courtship ; not because their affections cooled, but because all Austria's interests became temporarily concentrated on the possibility of reaching a direct truce with Hitler. This rather pathetic intermezzo begins with a conversation on the evening of the 12th of September under the painted ceilings of the Great Gallery of Schönbrunn Palace, Vienna. A resplendent congress of German-speaking Catholics had been held that day in the Austrian capital and, to close the festivities, the Government were giving a reception for the visiting Cardinal-Legate, Lafontaine. Towards 11 o'clock, Hitler's envoy in Vienna, Dr. Rieth, sought out Dollfuss with the words : 'Herr Kanzler, we must reach a truce. Things just cannot go on as they are and I am determined to do everything I can to improve them.' In the midst of the guests, Dollfuss named his three conditions — first, cessation of all hostile German acts against Austria ; second, the recognition by Germany of Austria's independence and third, the acceptance by Germany of the fact that 'no party can be allowed to exist in Austria which receives both its leadership and its orders from outside'. Rieth raised no objection to these terms and promised to convey them to Berlin.[12]

That the German envoy acted on instructions is plain enough, for we know that, only two months previously, he had received firm orders from his Government 'to refrain completely from conversations with Dollfuss at the present time'.[13] It is equally clear that Dollfuss thought the moment might at last be approaching for a direct heart-to-heart talk with Hitler on the Austro-German question. He had already sounded von Papen about this in April, when the two men had met in Rome ; Mussolini had faithfully pursued the matter on Vienna's behalf through his own Ambassador in Berlin, only to be told by the Foreign Minister von Neurath that such a Hitler-Dollfuss meeting was 'out of the question at the present time'.[14] The hope now flickered up that, impressed by Dollfuss's unexpected toughness and by Austria's new status as a military protégé of Italy, Hitler might agree in the autumn to the personal contact he had refused in the spring. At all events, in the weeks after that Schönbrunn conversation, Dollfuss bent all his energies to this aim — haunted, as a former *Nationaler*, by the thought of strife and bloodshed between the two German nations ; convinced, as a Christian, of his own mission to settle this fratricidal quarrel ;

and perhaps also encouraged as an Austrian by that typically Viennese belief that even the Devil can be slapped on the back with impunity after a glass or two of good Wachauer wine.

It was all in vain. The messages addressed to Hitler were promptly re-directed to Herr Habicht and by the end of the year even Dollfuss became gloomily convinced that his only road to Berlin lay via Munich. Significantly enough, it was in that city that the only really high-level contact did take place during the busy autumn of 1933 — the quite fruitless one hour's conversation on October 31 between Schuschnigg and Rudolf Hess, in the presence of Heinrich Himmler. The ground for this meeting had been prepared by Austrian and German agrarian leaders,[15] and it was intended in their eyes to lead up to a direct encounter between Dollfuss and Hitler. In fact, it seems doubtful whether Hitler had any knowledge of this particular project, while Habicht, who was well informed in advance, helped to torpedo it from the outside. Hess confined himself to the orthodox Berlin viewpoint that the suppression of the NSDAP in Austria was an 'affront to the honour of Germany'. Schuschnigg pointed out that a revival of the Nazi Party was now anyway ruled out by the new Austrian non-party constitution and made it clear that Austria's National Socialists could only be co-opted into the Government on the understanding that this was a purely Austrian affair. The rival standpoints never looked like coming nearer and Schuschnigg returned the same day to Vienna to report the failure of this totally unrealistic encounter.

After this fiasco, Hitler withdrew his principal lieutenants from the scene, and the only pretence at continuous negotiation which he allowed was through plenipotentiaries between Dollfuss and Habicht. As we shall see, even these two unequal partners were themselves prevented, in highly dramatic fashion, from getting together face to face.

The principal intermediaries in this strange business were two Austrian deputies of the Greater German Party, Franz

Langoth and Hermann Foppa. The Greater Germans were now just as dependent financially on Berlin as the *Heimwehr* were on Rome, payment usually being made by Dr. Rieth out of a 'special fund' held by his Legation.[16] Politically they had, by this time, joined forces with the illegal Austrian Nazi organization to form the so-called 'National Fighting Front'. Neither Langoth nor Foppa was a traitor. Both, at heart, were genuine advocates of the *Zusammenschluss,* or peaceful fusion between Austria and Germany. Like all the members of this particular camp, they were in a sorry state of mental confusion, unable any longer to see the Austrian wood for the German trees. It was a visual deficiency which suited Berlin far better than Vienna, and Habicht knew what he was doing when, at a secret meeting in Czechoslovakia on September 27, 1933, he appointed them Hitler's plenipotentiaries 'to negotiate with Dollfuss on behalf of the whole Fighting Front'.

These two well-meaning grave-diggers had their first talk with the Austrian Chancellor in Vienna on the following 13th of October, and put before him Habicht's 'peace plan'.[17] It was based on the maxim, laid down in Berlin, that there could be no improvement in external relations between Austria and Germany until Dollfuss agreed to an internal settlement with the Nazis in Austrian domestic politics. The suggested form of this settlement — the entry of the 'National Fighting Front' as a bloc into the Government — was congenial to Dollfuss, for it fitted in with his own resolve to prevent at all costs the re-emergence of the NSDAP as a separate Austrian party. But the hopeful mood created by these first contacts was rudely shattered at the end of the month when Habicht named his detailed terms.

These amounted to nothing less than a demand for complete equality between the two negotiating partners in any future Vienna government: the new Austrian Cabinet was to be made up 50 per cent of the 'Dollfuss group' (Fatherland Front plus *Heimwehr*) and 50 per cent of the

'Habicht group' (the Nazi-dominated Fighting Front). Dollfuss was to retain his post as Chancellor but Habicht was to
be made Vice-Chancellor 'with enlarged responsibilities'. In
addition, Habicht insisted on the immediate removal of the
ban on the Nazi Party, SA and SS in Austria, and the lifting
of all restrictions on Nazi propaganda activities. Almost as a
cynical afterthought, Habicht added another condition — his
own immediate naturalization, for the man who was proposing
himself as Austrian Vice-Chancellor was not even an Austrian
citizen! The secret memorandum of the German Foreign
Office which records these terms goes on to add: 'The
above points must be accepted or rejected *in toto* by Dollfuss,
though accommodations can still be made in the wording of
particulars'.[18]

These monstrous proposals made Dollfuss redouble his
efforts to circumvent the dreadful Habicht, and reach his
master in Berlin. But Hitler remained ruthlessly remote and,
at the same time, crushed every attempt made by amateur
diplomats to solve the crisis. Thus Hanfstaengl, his Foreign
Press chief, was severely reprimanded for presenting a private
'Nine-Point Peace Plan' to the Austrian Legation in Berlin.
And when a German aristocrat, Werner von Alvensleben,
who was Chairman of the still influential *Herrenklub*, started
up some unofficial discussions of his own in Vienna, Hitler
threatened to pack him off to a concentration camp 'if his
name should ever again get mixed up in Austro-German
policy'.[19]

Nor did Dollfuss at his end fare any better with official
diplomacy. After the failure of the Schuschnigg-Hess encounter, the Austrian Minister in Berlin, Dr. Tauschitz, was
again ordered to grope around for any contact that might lead
him to Hitler. On the 15th of December, 1933, Tauschitz did
contrive to have a discussion on the Austrian problem with
the German Minister of the Interior, Dr. Frick; but the result,
apart from thinly veiled threats, was simply a recommenda-

tion to talk the whole matter over with the inescapable Habicht.

By Christmas 1933 Dollfuss had reconciled himself to the apparently inevitable. On December 27 he instructed his envoy in Berlin to inform the German Foreign Office that he was now prepared to enter into personal negotiations with Habicht, provided that Hitler expressed his desire for such negotiations and specifically named Habicht as his spokesman. Hitler had now achieved what he wanted and promptly gave the required assurance via his Foreign Minister von Neurath on New Year's Day 1934. Preparations for the meeting began accordingly.

Apart from the patent futility of all his direct approaches to Berlin, there were at least two other developments which had persuaded Dollfuss to change his tactics. The first was the visit of the Italian Under-Secretary of State, Suvich, to Berlin on December 12-13. Dollfuss knew that the Austrian problem would be up for discussion, and he had a shrewd suspicion that the Italians, anxious to reach a common policy with Germany on the disarmament question, might offer short-term reassurances at his country's expense. Suvich was closeted with Hitler and his Foreign Minister for nearly five hours on December 13 and we now know, from von Neurath's memorandum on these talks,[20] that Dollfuss's fears were not unfounded.

Suvich tried, loyally enough, to persuade Hitler that 'Dollfuss was a thoroughly pro-German man who wanted nothing more eagerly than to reach a reconciliation with Germany', and he also put forward all Dollfuss's misgivings about an *Anschluss* in general and about Herr Habicht in particular. But when, at the end of the meeting, Hitler summed up by saying that 'Austria was too unimportant to be permitted to disturb relations between Germany and Italy', Suvich 'emphatically agreed and stated that this was also Mussolini's opinion'. Without abandoning their basic position on Austria, the Italians were, in fact, covering their bets, which is the oldest practice in diplomacy as well as in gambling. Dollfuss felt compelled to follow their example by at least opening up official negotiations with Germany, however distasteful the channel. The fact that Suvich was himself due in Vienna the following month only emphasized the urgency.

The second alarming development was the extent to which the *Heimwehr* itself had now begun to intrigue with Habicht, as with Mussolini, behind Dollfuss's back. On December 6 Habicht reported to Berlin that the leaders of all four *Heimwehr* groups — Fey, Starhemberg, Steidle and Alberti — were 'taking it in turns' to call on his representative in Vienna, Schattenfroh, with proposals for separate pacts. With understandable contempt Habicht added : 'Each tries to cut out the other and represent him as being impossible, yet none of them is in a position to take a decisive step. . . . All are united solely in being furious at Dollfuss, who is increasingly depriving them of influence.' [21] How far these schemes went in the disordered brains of certain *Heimwehr* extremists is shown by the suggestion which Alberti once put up to Munich of forming an 'Austrian-Fascist Front' by merging the Austrian Nazis with the *Heimwehr*. This front, to be headed possibly by Rintelen, would aim at by-passing Dollfuss's Fatherland movement and completing the process he was balking at — the introduction of a totally Fascist system.

Hitler, of course, knew full well that the basically patriotic instincts of the *Heimwehr* and the hopeless rifts in their leadership made them impossible allies ; Habicht was accordingly instructed to drag out these intrigues for tactical reasons without ever binding himself. Dollfuss suspected this but could not be sure of it. Partly to cut the ground from under the *Heimwehr*'s feet, therefore, he himself received the much-courted Austrian Nazi, Schattenfroh, shortly before Christmas 1933, at the same time sending word to Langoth and

Foppa that he would like to resume his interrupted conversations with them. The formal approach to the German Foreign Office followed a few days later.

That Dollfuss loathed the idea of negotiating with Habicht, whom he had expelled from Austria the previous summer and who had personally conducted the campaign of blackmail and violence against him ever since, was obvious enough. Even in his official telegrams to Berlin agreeing to the meeting, he had not been able to suppress a reference to his 'understandable personal reluctance' at the prospect. In private he gave full vent to his distaste. Forty-eight hours before the event was due to take place he told a close friend that, for him, the conference with Habicht was 'a journey to Canossa'. Dollfuss added bitterly : 'And tonight I have to go to a ball and show a smiling face when at heart I would rather die'.[22] The whole Habicht incident demonstrated indeed that Dollfuss was always prepared to put his country's vital interests above his pride as a man, and even above his pride as Chancellor.

As things turned out, the Nazis and the *Heimwehr* combined to save him from embarrassment. It had been planned that Habicht, accompanied by one or two adjutants, would fly on the morning of the 8th of January to Aspern airfield, near Vienna, and then be brought to the villa of ex-Chancellor Buresch at Langenzersdorf for the critical secret meeting with Dollfuss. In the first days of the New Year, however, a new series of Nazi bomb outrages had started up throughout Austria. Dollfuss at first ignored them, but when this wave of violence actually reached its climax on the very eve of Habicht's arrival, he had second thoughts.

Late on the evening of the 7th of January he called Starhemberg to his flat in the Stallburggasse, where the issue was debated until the early hours of the following morning. According to two eye-witnesses [23] the discussion was 'loud and heated'. Starhemberg was emphatic that it would be 'nonsensical and undignified' to receive Habicht in Vienna at the very moment when his own agents, acting under his own orders, were indulging in new acts of terror on Austrian soil. The *Heimwehr* Vice-Chancellor, who was probably reflecting Mussolini's influence as well as his own ideas, argued convincingly. Dollfuss at first hesitated, fearing the diplomatic complications of any last-minute reversal. But he was talked over in the end and, as usual, acted like lightning on the decision made. In the middle of the night Tauschitz was woken up in Berlin and Prinz Erbach was roused at the German Legation in Vienna to be informed that the visit could no longer take place. A party, headed by the Chief of Vienna Police, Dr. Skubl, was also organized to go down to Aspern airfield later that same morning to put Habicht politely but firmly back into the air again should he try to fly in after all.

And that, in fact, was precisely what Hitler's dreadful *Landesleiter für Österreich* tried to do. As early as he decently could on the morning of the 8th, the Austrian Minister in Berlin telephoned the German Foreign Office informing them that 'in consideration of the great deterioration in the situation in Vienna evident in the last few days, caused by the militant activity of the National Socialist supporters (outrages with explosives and the like), which had aroused great exasperation in the Austrian population, the Federal Chancellor considered it expedient to call off the conversation with Herr Habicht scheduled for today'.[24]

The harrassed duty official at the Wilhelmstrasse immediately telephoned to Munich with the news. Habicht seemed genuinely dismayed and, to gain time, asked the Foreign Office to tell the Austrian Government that 'it had not been possible to notify him'. As soon as he had put down the receiver, he drove at full speed to Schleissheim airport near Munich and took off in his special plane for Vienna, relying on Hitler to squash any later protests from the diplomats on both sides of the border. But, for once, the Führer was not to be won over for his pro-Consul's escapades. He was told at noon of the situation, when it seemed almost out of hand, and immediately ordered the plane to be turned back in mid-air. The radio message reached Habicht when he was deep in Austria, flying over the great baroque monastery of Melk, only twenty minutes from Vienna. The target was tantalizingly close, but a personal order from the Führer was quite a different thing from the telephone message delivered two hours earlier by the Deputy Director of Department II in the Foreign Office. Habicht had no choice but to turn back, and the Austrian 'reception committee' at Aspern, who were anxiously scanning the horizon for the secret plane, breathed again and went home to lunch.

Whatever the full background to this extraordinary episode may be, there is little doubt that Habicht himself did not wilfully sabotage the meeting. He appeared the very next day in Berlin, where the Foreign Office reported that he was 'exceedingly upset by the outcome of the affair and deeply disappointed'.[25] Moreover, in an attempt to renew the threads to Dollfuss without delay, he persuaded Hitler that same afternoon to send his (Habicht's) assistant, Prince Waldeck-Pyrmont, to Vienna on an 'exploratory mission'. The prince duly arrived in the Austrian capital on the 11th of January and was promptly arrested by the police when attending a midnight conclave of underground Nazi leaders. He flourished in his defence a photostat copy of the *laissez-passer* issued specially for the Habicht trip and, when this was taken away from him, commented with a cheerful grin : 'Don't worry, we have fifty more'. Altogether, not a very tactful reconnaissance!

It is, of course, very possible that Habicht, without wanting to wreck the meeting in advance, had organized a new terror wave in Austria in order to put Dollfuss in a subdued mood for the occasion. But it is also conceivable that the Austrian Nazis, who were often jealous of Habicht's overlordship from

Munich, had kicked over the traces in the first week of January in a deliberate attempt to create difficulties. An open feud was known to exist between Habicht and the leader of the Austrian SA, Reschny, who, at the end of the same month, was reported to be preparing his own private *putsch* in Vienna.[26]

Certainly, jealousy played a part in the decisive influence Starhemberg had exerted to prevent the negotiations. Like all the *Heimwehr* leaders, he dipped his own fingers in the Nazi pie from time to time ; indeed, less than a fortnight after the abortive Habicht trip, we find him probing around for a particular juicy plum. The German Foreign Office files record that, on January 20, Starhemberg approached the illegal Nazi headquarters in Vienna with a proposal that he should be nominated Federal President in a new regime, with Habicht as Chancellor. The prince was considerate enough to add that he would be pleased if a Cabinet post could also be found for his friend Dollfuss.[27] In short, the heavy atmosphere of intrigue and distrust which hung over Vienna at the time of the January 8 débâcle made the question of blame somewhat academic. Quite apart from Habicht's excessive demands, the same domestic factors which combined to prevent the talks would probably have wrecked them had they ever taken place.

For another month or two, the secret attempts to reach an understanding with Berlin went on, many of them with Dollfuss's knowledge and some of them at his initiative. Before the end of January, for example, the Chancellor had put out another feeler to Habicht through Gebhardt, the Christian-Social leader of the Western Alpine provinces. In February the ex-Chancellor Buresch tried through diplomatic channels in Rome, and in Vienna, Gilbert in der Maur, an Austrian journalist who had crossed the Bridge of Sighs between pan-Germanism and Nazism, made a brief and somewhat amateurish appearance as go-between. But by March the scheming Rintelen had moved into the foreground of the picture again, intriguing with the Nazis against his Chancellor from his post as Austrian Minister to Rome. And the reappearance on the scene of this political pirate from Styria marks the beginning of the end. From now on, the emphasis in these secret Austrian contacts with Germany is more and more on treachery and less and less on peace-making.

These, it must be recalled, were the weeks after the Civil War, when Fey was strutting around in Vienna as the hero of the hour and when there were many in Berlin and Rome who considered Dollfuss's days as Chancellor numbered. Even Hitler seems at this stage to have been toying with the idea of establishing direct contact with the triumphant *Heimwehr* leader. The German Foreign Office informed Dr. Rieth in Vienna on March 15 : 'Concerning the feelers which have now begun again to be put out by Austria in a more or less non-committal form — among other things, for example, the suggestion for a personal talk between Fey and Hitler — the Reich Chancellor takes the position that the greatest reserve is to be maintained . . . as long as one does not see clearly who has the power within the Austrian governmental front itself.'[28]

In all these cross-currents, the swastika seemed to many Austrian adventurers to be the only sure thing to steer by, and the conspirators set their sails accordingly. On the 7th and 8th of March, 1934, Habicht's Chief of Staff, Dr. Rudolf Weydenhammer (a name we shall hear much more of later), visited Rintelen in Rome. The opening words of Weydenhammer's secret report to Munich on these talks show how far the betrayal had already gone. Weydenhammer writes : 'Dr. von Rintelen, who, on the basis of last month's negotiations, stated that he was unconditionally prepared to follow the directives of Landesinspektor Habicht, asked me . . . for instructions so that he could arrange according to our wishes his activity and his conversations on the occasion of Chancellor Dollfuss's forthcoming visit to Rome'.[29]   From this stage, it was but a short and slippery slide down to the role Rintelen was to play four months later, in the abortive Nazi *coup* which ended his Chancellor's life.

Thus the only interlude of faint hope in Austro-German relations which Dollfuss was to experience, the period of *détente* that began with Dr. Rieth's remarks in Schoenbrunn Palace on the 12th of September, 1933, really ended when Habicht's plane turned back over Melk Monastery on that 8th of January, 1934. Everything that came later looked more and more like shadow-boxing as, on the one hand, the Austrian Nazis prepared themselves for outright betrayal and, on the other hand, the German Nazis got ready for open violence.

As always in the foreign policy of a small state which must balance itself between two powerful and mutually suspicious neighbours, the weakening of Austria's links with Berlin led automatically to a strengthening of her ties with Rome. Ten days after the Habicht fiasco, the Italian Under-Secretary Suvich paid his 48-hour visit to Vienna. The fateful effects of this visit on the Austrian domestic scene — notably the spurring-on of the *Heimwehr* to a battle *à l'outrance* with the Austro-Marxists — have already been described. Pressure on Dollfuss was also intensified, a sure sign that he was proving anything but a 'willing tool of Mussolini'. After returning to Rome, Suvich wrote to the Austrian Chancellor describing the impressions he had just passed on to the Duce about his trip. These impressions, he felt bound to point out, included 'a fairly widespread uneasiness (in Austria) concerning the inactivity of the Government and the delays which had set in over the reform work'. In order to mobilize, above all, Austria's youth behind him, Suvich urged Dollfuss to greater 'decisiveness and precision' in the tasks he had undertaken, namely 'the fight against Marxism, the reform of the Constitution in an anti-parliamentary and corporative sense, the abolition of political parties, and the strengthening of the Fatherland Front'.

Dollfuss agreed with every word of this exhortation without welcoming it, if only because anything which took the initiative from his own hands was distasteful. What he was far happier to read in the same letter was another passage in which Suvich categorically confirmed Mussolini's determination 'to support Austria to the end in maintaining her struggle for independence'. This was the only rock on which Austria's foreign policy could be built in 1934. To feel it under his feet again, Dollfuss was prepared to accept all the Duce's accompanying sermons.

Nor was Suvich himself idle in Austria's cause. The German Ambassador in Rome, Hassell, reported to Berlin on January 26 that, a few days after returning from Vienna, Suvich had taken him earnestly to task over Nazi interference in Austria. The Italian Under-Secretary stressed to Hitler's envoy the 'great bitterness' which Dollfuss felt about 'the extensive support which Austrian National Socialism constantly received from the Reich'. He referred to the 'voluminous evidence' which Austria possessed on this point and brandished under Hassell's nose 'a whole pack of photographs etc. which were meant to prove their German origin'.[30] Such pressure, which was supported by parallel steps in Berlin, showed that Italy was taking her role seriously as Austria's diplomatic patron.

In the next few weeks this patronage finally took on its official form. Suvich's letter in January had contained the first written reference to the Duce's plan for a triple conference to be convened in the near future in Rome between Italy, Austria and Hungary; the fruits of this plan were the so-called Rome Protocols, signed in the Italian capital on the 17th of March, 1934, between Mussolini, Dollfuss and Gömbös. Two of the three protocols were economic and simply extended those bilateral preferential trade agreements which Dollfuss had always favoured in the Danube Basin. Hungary, who received substantial concessions in the way of increased

grain exports to both her partners, profited the most ; Austria
was granted additional preferences in the export of finished
goods and agricultural produce ; Italy's emphasis, as befitted
a patron, was on giving rather than receiving.

But the pith of the Rome Treaties was in the first political
Procotol. This provided for a co-ordinated foreign policy
between the three countries and laid down that, to this end,
'the three governments would consult together whenever at
least one of them considered this desirable'. We now know
that these diplomatic links came as a rude shock to the Germans, which was the effect Dollfuss so earnestly desired. In
a telegram to Dr. Rieth in Vienna sent two days after the
event, the German State Secretary for Foreign Affairs, Bülow,
refers to the unexpected 'far-reaching commitments' made by
Austria and to the fact that the political clauses were un-
mistakably 'directed against Germany'. In a parallel telegram sent to Budapest, Bülow instructs his envoy there to
express the 'astonishment' of Berlin at the news. 'We are
compelled to state', this guidance message continues, 'that it
is not in accordance with the close friendly relations between
Germany and Hungary for Hungary now to join Italy and
Austria in an agreement that has an unmistakable tendency
against Germany.' [31]

This raising of eyebrows at the Wilhelmstrasse was understandable. Both Austria and Hungary, though knowing full
well what the Rome agenda would be, had played with some
success the usual game of reassuring the victim in advance.
Ten days before the Protocols were signed Dollfuss told the
anxious Dr. Rieth in Vienna that though 'for some time now
he had been discussing general questions of foreign policy
with the Italians in a friendly way, he did not intend to
commit himself unilaterally with Italy in this regard'.[32] And
only 48 hours before the announcement of the pact, both
Dollfuss and Gömbös were giving similar assurances to the
German Embassy in Rome. Neither, by their own lights,

was telling a downright lie, for they were describing the intentions of their actions, and not the effects. When Gömbös, on this occasion, declared that 'North of the Danube Hungary had a friend and south of the Danube likewise — namely Germany and Italy' and that 'these two factors stood in a 1 : 1 relationship for Hungary', he was simply expressing Budapest's dream of stability in an unstable world.

The Hungarian hope, which Dollfuss strongly echoed, was that, in time, Germany would herself become associated with the Italo-Austro-Hungarian bloc, thus creating a four-power co-operation in the Danube Basin to balance the French-sponsored Little Entente. But all such hopes conveniently dodged the issue that Hitler was just as determined as Mussolini to dominate Central and South-East Europe and that, in Germany's eyes, the Rome Protocols were a clear Austro-Hungarian vote for the opposition. However it was more important for Dollfuss than any Danubian pipe-dream, to demonstrate to the Wilhelmstrasse that Austria no longer stood alone and that, furthermore, she had found the one powerful protector in Europe to whom Hitler could have no ideological objection. This success was irrefutable. As Hassell, the German Ambassador in Rome, wrote to his Government in summing up the affair : 'Austria has thereby received a new and conspicuous pledge of her independence'.[33]

In March 1934, therefore, Dollfuss finally roped himself to the Fascist chariot in an attempt to escape the Nazi steamroller. But it is worth recording that, even before taking this seemingly inevitable step, the little Chancellor had sounded out every feasible alternative. The previous summer, for example, he had made a vain attempt to win Hungary over to the idea of a joint Austro-Hungarian association with the Little Entente, thus uniting the Danubian winners and losers of 1918 in a common front against Germany. However, Gömbös, during a visit to Vienna on July 9, flatly refused to entertain such schemes, rejecting any diplomatic alignment which would force Hungary to recognize her present frontiers with her neighbours. 'Austria's rapprochement with the French group has been blocked', noted the German Foreign Office with satisfaction after the Gömbös-Dollfuss talks. Budapest's revisionist obsessions had triumphed. Once again the withered hand of St. Stephen seemed to reach out from the past, protecting the sacred thousand-year-old Magyar homeland that was now only a bitter memory ; and once again in her history Vienna paid the price for Hungarian pride.

Finally, only six weeks before signing the Rome pacts, Dollfuss had attempted, against the strong opposition of Mussolini, to seek refuge in that mausoleum of righteous causes, the League of Nations. On the 17th of January Dollfuss had warned the German Government that this step was being contemplated in Vienna, and on February 5th, after receiving a particularly uncompromising reply from Berlin, he was given the necessary authorization by his Cabinet. The Civil War, which broke out a week later, intervened to paralyse Austrian diplomacy completely for a few days. Acting on Hitler's instructions, Habicht delayed a decision for longer by publicly announcing a brief 'truce' with Austria.

Both these developments dislocated the original plan. But the basic reason why the Austrian approach to Geneva never went through was that the three powers for whose sponsorship Dollfuss had formally applied could not agree among themselves over the course to take. As the German Ambassador in Rome telegraphed to his Government on February 15 : 'Suvich told me today that the reply to the Austrian *démarche* had been somewhat further delayed because no understanding had been reached between Rome and London and Paris. Italy had from the beginning taken a position . . . against placing the matter before the League of Nations. France from the start had been of a different opinion while England had originally been in favour but had latterly, under the pressure of public opinion, changed her course because she feared the

League of Nations would suffer a loss of prestige.' [34] The three Governments ultimately agreed among themselves to settle the issue with a joint declaration in Austria's favour. Published on February 17, this stated that the three Governments had received from Austria 'material which proved German interference in Austrian affairs'. England, France and Italy went on to record their agreement 'as to the necessity of maintaining the independence and integrity of Austria in accordance with the treaties in force'.

This was about as much publicity and as much sympathy as Austria could ever have achieved through the League of Nations (which Germany had anyway walked out of by this time) and the Austrian Government dropped the appeal to Geneva accordingly. Strong Italian pressure to accept the Three-Power declaration as a *pis aller* certainly played a major role in this decision ; on the other hand, the incident in itself is proof of Dollfuss's efforts, on the eve of joining the Rome-Budapest axis, to keep other diplomatic channels open.

Austria's abortive move towards the League of Nations in February and the signing of the Rome Protocols in March were, both of them, serious 'provocations' in the eyes of Hitler. But it was Dollfuss's domestic programme even more than his foreign policy which now stung the Nazis into drastic action against him. The proclamation of the new Austrian Constitution on May 1, 1934, with all its defiant patriotic undertones, was the signal for this final offensive, which claimed Dollfuss himself as a victim before collapsing as suddenly as it was launched. Unlike the Chancellor's opponents at home, the German Nazis abroad appreciated only too well what his desperate reforms meant to the cause of Austria's independence.

This final Nazi onslaught, which covered the last ten weeks of Dollfuss's life and office, surpassed everything that had gone before in intensity as well as in scope. It was no longer a case of swastikas smeared on garden walls or primitive cardboard-cased bombs being left in cinema cloak-rooms. A methodical sabotage campaign was organized against the vital utilities and communications of the country, so that scarcely a day passed without a dynamite attack against electricity or water power installations, railways, telephone networks or public buildings. The terrorists struck province by province. In May and early June they concentrated on Salzburg, where the famous old episcopal residence was among their targets. From the 10th to 12th of June, their attentions shifted to Lower Austria, where the entire telephone system was dislocated by hundreds of co-ordinated sabotage acts. Styria's turn came in the second half of June, with attacks against both of Austria's main southern railway routes (Bruck-Spielfeld to Yugoslavia and Bruck-Klagenfurt to Italy). Towards the end of June, the pressure shifted to Tyrol and Vorarlberg, where post offices, aqueducts and power lines were dynamited.

Soon after authorizing this wave of terrorism in Austria, Hitler went down to Venice on June 14 for his first meeting with the Duce. As the Austrian question was the only serious bone of contention between the two dictators, Mussolini was reluctant to let it force an open breach between them. Indeed, the secret records of these conversations which are now available show that, at this particular juncture, the Duce was seeking Hitler's co-operation on far wider issues. He needed German support for his disarmament plan which Italy had recently put before the Great Powers, and he was anxious to evolve with Berlin a common line of resistance against Russia's 'Eastern Locarno Pact' and the repercussions of Russia's possible admission to the League of Nations.

But those same records show that, within the framework of this global policy, Mussolini proved a loyal friend to Dollfuss, and argued his case with as much emphasis as the informal and friendly setting allowed. Hitler was shrewd enough to broach the Austrian question himself as soon as he arrived, in an attempt to banish the shadow from the start.

According to the account of the meeting given by his Foreign Minister, von Neurath,[35] the Führer immediately presented his host with a Five Point 'peace plan' for Austria. The sequence of Hitler's case ran as follows :

1. The question of the *Anschluss* was of no interest since it was in no way acute and, as he was well aware, not internationally feasible.
2. It was not possible for him to come to terms with Dollfuss, who should be replaced by a 'neutral' person. (When asked by Mussolini whether he had anyone in mind, Hitler replied he had not.)
3. This 'neutral' Chancellor should then proclaim early elections in Austria.
4. The Austrian National Socialists would then be taken into the Vienna Government.
5. In general, all questions concerning Austria should be decided by Germany and Italy in agreement with one another.

Mussolini at first merely took note of these proposals, and the talk proceeded to other and larger issues. But, according to a verbal account of the meeting given a few days afterwards by Suvich to Hassell, the German envoy in Rome (no written record was kept on the Italian side), the Duce returned to the Austrian question later in words which showed he had no intention of letting down his little protégé in Vienna.

Hassell reported to Berlin : [36] 'According to Suvich's account, Mussolini replied that such a programme (*i.e.* Hitler's five points) could only be considered after a period of peace had set in, as there could hardly be any thought of negotiating under the present conditions of conflict in Austria. After all, Dollfuss, who, incidentally, was anything but anti-German and urgently desired an understanding with the Reich, could not be blamed for defending himself by all available means and, in view of the method of fighting used against him, was not inclined to take the initiative in starting negotiations.'

There was, in fact, as Hassell noted, an 'evident divergence of opinion', and von Neurath was telling a bald untruth when he circularized German missions abroad after the Venice meeting suggesting that agreement on Austria had been reached. All that had been reached was agreement to differ, for, in diplomatic parlance, the Duce's defence of Dollfuss and his policy by name spoke a plain enough language.

However, as the Austrian Government noted with regret, it was not plain enough to halt the Nazi wave of sabotage. The only breathing space the luckless Austrians got was after the 30th of June, when the so-called 'Roehm Putsch' in Germany caused Hitler to concentrate all his energies on preparing a bloodbath for his rivals at home. Yet even this respite, however welcome on the security front, was politically bitter for Dollfuss. Secret reports had been reaching Vienna for some months of growing opposition to Hitler among German Army and SA circles, and though there is no evidence to suggest that Dollfuss was in actual contact with the rebels, it is known that he half-expected their action and set all his hopes on its success.

The first news of the upheaval reached Dollfuss while on a visit to Innsbruck, when his secretary telephoned breathlessly from Vienna to say that all communications with Germany had been cut for several hours and that all the frontiers were closed. Close friends of the Chancellor's have described how his exultation gradually turned into dejection when, the following day, it became clear that Hitler was firmer than ever in the saddle. It was as though Dollfuss sensed that Austria's last hopes of survival, and his own, had somehow been extinguished in the July massacre.

This note of desperation was sounded in the Cabinet re-shuffle — the last he was to make — which Dollfuss carried out on July 11. Profiting by the temporary lull, he reorganized his Government on what was in fact an emergency battle basis. He again took over himself the Ministries of Defence and Security, and appointed as State Secretaries for these departments two officials, General Zehner and Baron Karwinsky, in whom he could place his absolute personal trust. Fey, who had been under special police watch since June and about whose loyalty even the over-trusting Dollfuss was beginning to have serious doubts, was dismissed at last from the front ranks of power. He was nominated 'General State Commissioner for the suppression of anti-government tendencies in private industry', a truly comic-opera post created specially to cushion his fall. Dollfuss now had in his hands the direct control of police, gendarmerie and Army, and stood with gathered forces awaiting the blow. In these last weeks, he resembled a garrison commander rather than a Chancellor, and Austria herself seemed less like a state than a fortress, pounded with heavier cannon than it could take from outside, its already battered walls undermined by treason from inside.

Those days before the end were full of symbols, omens and ironies. That final regrouping of forces against the Nazi menace, for example, had been decided on July 6 in Mariazell, where Dollfuss had gone, with a group of friends and advisers, to attend the traditional 'Men's Pilgrimage Day'. In the evening, after the service in the great twin-spired yellow church, there was the usual candlelight procession around the narrow streets of the town. But as the political pilgrims formed up with the others in rows of eight outside the church door, shielding their flickering flames from the breeze, a huge image of the swastika, secretly erected on a peak of the surrounding mountains, burst into flames in the darkness high above them and continued to crackle and blaze away in defiance throughout the procession — as malignant and un-reachable as Hitler himself.

And the last week-end of Dollfuss's life found him getting ready for a holiday visit to his protector Mussolini, to join his wife and family who were already in Italy as the Duce's private guests. Dollfuss was preparing himself in a very special way for the visit ; he was, in fact, learning to swim, for the peasant boy from Kirnberg had neither known a swimming pool nor ever seen the ocean. As it was, he knew he cut a diminutive enough figure in a bathing suit beside the massive Mussolini, and he resolved not to bring unnecessary shame on himself or on Austria by being unable to follow the athletic Duce into the Adriatic waves. So he repaired for three days to an isolated villa which belonged to some boy-hood friends [37] on the shores of one of Salzburg's quietest lakes, the Mattsee. And here, under the expert guidance of a police instructor specially summoned for the purpose, Engelbert Dollfuss finally mastered his breast-stroke. He could have saved himself the trouble, for while he was splash-ing earnestly in the waters of the Mattsee, his assassins were gathering in the cafés of Vienna.

CHAPTER EIGHT

Hitler's First Victim

THE 25th of July, 1934, is a memorable date in world history as well as an unforgettable date in Austrian history, for the Nazi *putsch* launched that day in Vienna was Hitler's first act of gangsterdom outside his own borders. Furthermore, until that fatal and final error of attacking Russia instead of invading Britain, it was about his only serious blunder.

There can be no doubt that the blow struck at Austria was prepared with Hitler's previous knowledge and consent. We have seen how the specially appointed Nazi *Landesleiter* for Austria, Theo Habicht, was kept firmly under the Führer's thumb in all his major escapades, while the German Foreign Office documents of the time abound with references by State Secretary Neurath or his deputy Bülow to the fact that 'the Reich Chancellor has reserved all final decisions on the Austrian question for himself'. Indeed, barely three months before the abortive *coup*, Bülow prefaced a secret memorandum on developments in Austria with these words : 'Only the Reich Chancellor can settle the question of how to distinguish the former Nazi party from the future Nazi movement in Austria ; what guarantees for the continued existence of the Austrian Nazi movement can be demanded ; and how the dividing line between the German and the Austrian party is to be drawn'.[1]

But it does seem likely that Hitler was totally bamboozled, via Habicht, as to the nature of the July *putsch*. What a small group of Austrian and German Nazi plotters had virtually promised him was a national uprising, based on Austrian Army support, in which the obstinate Dollfuss and his followers would be swept away like ninepins. With equal smoothness, they were to be replaced by a new pan-German Government which would roll out the red carpet for its spiritual Führer all the way to Passau on the Austro-German border before Mussolini or the Western Powers could collect their wits.

What actually took place in Vienna was a bold but isolated stroke of 154 desperadoes, enacted against a background of muddle and improvisation. Moreover, it was doomed to failure from the start by that same creeping paralysis which had struck down all previous *putsch* attempts in Vienna, whether launched by Austro-Fascists or Austro-Marxists — an utter lack of popular response rooted in the ordinary Austrian's refusal to commit himself too far to any radical course. That same Austrian 'curse of half-measures', for which Grillparzer had once so eloquently arraigned the Habsburgs, hung like a soggy Danube mist over the July disaster. The plot itself was half-implemented and half-abandoned by its Austrian supporters. The capital on that day was full of semi-bravery and semi-cowardice, of hesitant treachery and of dubious loyalty. There was but a small handful of men, among either the conspirators or the Ministers and senior officials involved, who followed a resolute and consequent course from beginning to end. And, at the close of that long day, among the very few Austrians whose case seemed crystal clear was Dollfuss, who had been murdered, and Planetta, the Nazi rebel who had murdered him. Most of the other actors had demonstrated, consciously or unconsciously, how right the dead Chancellor had been to concentrate above everything else on trying to kindle an Austrian patriotism. They had also shown how far he had still been from his goal when Hitler's bullets struck him down.

*   *   *

The *putsch* plan itself was more than a year old. The Austrian Nazis had begun to discuss desperate remedies of this sort among themselves soon after Dollfuss drove them underground by banning the party in June 1933. At the beginning of 1934 the illegal leadership in Vienna decided to collect all Nazis expelled from Austrian military service in a special 'Commando' unit, the so-called 'SS Standarte 89', and a striking arm to implement these schemes thus became available. The planning grew more detailed accordingly. But it remained essentially an *Austrian* Nazi affair ; and the plan without German approval was like a shell without its fuse-cap.

The introduction by Dollfuss in May 1934 of his new constitution, with its unmistakable note of raw patriotic defiance against Berlin, seems to have decided Hitler that strong-arm methods would have to be applied to remove this unyielding little 'Germanic traitor' from the scene. At all events, the Führer's henchmen got down to business the very next month.

We now know [2] that it was in Zürich on the 25th of June, 1934, that the first top-level conference of Dollfuss's assassins was held. In attendance were Landesinspektor Habicht from Munich ; his Chief of Staff, Dr. Rudolf Weydenhammer, from whose secret report to Hitler on the July *putsch* many of the following details are taken ; another of Habicht's lieutenants, Dr. von Wächter, who became the chief organizer of the revolt ; and the leader of the recently formed SS Standarte 89, SS Sturmbannführer Fridolin Glass. Of this quartet, only Glass was Austrian ; the other three were all German citizens, a sure sign that the reins had now been taken over by Berlin.

But there was at least one prominent Austrian who was sitting in that Zürich hotel room in spirit, and who would have been sitting there in the flesh had it been safe to do so. This was Dr. Anton Rintelen, the former Provincial Governor of Styria, the then Austrian Minister in Rome, and the most morbidly and ruthlessly ambitious citizen of the First Austrian Republic. We have seen how Rintelen had already placed himself unreservedly under Hitler's orders in the spring of 1934, against a promise of the Austrian Chancellorship after Dollfuss's removal ; and Weydenhammer has described [3] how he paid no fewer than fourteen clandestine visits to Rome during the first six months of the year to discuss the problem with him.

At the Zürich meeting, Glass explained his favourite *putsch* plan in detail to his German masters. Its central objective was to capture both the Federal President and the entire Austrian Cabinet at the same moment, thus creating a total vacuum of state authority into which the pro-Hitler Government of Rintelen would move like a tempest. The SS Standarte 89, who were to carry out the kidnappings, would also seize the Austrian radio transmitter RAVAG and the Vienna telephone headquarters in parallel actions. A pre-condition of the Glass plot was active assistance from Austrian Regular Army units, to be directed by Nazi officers still left undetected or un-watched in their ranks. The conspirators were originally supposed to assemble in the actual premises of the Vienna Garrison Headquarters (*Stadtkommando*), and Glass promised the services in this connection of a 'higher General Staff officer'. [4] (It should be made clear in advance at this point that though two or three Austrian Army officers did conspire with the rebels, Glass's expectations of military support were to prove wildly exaggerated, while Weydenhammer de-liberately over-emphasized the military side in retrospect in order to cover up his own failure.) The Zürich meeting ended on a confident and practical note. Glass's plan was approved in principle and he was told to return to Vienna to prepare the action in detail, concentrating above all on ex-tending his contacts with any Nazi sympathizers he could find in the Austrian Army and police force. Further deliveries of weapons were promised from Habicht's headquarters in

Munich ; but no dates for the operation, even provisional, were mentioned.

It was Rintelen who now began to put on the pressure. On July 11 Weydenhammer paid yet another visit to Rome. He found the treacherous diplomat and would-be Austrian Chancellor consumed with impatience. In his post-mortem report to his Führer, Weydenhammer writes : 'Rintelen urgently requested that the operation should be carried out before the end of July. He referred to the imminent Dollfuss-Mussolini conversations [arranged in Riccione for August] and to the Dollfuss-Barthou meeting [a conversation between Dollfuss and the French Foreign Minister took place in Vienna on June 19] whose outcome could endanger German policy. Rintelen stated that he could not possibly postpone his leave [in Vienna] beyond the end of July and said it was unlikely that he would be returning to his post in Rome afterwards.' [5]

As the only 'legal' Austrian cover-man in the great conspiracy, Rintelen's arguments were weighty enough. But the issue was really decided a few days later when the plotters in Vienna reported that a senior Austrian Army officer holding a key position for the operation had promised his support. This important addition to the conspirators' ranks was Lt.-Colonel Sinzinger, Chief of Staff at the Garrison Headquarters in the capital. Rintelen's impatience and Sinzinger's treachery (which, typically enough, was never consummated) seem to have persuaded Hitler via Habicht to strike while the iron of opportunity was hot.

At 10 o'clock on the morning of the 16th of July what Weydenhammer describes as 'the last and decisive conference' was held in Habicht's flat at 60 Kunigundenstrasse, Munich. The circle was a little wider than at previous meetings and, for once, Austrian Nazis and their sympathizers predominated. Habicht and Weydenhammer represented the German end of the business. From Vienna had come : Frauenfeld, Nazi Gauleiter-designate for the capital ; Reschny, the head of the

Austrian underground 'SA' organization ; Glass, the field-commander for the proposed *putsch* ; and a Major Egert of the De-coding Department of the Austrian War Ministry, who turned up as the 'personal representative of Lt.-Col. Sinzinger'.[6]

Glass reported to the meeting that he had in the meantime concluded 'positive negotiations' with Dr. Steinhäusl, a senior pro-Nazi official of the Vienna police ; with the commander of the police Emergency Squad (*Alarmabteilung*) ; and with two more unnamed Army staff officers. The final details of the action were now hammered out and a firm time was fixed — the afternoon of July 24, when it was generally assumed that the Austrian Cabinet would foregather for the last time before scattering for the long *diaspora* of Austria's summer holidays.

Glass was despatched back to Vienna with two false passes — one Austrian and one German — to get him through Dollfuss's steadily tightening police controls. Weyden-hammer remained for the time being in Munich, to tie up the last threads of intrigue between Berlin and Rome. The stage for Hitler's first foreign venture was set.

Before following the conspirators to Vienna, it is worth noting that the plot now afoot was strictly a Nazi Party affair. The German Government, as represented in this instance by one or two senior officials of the Foreign Office, appears to have been only sketchily informed, and at a relatively late date. Throughout the early summer of 1934 the Wil-helmstrasse continued to preach and practise the doctrine of the 'peaceful' penetration of Austria by propaganda and blackmail pressure. The outlines of this programme had been laid down in the spring, in a secret memorandum circulated on April the 9th by State Secretary Bülow. This reads : 'It is presumably clear that Germany is not in a position now to put through internationally a solution to the Austrian question in a German sense. By solution in the German sense is meant not only the direct achievement of the *Anschluss* but even *Gleichschaltung* on the Danzig pattern. All German attempts in this direction will founder on the solid opposition of all the European Great Powers and the Little Entente. In these circumstances we shall have to take the position that in the Austrian question we want nothing except that natural political developments should continue to be given free play. We can, for our part, calmly renounce all militant methods . . . but we must naturally demand that all other governments conduct themselves accordingly.' [7]

And only ten days before the blow fell in Vienna the German Minister, Dr. Rieth, had shown genuinely shocked disapproval when a certain Hans Köhler, a veteran Austrian Nazi and retired post official from Hainfeld, sent him, for onward transmission to Hitler, a proposal to take the Austrian Federal Government prisoner. Dr. Rieth comments, in his telegram to Berlin on the incident : 'Herr Köhler was told by the Legation that the ideas contained in the memorandum were prejudicial to the policy of the Reich and he was requested, moreover, to prevail on his collaborators to desist from the plan. The memorandum was retained to prevent it falling into the wrong hands. Since it cannot be ascertained here whether Herr Köhler is pursuing his plan further in spite of the fact that he was warned against it, I suggest that appropriate steps be taken to stop this action.' [8] The German Foreign Office duly urged Habicht in Munich 'to prevent any such plans that might possibly still exist'. Habicht must have thrown this request into the fireplace of 60 Kunigundenstrasse with a broad grin on his face. By this time, Weydenhammer had already had about half a dozen meetings with Rintelen to prepare for the very operation which the humble Hans Köhler had been shooed away from.

Nor was the German Army informed any better or any earlier. On May 24, 1934, Hitler's Military Attaché in Vienna, Lt.-General Muff, had a long and earnest conversation about Austria with General Werner von Fritsch, while on a visit to Berlin. He pointed out that Dollfuss's position had been strengthened by the introduction of the new Constitution and went on : 'German aspirations have failed for the present, due to Italy's intervention. Italy has great influence in Austria. The Italianization of the army, the economy, aviation etc. is making headway.' General Muff unwittingly put his finger on Dollfuss's hopes and on Hitler's fears, and thus on the irreparable breach between the two German capitals, when he added : 'And yet the Austrian problem is very important for us for the reason that Austria is the rallying-point of all opposing forces. There is already talk of a Fourth (Austrian) Reich, and already signs that the clergy is preparing an offensive to recapture Southern Germany.' Finally, the worried General complained bitterly to his superior about 'the lack of a clear line with respect to the Austrian problem'. 'People', he said, 'do not know who makes this policy, the Party or the Foreign Ministry.' 9

It seems likely, in fact, that the Foreign Ministry was not properly enlightened on this subject by Hitler until the July *coup* was almost under way. As we shall see, the painstaking Dr. Rieth seems to have been left without proper instructions until the very end, and he scampered around Vienna on the fatal day like a startled and not very intelligent rabbit. The fact that the conspirators had close contact with at least one member of his staff does not necessarily mean that the Minister himself was always fully informed in advance of the events which were to cost him his career. The walls of all diplomatic missions contain officials camouflaged in striped trousers who do not answer to their Foreign Offices ; and, in the dichotomy of the Nazi state, this hallowed practice grew more pronounced than ever. But it is time we returned to the scene of action.

* * *

Weydenhammer, disguised as a British business man 'Mr. Williams', joined Wächter in Vienna at 7 P.M. on the evening of July 23. The two men met to discuss the situation in the offices of Herr Blaschke, an Austrian Nazi lawyer who was rewarded for his services after the *Anschluss* four years later with the post of Deputy Burgomaster of Vienna. All arrangements seemed to be tied up except for the provision of lorries to transport the 'Standarte 89'. (This vital gap was duly filled the next day by Herr Lohner, a well-known Austrian industrialist, who equipped the 'putschists' with vehicles from his own firm.)

Rintelen was already in the Austrian capital, residing quite openly at the fashionable Hotel Imperial on the Ringstrasse. There was, of course, no need for him to disguise his presence. The pretext for his journey — to report to his Government on the position in Italy before the summer recess — was a plausible one. Furthermore, it was common knowledge that this Styrian freebooter had intrigued to replace not only Dollfuss, but each of the five Austrian Chancellors before him. This meant that the political pundits of Vienna were quite used to seeing Dr. Rintelen, squatting like a puff-adder over the marble-topped tables of the Imperial Café, whenever a crisis was in the air.

The *Landbund* leader and former Vice-Chancellor Winkler, whom Dollfuss had dropped from his Government the previous year at Mussolini's suggestion, was also in the capital and in contact with the rebels. Here again we strike against that reef of paradox on which the Austrian Republic foundered: its patriots could never be democrats, and its democrats could never be patriots. Winkler, like Dollfuss, was a peasant leader of distinction and integrity. What is more, unlike Dollfuss, he clung to the belief that Austria could weather her terrible foreign political storms with her unwieldy Parliament lashed somehow onto the ship's decks. He thus opposed what he thought was the dictatorship of Dollfuss and, in doing so, ran straight into the arms of the super-dictator whom Dollfuss was struggling against. Unlike Rintelen, who was a plain case of the ambitious intriguer common to all countries and races, Winkler belonged to those hopelessly muddled and disorientated politicians whom only Austria seems to have produced in such quantities.

Having left word for Rintelen at his hotel, Weydenhammer joined Wächter and Glass for another council of war, this time held over dinner at an obscure restaurant of the capital. A plan to strike immediately in the early hours of the following morning was abandoned. The action was fixed for the afternoon of July 24, and the night was devoted to settling several outstanding problems. The trickiest of these was the Federal President Miklas himself, who had upset the whole rebel timetable by blissfully sailing down to Velden in Carinthia to begin his holidays, as befitted the first citizen of the Republic, a day or two before any of his Ministers. Wächter who, even in Weydenhammer's subjective account, emerges as the organizational brain of the conspiracy, had already taken steps to meet this unexpected hitch. A small task force headed by a certain Grillmayer, one of the most resourceful of the Austrian 'activists', was despatched that same night to Velden with orders to hold the President prisoner by the warm blue waters of the Wörthersee until further instructions. (As it turned out, Grillmayer and his party failed in their task and thus contributed substantially to the failure of the entire operation, for there were moments on the afternoon of the 25th when the real voice of Austria was President Miklas, screeching angrily down the telephone from Velden.)

According to his own story, Weydenhammer drove out after dinner with Glass in an SS car disguised as a Vienna taxi to Klosterneuburg, the beautiful abbey town on the western outskirts of the capital. Here, in a copse near the local Danube swimming pool, he conferred with the military end of the conspiracy, Lt.-Colonel Sinzinger and two other Austrian

Army officers. It was agreed that the 'Standarte 89' should assemble in the courtyard of the Vienna Garrison Head-quarters any time after 4 P.M. the following day, and Weyden-hammer claims that these three military traitors also promised that the First Brigade (Vienna) and the Second Brigade (Lower Austria) of the Regular Army would be ordered to turn out in his support. Either the officers concerned had undue hopes on the eve of the revolt or cold feet during the course of it, for the only Austrian units to leave their barracks marched against the conspirators. But a military treachery of sorts there undeniably was, despite the fact that, judged as a whole, Austria's Army officers probably saw more clearly than her police force or her politicians where their duty lay.

At 11.15 that night Weydenhammer and Glass rejoined Wächter at a wine-garden in the nearby village of Nussdorf and reviewed the position again at a wooden table under the trees, each innocently clutching a glass of new wine in his hand. From there, Weydenhammer returned to the swim-ming pool at Klosterneuburg to inspect the troops for the impending action — the desperadoes of the 'SS Standarte 89' under their leaders Glass, Holzweber and Planetta. These were all assembled, furtively and somewhat incongruously, between the clothes-pegs of the deserted changing-room.

After an emotional parting and a whispered 'Heil Hitler', Weydenhammer drove back to Vienna where he at last met up with Rintelen in his hotel room. Here the two men dis-cussed at length 'all necessary measures and announcements which would have to be made after the action was completed and also the reconstruction of the Cabinet'.[10] Without sug-gesting that Schuschnigg was in any way involved in the plot, Rintelen said he had spoken that day to Dollfuss's colleague and successor, and claimed that Schuschnigg had given him to understand that he, too, was dissatisfied with the present system. This has been most categorically denied by Dr.

Schuschnigg [11] and the truth of the matter seems to be that, if the unscrupulous Rintelen did make the alleged remark, he was merely trying to invent non-existent support in order to impress his German sponsors. When one compares the personal character and record of Schuschnigg with that of Rintelen, it is difficult to decide any other way when faced with a clash of evidence between them.

From the Hotel Imperial, the indefatigable Weyden-hammer went for another two hours to the all-night wine restaurant St. Pauli, to brief the departing 'Velden task force', and got to his bed at the Hotel Cobenzl in the Vienna Woods at 4 A.M. He had had the sort of frantically exhausting day for which conspirators have only themselves to blame.

*　　*　　*

As it turned out, it was all in vain ; at least as regards July 24. The day began briskly enough with a conference at 8 A.M. between Weydenhammer and ex-Vice Chancellor Winkler at the latter's flat in the Rathausplatz. Winkler's role in the conspiracy was to proceed immediately to Prague, where he would reassure his contacts in the Czech Government, and particularly Beneš himself, that the forcible removal of Dollfuss had been inevitable and that the new Rintelen administration represented that solid barrier against Nazi aggression which the Czechs demanded above all else, in Vienna. Undeterred by the patent lunacy of this, the sound democrat and unsound patriot Winkler set off. He now disappears, in a fog of earnest confusion, for ever from our sight. Rintelen turned up unexpectedly at the Rathausplatz to wave him goodbye.

At midday the conspirators were informed by Rintelen that the Cabinet meeting would take place as scheduled that afternoon. According to Weydenhammer's report, the informant was the Christian-Social former Chancellor and then

Finance Minister in the Dollfuss Government, Dr. Buresch. (Without stating that Buresch was knowingly involved in the plot, Weydenhammer claims that the Minister was 'in close contact'—'weitgehende Fühlung'—with Rintelen.) The buttons were pressed to start up the action and the lorries were already rolling to the rendezvous, laden with weapons and Austrian Army uniforms for the striking force, when, shortly before 3 P.M., Rintelen and Weydenhammer were rung up at the Hotel Imperial to be told that the Cabinet meeting had been 'suddenly cancelled' and postponed until noon on the following day. According to Weydenhammer, the informant was again Dr. Buresch. Winkler's secretary confirmed the appalling news a few minutes later.

A retreat is notoriously the most difficult operation of all to control. Wächter and his team, operating from a café in the Alserstrasse, with the No. 5 trams clanking noisily past the windows, now worked a small miracle of organization by bringing the whole action silently to a standstill and dispersing everyone back to their hide-outs within the next hour and a half. Before 5 o'clock, Weydenhammer records with justifiable pride, even Velden, Prague and Munich had been brought to the same smooth full-stop. A betrayal was suspected as the cause of this last-minute hitch and a betrayal did actually take place on that afternoon; yet, according to the official Austrian records, it reached the authorities long after the Cabinet session had already been cancelled.

The official Austrian 'Brown Book' on the revolt [12] describes how, around 4.30 P.M. on the 24th of July, a police commissioner was informed 'privately' at his home that the Nazis intended to descend on the Ballhausplatz that very same day and take the entire Austrian Government prisoner. The informant, one of the rebels called Paul Hudl, had added that 'for his part he would prefer to have nothing to do with the affair, but that for moral reasons he could not back out, as this would make him appear a coward in the eyes of his comrades'.[13] It would be difficult to imagine a more determined or more typical attempt to sit between two stools.

The police official hurried to his headquarters where he solemnly recorded the information in a file. (His worship of paper was apparently so great that it does not seem to have occurred to him to pick up a telephone.) The precious file was then handed to the State Police, who duly informed the headquarters of the Inner City, who duly informed their detachment on duty at the Chancellery. It was just as well that Dollfuss was not dependent for his safety that day on his bureaucrats, for it was now early evening, and the *putsch* referred to had been cancelled three hours ago and was already being busily reorganized for the following day.

The Vienna Police Headquarters committed another error that day which probably had as much to do with the traitors in their midst as with any general inefficiency. Neither Dollfuss nor any other member of the Government was given even formal notification of the incident and no orders whatsoever for extra precautions at the Ballhausplatz were issued. The effect of this was felt the next day. Dollfuss was already nervous and seems to have sensed that something sinister was hanging in the air ; he had ordered a special police guard to watch Rintelen in his red plush headquarters at the Imperial Hotel, while the *Heimwehr* Minister Fey was now being shadowed night and day by no fewer than three detectives. False alarms of plots were common in Vienna at the time. Yet, despite this, had the Chancellor, in his anxious mood, been told of the threat on the 24th, he might well have saved his own life the following day — instead of merely giving his country another four years to live.

Meanwhile, if the police were wasting time, the conspirators were not. They were frantically at work recasting their whole operation to match the altered circumstances. Weydenhammer describes how, for greater security, they were now obliged to use the flat in the Rainer Palace of von Altenburg, a member of the German Legation staff. As Altenburg is described as 'helping to draft the proclamations and announcements for the following day' [14] it is plain that, by this stage, at least one German diplomat in Vienna was standing up to his starched white collar in the plot, even if Dr. Rieth himself may not have known all the details.

The 'putschists' were up until 3 o'clock in the morning revising their plan. It was agreed that, as the action would now have to take place at noon, the courtyard of the Vienna Military Garrison headquarters could no longer serve as an assembly point, for it would be crowded at that hour with officials and visitors (Austrian Government offices, then as now, normally worked from 8 A.M. to about 4.30 P.M.). It was Holzweber, the leader of the Vienna task force, who suggested instead the gymnasium in the Siebensterngasse, a building which backed onto a military barracks less than a mile away from the Chancellery. The proposal was adopted and the conspirators, unaware they had been betrayed once already on the 24th, then made final emergency arrangements in the event of treachery on the morrow. Sure enough, that treachery cropped up again. This time, the traitor had the decency to start work early in the morning ; but he ruined everything for both sides by being much more hesitant than his comrade Hudl, and twice as bureaucratic.

*   *   *

The Austrian Nazi who achieved this remarkable feat of leaving both Hitler and Dollfuss in the lurch on the 25th of July was Johann Dobler, a district inspector (*Polizeirevierinspektor*) of the Vienna police force. Dobler had agreed to join the conspiracy on the 23rd, when assured by another Nazi police comrade that the Army were supporting the rebels and that one of his high-ranking superiors, Dr. Steinhäusl, was also committed and was, in fact, the new Police President-designate. But, the very moment he joined the rebels, Dobler also decided to betray them, in an effort to guarantee his future either way and to salve his half-drowned Austrian conscience. (This conscience was to prove too much for him a few days later : on July 29 he committed suicide by leaping through the window of his prison.)

Unfortunately, Dobler was nearly as unsatisfactory as a traitor as he was as a conspirator. His performance on the morning of the *putsch* and the pointless scurry of events which it started up, can only be likened to Viennese comic opera, despite the great and tragic issues at stake.[15] Dobler decided, perhaps wisely, to avoid acting through his own police force, which he knew to be peppered with Nazi sympathizers. But, for some reason, he also avoided a direct approach either to the Chancellery, the Security Ministry or the Defence Ministry, the three other departments involved. Instead he began, soon after 8 A.M., by ringing the headquarters of the Fatherland Front and asking for its leader Dr. Stepan, whose loyalty to Dollfuss and to Austria was one of the few rocks in Vienna's political quicksands. By a tragic misfortune, he was not in his office, and Dobler did nothing more than ask Stepan to meet him in the Café Weghuber 'for an important communication'.

Once at the café, however, the panic-stricken Dobler, bubbling over in frustrated betrayal, poured out his heart to the first sober-looking stranger he chanced to meet there. This turned out to be, of all people, the cashier (*Inkassant*) of Fey's Vienna *Heimwehr* organization. At this stage, the operetta threatened to get quite out of hand. For the cashier, being like most Austrians, a good bureaucrat at heart, went through proper channels and rang up the *Heimwehr*'s Chief Accountant with the news. The Chief Accountant summoned his excited cashier to the *Heimwehr* headquarters in the

Renngasse, heard his story, and asked Fey's personal military adjutant, Gendarmerie Major Wrabel, to receive him. It was now after 10.15 A.M. and Dollfuss was due to assemble with all his Cabinet at the nearby Chancellery in less than 45 minutes' time, the meeting having been put forward one hour.

This thought seems to have stirred Dobler into fresh frenzies of treachery, for, back at the café, he was busy disclosing the Nazi plot to any *Amtsperson* or official personage he could find. Fortunately, the Café Weghuber boasted many such figures among its regular customers. As a result, long before 11 A.M., a retired Army officer, Lieutenant Schaufler, was in on the secret and, far more important, the Commander of the 5th Vienna *Heimwehr* Regiment, Captain Ernst Mayer. It was Mayer who, at last, took direct action. He rang up Fey as the latter was preparing to leave for the fateful Cabinet meeting in his capacity as Minister without Portfolio, and told him, without giving details, of a plot against the Government which 'sounded fantastic but which might well have a real basis'.

The next hour was crucial, not only for the revolt itself, but also in connection with that oft-posed riddle : to what degree, consciously or unconsciously, did Major Emil Fey betray his country on that 25th of July, 1934? As with the mystery of the great Wallenstein, of whom Fey was in some ways a 20th-century miniature, the full answer may never be known. But, from the evidence now available, two things are certain and a third highly probable about Fey's behaviour in this critical midday period. The first hard fact is that Dollfuss and the assembled Cabinet did not even glimpse their Minister without Portfolio until at least 70 minutes after Fey had received the first *putsch* warning. The second hard fact is that, in this interval, Fey was conducting his own private investigation into the alleged plot and had collected detailed evidence, well before noon, both of its seriousness and of its imminence. The strong probability, which fits his ambitious, energetic character and his embittered mood at the time, is that he also attempted in this period to suppress the revolt single-handed with his own Vienna *Heimwehr* forces, in order to appear once again, like after the February Civil War, as the shining hero of the hour.

Since the Cabinet changes a fortnight before, Fey had lost all official control over the security forces. Even the Vienna *Heimwehr* regiments could now only be ordered into action by the Chancellor or his newly appointed State Secretary for Security, Baron Karwinsky. But for Fey, the latter point would have presented no difficulties nor, from what we know of him, would it have caused him any scruples. He was still the undisputed leader of all *Heimwehr* units in the capital and, in an emergency such as the 25th of July presented, his word among his own men would have been as good as unchallenged. A general judgement on Fey's behaviour must be postponed until the long day has ended with the final surrender of the rebels at 7.30 in the evening. Yet the above remarks will serve to simplify the tangled chain of events which preceded Dollfuss's murder, and to which we can now return.

Fey's first act after receiving the mysterious phone call was to go across to the Chancellery from where, without joining or even contacting his assembled colleagues in the Cabinet room, he set part of the *Heimwehr* apparatus in action. Soon after 11 A.M. he learned the general outline of the plot through the excited *Heimwehr* cashier from the Café Weghuber who had now hurried to the Ballhausplatz with his tale. No contact had so far been made with the original source of all this wisdom, Inspektor Dobler, for this reluctant rebel and inefficient traitor was refusing to expose himself by entering any government building. Fey accordingly sent out his adjutant Wrabel to speak to Dobler (who had meanwhile transferred his headquarters to the Café Central) in order to establish, if possible, the truth of all his allegations. It was by now about 11.15 A.M., and the Cabinet meeting upstairs had already begun.

Half an hour later Fey held the conclusive proof in his hands that a Nazi *coup* was planned against the Chancellery before lunch-time. The evidence was a slip of paper which Dobler had collected at Wrabel's request : the traitor's own orders, issued that morning under the code sign '89', to assemble at 12.15 in the Siebensterngasse Gymnasium for the action. Two policemen attached to *Heimwehr* headquarters were now despatched by Fey's adjutant to observe developments in the Siebensterngasse and told to report direct to him.

It was at this point that Fey seems to have decided to summon his own reinforcements onto the scene. An order was sent — by whom is not clear — to a *Heimwehr* regiment manœuvring that morning in the Vienna Prater three miles away to march immediately back to town. The order was an illegal one and the troops arrived too late, as might have been expected. But their commander, Lt.-Colonel Pollaczek-Wittek, did in fact turn up in the Chancellery with all his staff officers about forty minutes after the summons and was seen reporting to Fey in the 'Chamber of Columns' there.[16] They were just in time to be taken prisoner by the rebels.

Until this moment, every single action of Fey's had been confined to his own *Heimwehr* circle. But it was now nearly noon ; he was an hour late for the Cabinet ; the rebels would begin assembling in only fifteen minutes' time ; and he had anyway done all in his power to call a private counter-action into play. A minute or two before 12 o'clock, Fey accordingly entered the Cabinet room and, after excusing his lateness, called Dollfuss over to a corner where he whispered something in the Chancellor's ear.

What those words were nobody will ever know. But two eye-witness accounts are available of the scene which followed.[17] Dollfuss at first shook his head as if in doubt, then moved back into the room and addressed the curious company in these words :

'Fey has just told me something and I don't know yet

whether there is anything behind it or not. But it's perhaps better that we interrupt the session and that every Minister goes back to his own office. I will let you all know when we can continue.' Fritz Stockinger, the Trade Minister, and one or two of his colleagues urged that the Cabinet should remain where it was in the Chancellery. But Dollfuss insisted on the dispersal, retaining with him in the building only Karwinsky, his deputy for Security matters ; General Zehner, the State Secretary for Defence ; and Fey himself. With that single decision Dollfuss sealed his own fate but probably saved that of Austria. The order to scatter meant that more than half of the existing Government remained at liberty and in opera- tion in the capital, thus preventing that total vacuum of state authority on which Hitler and Habicht had staked everything.

It seems to have been the Chancellor's peasant instinct, rather than the preciseness or urgency of Fey's whispers, which prompted Dollfuss to act as he did. For when, immediately after the others had left, he called Fey into his inner office and asked him to repeat his message aloud in front of Zehner and Karwinsky, all that Fey produced, in his clipped Viennese dialect, were the following two casual sentences : 'I've had a report that something is planned against the Ballhausplatz. There is a gymnasium in the Siebensterngasse which is sup- posed to have something to do with it.' And not another detail, then or later, did he reveal ; no mention of the time, the proof, nor of his own actions. Fey was often tight-lipped with his colleagues. But, as a description of a plot whose details he alone knew, which was being launched almost as he was speaking, and which he had been busy trying to block for the past hour, the inadequacy of those two sentences went beyond mere taciturnity. It is difficult to resist the conclusion that this vagueness was deliberate and that Fey was unwittingly condemning his Chancellor to death by trying to save him single-handed.

No such disastrous ditherings afflicted the rebel camp. They had duly been passed word that the Cabinet meeting was beginning at 11 A.M. instead of noon, and the hour lost to Dollfuss by Fey's manœuvres was put to good use by Wächter and his task force. At 11.45 the Gymnasium was 'requisitioned' by Austrian policemen in league with the conspirators and, soon after midday, the 150-odd members of the 'SS Standarte 89' streamed into the assembly point from all over the town, some already dressed for the part, some to collect the stolen Army uniforms and weapons brought there for them in Herr Lohner's lorries. According to Weyden-hammer's account, it had also been arranged early that morning for Glass, the commander of the 'Standarte', to inform personally the traitors in the Vienna Garrison H.Q. the moment the Ballhausplatz had been stormed, 'so that the supporting military action could be put into motion'. From the Nazi side, in fact, the wheels of the conspiracy were now running as swiftly and smoothly as on the previous day.

But the two policemen sent by Fey half an hour before to observe happenings in the Siebensterngasse had also not been idle.[18] One of them, Anton Marek, managed to telephone three reports to Major Wrabel in the Chancellery before he was himself seized by the rebels and forced to mount one of their lorries. His first message, sent at 12.10, described a 'brisk flow' (*reger Zuzug*) of people in uniform and civilian clothes into the Gymnasium. The second, sent only five minutes later, said that Army uniforms were being donned and arms distributed, and that a lorry was being loaded up outside the Gymnasium with various cases and sacks. Marek's third and final message, which reached the Ballhausplatz shortly after 12.30, reported that four more lorries had now formed up outside the suspicious building. 'There is no time to lose', were the last words he shouted into the telephone. All three messages were passed on by Wrabel, as soon as received, to Dollfuss and the three Ministers who were waiting uneasily

in the Chancellor's study. Only one of the group — Fey —
knew their full significance.

It should have taken about four minutes for units of the
alarm squad standing by at the main police barracks to reach
both the rebel centre in the Siebensterngasse and the Ballhausplatz in order to neutralize the one and protect the other.
That neither measure was in fact carried out seemed only
possible in the Vienna of the day and was due to a blend of
Nazi sabotage in the police network combined with dilatori-
ness or confusion almost everywhere else. Neither Karwinsky
nor the Vienna Police President, Dr. Seydel, can be entirely
cleared of the latter charges, though the loyalty of both men
seems beyond doubt. Karwinsky always ordered too little
action too late and Seydel always delivered even less even
later. What was worse, both men sat all the time at their
telephones while the dagger was being driven into their
country's back.

Thus, after Marek's first report had come in, Karwinsky
simply ordered a reconnaissance in the Siebensterngasse by
one single police car. Ten minutes later, after Marek's second
report had arrived, Karwinsky rang up Dr. Seydel for news,
only to be told by the apologetic Police President that the
reconnaissance car had not yet been sent because 'all available
forces' had been despatched to the Michaelerplatz outside the
Imperial Winter Palace, where another plot had been reported
to murder Dollfuss as he walked home to lunch. Even now,
Karwinsky did no more than try to urge on his original
instructions. It was not until 12.35, after hearing Marek's last
message, that Karwinsky finally issued direct orders to the
State Police to send alarm squads both to the Siebensterngasse
and to the Chancellery and bring the position forcibly under
control.

This was late enough in the day, as the rebels were already
mounting their lorries. Even at 12.35, however, the situation
could have been saved had Karwinsky's belated call for action

been promptly followed up. But journeys which should have taken less than five minutes mysteriously took more than fifteen. The squad ordered to protect the Chancellery arrived at the scene just after the rebels had stormed the building ; the squad ordered to clean up the Gymnasium never seems to have got to its destination at all. Even more suspicious, Seydel's solitary reconnaissance car, which finally got to the Siebensterngasse just as the rebels were moving off in their lorries, decided to regard the vehicles as a column of ordinary Regular Army troops, and took no action.

In fact, the sight which met Karwinsky's horrified gaze as he looked out of the Chancellery window a few minutes later had revolution written all over it. As he described it later : [19] 'Standing on old open lorries, some with the names of business firms still painted on their sides, was a mixture of men in police and military uniform . . . the "soldiers" were obviously incorrectly dressed. Some had rifles, some pistols ; some had rifle straps and some were without. Several had their weapons hanging simply by cords from their necks. In the middle of all this riff-raff stood a man in staff officer's uniform with the Order of the Iron Crown on his chest.'

And under his eyes, this motley band of cut-throats sailed smoothly into the Chancellery courtyard without a shot being fired, despite the fact that Karwinsky had ordered the great door to be closed at least a quarter of an hour before. Treachery may have also played a role here. But the main reason for this final disaster was ingenious planning on the rebels' part. The military guard on the Chancellery building was relieved every day at 12.50 by a fresh detachment from outside. This detachment, and the 'putschists', seem to have been the only people who strictly kept their appointments in Vienna on the 25th of July. Dead on time, the relief guard marched into sight and were admitted ; and right behind them, through the still open gates, roared the lorries of the 'SS Standarte 89'. The first act of the bogus soldiers was to disarm the genuine ones as they were peacefully carrying out the formalities of guard-changing. The rebels need not really have bothered. For the ultimate lunacy of the day was that the Chancellery's military guard, even in these desperate times, was still considered 'ceremonial' and therefore carried no ammunition in its rifles.

It was now exactly 12.53. The seat of the Austrian Government which, until then, had been occupied by a strange assortment of people who did not know quite what to do, was now under the control of 154 armed Nazi 'putschists' who knew precisely what they were aiming at. The pace of events quickened accordingly and Dollfuss himself soon became its victim.

When the rebels broke in below, the Chancellor was alone with Fey and Karwinsky in his cream-and-gilt first-floor office. (General Zehner had been sent away over half an hour before to investigate reports that 'soldiers' were among the mysterious crowd in the Gymnasium. This was Dollfuss's last known order, but with it he helped to seal the fate of his assassins by putting the Army Commander, as well as the rest of the Cabinet, beyond their reach.) Karwinsky, his first thought for the Chancellor's safety, pulled him by the arm through the adjacent 'Chamber of Columns', intending to rush him up to the third floor and hide him in a remote cloakroom he remembered seeing there. But Hedvicek, Dollfuss's personal attendant, suddenly appeared to bar their way. He pulled the Chancellor by the other arm, urging him to retrace his steps and try and escape from the building altogether through a side entrance at the opposite end of the main floor which led out onto the Minoritenplatz. Confusion to the very last, and this time fatal.

Trusting to the attendant's closer knowledge of the labyrinthine corridors, Dollfuss left Karwinsky and ran back with Hedvicek through his office and into the so-called Corner Room beyond it. They reached the door to safety, found it, to their horror, locked, and were just turning on their heels

A memorial statuette in the so-called 'Corner Room' of the Vienna Chancellery marks the exact spot where Dollfuss was shot down

Special Editions of the Vienna press announce Dollfuss's murder and the formation of Schuschnigg's emergency Cabinet

Full military honours — too late. The body of the murdered Dollfuss is borne
out of the Vienna Chancellery the morning after the abortive Nazi *putsch* of
July 25, 1934

again in despair when a group of rebels led by Otto Planetta broke into the room from the grand staircase. Planetta rushed up to Dollfuss and, without uttering a word, fired two shots at him from close range. They lodged in the Chancellor's neck and armpit and he fell, heavily bleeding, on the floor. The time was now shortly after 1 o'clock. In seven minutes the rebels thus accomplished more than the entire Austrian police force had organized against them in an hour.

It is not possible to give a firm answer to the question : Were the rebels ordered by Hitler to kill Dollfuss, or did the assassin act on an impulse ? Such evidence as has become available to date allows of either interpretation. We must first jump in this connection to December 1936, when a number of Austrian Nazi refugees who had taken part in the Vienna *putsch* and who had subsequently fled to Germany, were interrogated at length by the NSDAP 'Refugee Organization' in Berlin. The interrogations formed part of an official enquiry into what had gone wrong on that 25th of July two years before. The signed originals came into Austrian hands after the war ; [20] they throw several interesting and one or two startling spotlights on the plot and the actors involved.

On the question of assassination, nearly all the ex-rebels testified that, on being issued with their arms and final instructions in the Siebensterngasse, they were told not to use their weapons unless this was absolutely essential, and even then to avoid any unnecessary bloodshed. One of them, Armin Kraupatz, described how he was ordered by his particular detachment commander, Sturmführer Grondinger, 'to shoot as far as possible at the legs of anyone who offered armed resistance'.

Another of the escaped 'putschists', the Austrian engineer Fritz Lehrer, with the NSDAP party number 685,000, gave evidence which tended to exonerate Planetta of wilful murder. He described how he met Planetta in the corridor outside

Dollfuss's office a few minutes after the fatal shots had been fired. Planetta immediately admitted, in reply to Lehrer's question, that he had done the shooting and added that it had been in self-defence : Dollfuss, he claimed, had jumped at him and, in raising his hand to ward off the blow, Planetta had accidentally pulled the trigger of his pistol. How a second shot was 'accidentally' fired into the Chancellor's body was not explained ; but Lehrer's version is worth recording here since, in the same Berlin report, he alleges that the Austrian police refused, five days after his arrest, to record these remarks in defence of Planetta on the grounds that they were 'uninteresting'. If this be true, then Austrian justice, admittedly under severe provocation, was making another of its periodic bows to politics.

There is no reason to doubt the general accuracy and sincerity of the statements made in these 1936 Berlin investigations, since the ex-rebels involved had nothing to fear from their hosts and were only concerned, where possible, to exaggerate the difficulties they had faced and, where plausible, to place the blame for the fiasco on someone else. Yet, on the other hand, whatever instructions the rank-and-file of the 'SS Standarte 89' may have been given on the 25th July, we know that the German organizers of the plot had at least made provision for the fact that the operation might well cost Dollfuss his life.

The very day after the revolt, an Austrian border patrol at Hanging in Upper Austria captured a German courier who was carrying, stitched to his shirt and his shoe soles, copies of complete instructions for a nation-wide 'spontaneous' Nazi uprising in the event of the Dollfuss Government 'being forced to resign'. These papers, which became known as the 'Kollerschlag Documents', included a list of code signals by which the rebels were supposed to report back to Germany on the progress of events. The two parts of the plan, the Vienna *coup d'état* and the national revolt in sympathy, were described, with grim Teuton humour, as 'Summer Festival' and 'Prize-Shooting' (*Sommerfest* and *Preis-Schiessen*). Telegrams with these identification words were, in fact, despatched from several post offices in Austria on the 25th. More important for our present purpose is the list of 'special contingency' codes attached to the general instructions. The very first of these was to signal the death of Dollfuss. It was not very dramatic. Hitler was to be informed that his little challenger in Vienna was for ever out of the way with the mundane words : 'Old cutlery samples arrived'.[21]

But, premeditated or spontaneous, Planetta's two bullets found their mark a few minutes after 1 o'clock on the 25th ; and, before he drew his last breath over two and a half hours later, the mortally wounded Chancellor was to suffer such agonies of body, mind and spirit as many men are not called upon to endure throughout their lifetime. To begin with, he was allowed to bleed slowly to death on a sofa by his assailants, who refused all his pleas for proper attention and even rejected medical aid when it became available. (One of the Berlin interrogees, Bruno Pouchly, testified that a doctor with an ambulance made two attempts to gain admittance to the building during the afternoon. On the first occasion, he was roughly turned away by the rebel guards ; on the second, he was told that it was now 'too late for his services'.) [22]

The greatest suffering, however, was not physical. A far sharper pain which throbbed in the heart of the dying Dollfuss was the tormented feeling that everything he had striven to achieve for his country during his two years of office had been destroyed in less than two hours by this handful of desperadoes who were now hovering over him. For he died not knowing that the Federal President and the bulk of his own Cabinet were at liberty, and Austria with them. He died believing that Rintelen, the embodiment of ruthless evil in the politics of the day, was now at the helm and that, behind this power-crazed puppet, Hitler's shadow already stood over Vienna.

That was his grief as an Austrian patriot and statesman. His grief as a devout Christian can only be imagined by a fellow-Catholic. Though there were certainly others of his faith among his captors, it was in vain that he begged them, time and time again, to be allowed to see a priest. And thus the little sacristan's assistant who had carried the cross in the church at Kirnberg, and who had tried to carry it by his life ever since, died without its final consolations.

Yet, even under these great weights of suffering, Dollfuss did not allow any hate or bitterness to break through in his last hours. Indeed, towards his murderers he showed the mildness of an early Christian martyr. Viktor Stiastny, another of the Ballhausplatz task force who fled to Berlin after his release from prison, described this to his Berlin questioners with an eloquence that was all the more remarkable for being unintentional. He had entered the Corner Room of the Chancellery only a second or two after the fatal shots had been fired. Planetta was still standing over the prostrate body of Dollfuss, the smoking pistol pointing down at him. Stiastny seems to have been an unusually cold-blooded cut-throat who, even at this moment, was more motivated by animal curiosity than by human compassion. He tells how his first action was to unbutton the Chancellor's coat and waistcoat, not to make the victim more comfortable, but simply to discover whether he wore a bullet-proof vest, as Nazi propaganda leaflets had alleged. Stiastny was disappointed to find that Dollfuss wore 'only normal clothes'. He then proceeded to search the unconscious Chancellor, and handed his wallet over to Holzweber, the leader of the SS task force, who had now appeared on the scene (without, incidentally, reproaching Planetta for his deed or even commenting on it).

At this point, Dollfuss came to his senses, and Stiastny describes a curiously placid political discussion which took place with the rebels standing grimly around. One of them,

whose conscience appeared to be troubling him a little, reproached the Chancellor that he had, after all, caused 'misery
and distress' to many Austrian Nazis himself. Dollfuss
answered : 'I tried always to do the best I could, and I always
wanted peace'. Another Austrian SS man broke in at this
point with the retort that it had been in the Chancellor's power
to bring about peace with Germany. Dollfuss looked up at
the tense young faces above him and said quietly : 'Children,
you simply don't understand'. To that there was, apparently,
no reply.

These rebel eye-witness accounts confirm the impression
given by the official Austrian version of events that the wounded
Chancellor's main concern, in July as in February of that
terrible year, was to put an immediate end to the strife, which
he imagined to be raging all over Austria again. They also
confirm that the first and only person he desired to act in his
name was Schuschnigg. He began by simply asking to see
his senior colleague, only to be told that this was 'not possible'.
Instead, after an interval for consultation among themselves,
the rebels brought in Fey who, until then, had been held under
close guard with Karwinsky and the other principal 'hostages'
in the nearby Chamber of Columns. For the second time
that day, though in very different circumstances, the Chancellor and his Minister without Portfolio held a whispered
conversation in the Chancellery, the exact content of which
will never be known.

According to Fey's own version, given from memory
afterwards, Dollfuss's first request was that Mussolini should
look after his wife and children, who were already in Italy as
private holiday guests of the Duce. Dollfuss next asked about
the fate of the other Ministers and said that Schuschnigg should
deputize for him. Then, probably because he had been told
by the rebels of their 'victory' radio announcement, he added
that there should be no bloodshed and that 'Dr. Rintelen
should make peace'.[23]

It is not possible to fix the exact time of this episode, but according to Karwinsky's account of the day's happenings, it must have taken place shortly after 2 P.M. Karwinsky suggests, without offering evidence, that the Chancellor asked originally to speak with him ; and he describes how, shortly before two o'clock, the rebels tried to draw him into conversation, presumably to sound out his views before accepting him as an intermediary. Only after he had brusquely rejected all overtures from the 'putschist' leaders was Fey fetched from the room and led out to Dollfuss instead.[24]

Those few words exchanged with Fey were the first and last contact which the dying Chancellor had with a member of his Government. After that, he saw only his captors and heard through the shuttered windows only the confused noises and muffled commands of the Government forces assembled in such strength and such masterly inactivity just below. His own ordeal was now drawing to a close, for the bouts of coma became longer and more frequent and the fits of blinding consciousness mercifully fewer and shorter. In the last of these, he turned to his guards who, more subdued as the afternoon dragged on, had started to wipe his brow at intervals and place pads of cotton wool over his open wounds. The final words he uttered were in a whisper to them : 'Children, be good to one another. I always wanted to do only the best.' It must have been about 3.45 P.M. when death came as a friend to release him, and the heart of the new Austria stopped beating.

One final thing, a sadly ironical touch, can be noted here about his assassination. He was killed by a fellow *Kaiserschuetzen*. The German police dossier on Otto Planetta [25] shows that he joined Dollfuss's beloved Kaiserschuetzenregiment No. 1 in 1915 as a sixteen-year-old volunteer, and was also decorated for bravery on the Italian front. One wonders whether the lieutenant who became Chancellor and the private who became his murderer ever fought side by side in the service of their Emperor, in the days before the party politics of the Republic had raised Austrians up in arms against each other.

*   *   *

Following Dollfuss to his end in the shuttered Chancellery has led us ahead of that twisting stream of events outside which, for an hour or two, was indeed unaffected by his death. The storming of the Government headquarters had been the rebels' first success. Their second was the seizure soon afterwards of the main Austrian RAVAG studios in the Johannesgasse from where, at lunch-time, they managed to broadcast a brief message announcing the 'resignation' of Dollfuss and the appointment of Dr. Rintelen as his successor. This was also their last success. For, between 2 P.M. and 7.30 in the evening, the *putsch* fizzled slowly but surely to extinction, snuffed out by the damp air of half-heartedness and indecision all around. Much, however, was to happen in those five and a half hours.

The situation outside the Chancellery after the shooting of Dollfuss was as follows : Wächter had moved to a café near the Ballhausplatz from where, according to the plan, he was to enter the building and personally conduct the negotiations with the captive Cabinet. (The rebel leaders had no idea at this stage that most of the ministerial birds had already flown out of their gilded cage.) Glass, having organized the military supporting action, was to join him in this task, though, in fact, there is no evidence that Glass ever succeeded in making contact again with Lt.-Colonel Sinzinger before he was himself arrested outside the Chancellery later in the afternoon. The third of this choice trio, Dr. Weydenhammer, had meanwhile moved over to the Hotel Imperial, where he was to guide the new 'Chancellor-elect', Dr. Rintelen, in his first governmental steps.[26]

It was soon clear to these two hopefuls in the hotel that something had gone sadly astray. True, after the RAVAG announcement, Rintelen was rung up by one or two prudent Austrians and congratulated on his appointment. But that was all. No delegation came to collect him in triumph. No sense could be got out of the 'garrison' in the Chancellery, and soon after its rebel fanfare the wireless started playing light music, which more or less signified playing for time. (A confused hand-to-hand battle was, in fact, going on with the Nazi task force in the RAVAG building which the police eventually won.) Worst of all, the Ringstrasse outside the Hotel Imperial presented its normal July picture of stolid leafy tranquillity, and the only signs of unusual activity were ominous ones — police cars driving rapidly past into the Inner City. The Austrian SA and SS units who were supposed by now to be parading the streets under 'Operation Prize-Shooting' were conspicuously absent, as were all those 'fraternizing' Austrian Army troops which Colonel Sinzinger had promised.

Had Rintelen only known it, the answer to the riddle was in the Austrian Defence Ministry, only a mile away down the Ringstrasse from where he was sitting. For, safe inside the massive walls of this former Imperial headquarters, the bulk of the legal Austrian Cabinet of the day were already collecting, including General Zehner and the whole of his staff. Whatever hopeful plans a few pro-Nazi Austrian officers may have cherished for a military *coup* in the rebels' favour were dashed to the ground by the appearance of this complete Army command. Indeed, slowly and somewhat nervously, a counter-action now began. Schuschnigg, as the senior among the Ministers at liberty, telephoned President Miklas in Carinthia to report on the alarming events of the day. He found the Head of State enjoying the holiday sun, for the Carinthian kidnapping plot had been frustrated by yet another betrayal. Miklas, remote though he was from the scene of crisis, supplied some badly needed energy and action. He declared he would not recognize a single decision announced on behalf of the Ballhausplatz captives, nor would he accept any political conditions offered by the rebels. He swore Schuschnigg in over the telephone as provisional Austrian Chancellor and provisional head of all other departments in the Dollfuss Cabinet and ordered him to bring the situation under control immediately and by force, and punish the rebels. The actual method he left to Schuschnigg and, for that unenviable man, the sting in the President's instructions came at the tail. For Miklas directed his new emergency Chancellor 'above all to free the captive members of the Government, and liberate them safe and sound from the Chancellery'.[27]

This is one key to the intermezzo of almost unbelievable inactivity which now followed. The rebel 'garrison' in the Chancellery had been virtually taken prisoner itself soon after entering the building. Before two o'clock, the whole Ballhausplatz was jammed with cordon after cordon of Austrian police (who hastened to do their duty when it was too late), backed up by *Heimwehr* units of Fey's Vienna force and Regular Army troops. Yet the whole massed might of Austria's 'Exekutive' held back until dusk before 154 rebels, parleying by shouts up to the balcony or whispers through a chink in the Chancellery gates. Fear for the lives of Dollfuss and the other hostages was, of course, the principal deterrent to action and, to some extent, an understandable one. Schuschnigg, whose dilemma was far worse than that of the local commanders, has pointed out that he did not, in fact, learn about Dollfuss's death until late in the afternoon and was forced, for this reason, to negotiate with the rebels instead of attacking them.[28] But somehow the picture is still not completely convincing : there are other ways in which an overwhelming majority of resourceful and determined people can take a rabbit warren of a building except by frontal assault. However, the 25th of July was just not a good day for either resourcefulness or determination in Vienna.

It was around the mysterious figure of Emil Fey that these parleys centred, and indeed the further course of the revolt, both inside and outside the beleaguered Chancellery. As the senior captive, he carried the greatest responsibility. He admitted afterwards that he deliberately accepted this responsibility by agreeing to act as the rebels' spokesman and intermediary with the Government commanders outside, and argued that this had been the only way to save the lives of the prisoners and perhaps exert some influence over the situation. It was a controversial decision to take. Moreover, considering that he was armed when the attack began, it was a strangely passive one for the most decorated officer of the Emperor Franz Josef (Fey held all three highest Austrian medals for bravery in the First World War, besides a dozen lesser military decorations and six wound stripes). Even according to the carefully varnished account of his behaviour given in the 1934 Austrian handbook, it led the gallant Major into some very unheroic performances during that long afternoon.

The first thing the Nazi 'garrison' made Fey do, for example, was to prevent any action being launched to liberate the Chancellery by the forces massed in such overwhelming strength just the other side of the gate. Twice between 3.30 and 4 P.M. Fey appeared with the rebel leaders on the little semicircular stone balcony over the front entrance of the building, a pistol trained on his back and his ankles held to stop him leaping over, and summoned the military and *Heimwehr* commanders standing below to enter the Chancellery for a parley. Inside the building, both men were received in the presence of the rebel leaders by Fey, who told them that Dollfuss was wounded and had begged that there should be no more violence. This much was true. But Fey was merely acting as a tool of the 'putschists' when he went on to add that the Federal President had authorized Dr. Rintelen to mediate in the dispute and that, until his arrival on the scene, no aggressive action should therefore be undertaken.

Soon after 4 o'clock Fey was prodded even further down his dark path of collusion. Holzweber, the commander of the Nazi task force, persuaded him to write a note addressed to 'The Armed Forces and people of Austria' for distribution outside the Chancellery. This missive repeated the falsehood that Rintelen was Chancellor, adding that his orders should now be obeyed and repeating that no attack against the building should be attempted. Fey passed similar messages by telephone on the rebels' behalf both to the Vienna Police Praesidium and to Schuschnigg in the Defence Ministry. It was from one of these conversations in the late afternoon that Fey learned over the telephone from his colleagues that a proper provisional government had been formed and was functioning in Vienna with the full authority of a President who was himself at liberty. From this point onwards, both Fey and Holzweber seem to have realized that the revolt was doomed and, in the official 'Brown Book' account of events, Fey only appears on the scene once again to negotiate the rebels' terms of surrender, in particular the disputed issue of their guaranteed safe-conduct to Germany. So much for the published version.

But, as has been indicated, the Austrian Government brochure on the July revolt, published only a month or two later to satisfy raging public curiosity, was deliberately in-complete. It is now clear that several of these omissions were made in order to 'beautify' the role of Fey. Colonel Adam, who compiled the publication, himself admitted as much to Baron Karwinsky several years later, when both men were exchanging reminiscences in a Nazi concentration camp.[29] Dr. Schuschnigg, under whose authority as Dollfuss's successor the Brown Book appeared, has confirmed this, stating that the suppressions were made to meet 'strong *Heimwehr* pressure' in the Cabinet.[30] According to Karwinsky's version of events, Starhemberg led this pressure, despite the fact that, two days after the revolt, he had even agreed to the arrest of both Fey and Wrabel on charges of high treason. He seems, on reflection, to have been worried about the effects on the reputation of the *Heimwehr* movement as a whole of any drastic action against his rival.

The Berlin interrogations and the Weydenhammer report suggest what the full weight of incriminating evidence against Fey might have been. On December 23, 1936, for example, the ex-putschist Fritz Lehrer told his German hosts how, shortly after the shooting of Dollfuss, he had joined the other rebel leaders upstairs in the Chancellery telephone exchange. In this crowded cubicle, a terrified girl operator was putting through some of the oddest calls of her life. Lehrer testified that he was standing next to Holzweber when the rebel commander suddenly offered Fey the post of Minister of Security in the non-existent 'Rintelen Government'. Fey hesitated, asking exactly what powers he would be given. When told he would have the Austrian SA and SS as well as the entire police and gendarmerie under his command Fey promptly replied : 'Good ; then I accept'.

It is of course possible to interpret this episode as meaning that Fey was simply leading the rebels on, while secretly intending to use any powers he was given against them. But just as likely an interpretation is that Fey was genuinely seizing the chance of regaining that coveted control over the 'Exekutive' which Dollfuss had taken away from him only a fortnight before. The powers Holzweber had mentioned, combined with Fey's existing leadership of the Vienna *Heimwehr*, would have made him undisputed master of the capital. For someone who had dreamed of nothing else for months and, during the past few weeks, had been fretting in a mood of revengeful bitterness, this was a dazzling and tempting prospect. It is at all events suspicious that no mention of this important episode was made in the 1934 Austrian Brown Book, despite the fact that the incident was immediately known outside the Chancellery. Lehrer, who was an educated man and a calm witness, testified that Fey rang up Dr. Seydel, the Vienna Police President, and informed him straight away of his 'appointment'. Seydel's anxious flood of questions were met by Fey with a taciturn 'Yes', 'No' and 'Perhaps'.

Another strange and rather ominous episode concerning Fey's behaviour on that afternoon is revealed by Weydenhammer in his post-mortem report to Hitler on the *putsch*. Between 2 and 4 o'clock Wächter, Weydenhammer and Glass all seem to have spent most of their time trying to get into the Chancellery, in order to take over political control from the task force inside. Their efforts were in vain. There is no record that Wächter and Glass ever got through the police cordons which surrounded the building. Weydenhammer claims he succeeded in this but was mysteriously refused admission, even though he yelled the prearranged pass-word 'Eighty-nine' several times through the barred door.

Guided by Wächter, this frantic trio then tried to steer the derailed action from outside. Wächter first sought out Dr. Steinhäusl, the Nazi traitor in the Vienna Police Headquarters, and urged him to try and start up an armed police move in the rebels' cause. But Steinhäusl had shot the last poisoned arrow in his quiver. Despite the many ditherers in their ranks, the police were now under the control of Dr. Seydel who, by this time, also seemed to be in control of himself.

Wächter's next thought was to bring Dr. Rintelen in person onto the scene of action, hoping that the mere appearance of the 'Black Knight of Styria' on the tense and crowded Ballhausplatz would cause all weapons to be lowered and all doors to be opened in a spontaneous surge of Nazi ecstasy. He rushed back to the Hotel Imperial with Weydenhammer and pleaded with Rintelen accordingly. Yet even that unscrupulous arch-traitor was now having second thoughts. He knew by this time that the real Government of Austria was not that handful of thugs in the Chancellery telephone exchange but a legal Cabinet sitting just down the road in the War Ministry who could be counted on at any moment to ask him to declare his hand. Sure enough, before this agitated conversation had ended, a messenger from Dr. Schuschnigg was announced from the hotel foyer downstairs. Wächter and Weydenhammer barely had time to hide themselves behind a curtain in Rintelen's sitting-room when in walked Dr. Funder, a respected Catholic journalist and a City Councillor of Vienna, to parley. Rintelen hesitated for a few minutes, his fear balanced tremulously against his ambition. Then he followed Funder back into the War Ministry and, as it turned out, into captivity. (His case was too blatant to be smothered over and, equally important in the Austria of the day, there was no pressure group, apart from the illegal Nazis, willing to plead for him. He was duly tried and sentenced to 25 years imprisonment, and the leaders of the July *putsch* did not see their Styrian man of straw again until Hitler opened the doors of his gaol in March 1938. He then suffered a fate which, for him, was far more bitter than the death he once tried to inflict upon himself : oblivion.)

For the Nazi leaders left behind in the hotel, the shadow of the gallows now began to fall across the whole escapade. No word came from Rintelen, and all attempts to reach him by telephone failed. (He was, in fact, arrested a few minutes after entering the Defence Ministry.) Wächter and Weydenhammer hurried out into the streets to try any last desperate gamble which might present itself. They ran into one of their Austrian Army contacts in the Vienna Garrison Headquarters, but this worthy could now offer them nothing but excuses and specious explanations. The pro-Nazi officers, he alleged, had never even received the news of the successful storming of the Chancellery, which was supposed to be the signal for their action ; and now, with General Zehner firmly installed in his own Ministry, it was hopeless to contemplate starting anything. The Austrian Army, whose role Weydenhammer over-estimated before the *putsch* and exaggerated afterwards, thus failed to let off even a ceremonial firework in the rebels' honour.[31]

The only hope left was the Austrian Nazi SA organization, who were anyway supposed to be standing by, their fingers on the triggers, for the start of 'Operation Prize-Shooting'. Wächter hurried to SA's Vienna headquarters, and discussed the position with their leaders — *Brigadeführer* Türk, Count Hardegg and Messrs. Dax and Hamburger. According to Weydenhammer's account, these gentlemen solemnly promised to mobilize all available forces to march on the Ballhausplatz and raise the siege.

As late as 6 o'clock, Wächter still cherished fond hopes that they would keep their word. At their final marble-topped table conference in the Café 'Viktoria' near the Chancellery (where the plotters successfully avoided suspicion by going through the motions of a noisy game of cards), Wächter assured his colleagues that the SA action would 'shortly take place'. It was also decided to try and strike an emergency eleventh-hour pact with the *Heimwehr*, and thus save the revolt by dividing the spoils with the only non-regular armed forces on the scene. Fey's association with Holzweber, and his nominal pledges of support, had evidently encouraged the rebels to stake everything on this last-minute approach to their sworn enemies.

Again according to Weydenhammer's version, the desperate manœuvre at first showed considerable promise. The indefatigable Wächter managed to contact a 'confidant' of Fey, Captain Kuglmayer, and raise the question of joint action with him. (The fact that this meeting took place has been confirmed by other sources.) Kuglmayer seemed to show willingness and allegedly informed Wächter of the following four 'orders' issued by Fey from within the surrounded Chancellery as the initial steps in this Nazi-*Heimwehr* co-operation. The first three of these orders were : that Major Reichl, a right-hand man of Fey, should deputize for him 'for the time being' as head of the Vienna *Heimwehr*; that there should be no firing on the rebel forces; and that immediate contact should be made between the *Heimwehr* and the Nazi leaders to 'discuss common action'.

Fey's last alleged 'order' has a real ring of authenticity in the intrigue-ridden Vienna of the day. It concerned his *Heimwehr* colleague and opponent Prince Starhemberg, who had been promoted over his head as Vice-Chancellor in the Dollfuss Government and who — true to form as ever — had picked this very time to be amusing himself again on the sands of the Venice Lido. By now, however, the gallant prince had torn himself from the beaches and was on his way back by air to Vienna. Fey's last condition was that his rival should be arrested on landing at Aspern airport that same evening.

This whole episode, which compromises Fey far beyond the excusable limits of a helpless captive, again finds no place in the official Austrian record. And again, though independent confirmation is lacking, it is difficult to see why Weyden-hammer should have invented such a detailed story in an account of events which he knew would be subject to the closest cross-checking. The moment has perhaps arrived to sum up the oft-disputed question of Fey's real role in the July *putsch* as far as the fresh evidence available allows of any solid judgement.

It can be said with virtual certainty that Fey had no previous knowledge whatsoever of the Nazi revolt and that he was not therefore in any sense a deliberate traitor. The Nazis them-selves have unconsciously cleared him of this suspicion. To begin with, Weydenhammer's elaborate report on the lengthy preparations for the plot shows not a single mention — direct or indirect — of Fey as a collaborator or sympathizer, though several other prominent Austrians are mentioned in this con-nection. Even more conclusively, the written instructions

ss's grave-digger, Theo Habicht, Hitler's 'pleni-
ciary for Austria' who organized the July *putsch*
from Munich

And his assassin — Otto Planetta, as an Austrian
soldier in the post-1918 Austrian Army. By a
strange irony, he served in Dollfuss's own regiment

The chief mourners at Dollfuss's funeral : Right (heavily veiled) his widow.
Centre, the *Heimwehr* leader, Prince Starhemberg — his rival but not his enemy

Hitler and Mussolini come to terms. The handshake Dollfuss died to prevent :
it sealed the fate of Austria and of Europe

sent from Germany to organize the 'nation-wide Nazi uprising' on the 25th prove that Fey was regarded as being just
as great a danger to Hitler's plans as Dollfuss. Point 10 of
those 'Kollerschlag Documents' referred to already reads :
'Should Fey seize dictator's powers on the resignation of
Dollfuss, the same procedure (*i.e.* universal armed resistance)
is to be adopted against him'.

That Fey may well have harboured precisely these plans
is suggested by a remark which his personal adjutant Wrabel
allegedly made to one of the rebels on the fatal day. Viktor
Stiastny, whose 1936 Berlin testimony has been quoted above,
claims that, shortly before the defeated 'putschists' were led
away under guard from the liberated Chancellery, Wrabel
turned to him and said : 'A pity you struck now. We in the
Heimwehr were planning a similar sort of thing for the
autumn of 1934 and it would have been more successful if
we could have done it together.' If this remark were indeed
made it was, to put it mildly, an extravagant way to try and
console a prisoner. But the point at issue is that, even if Fey
had been toying with the idea of an early *Heimwehr putsch*, it was
his own independent action he would have launched against
Dollfuss, and not a palace revolt dictated from outside Austria's
borders.

However, though Fey can be cleared of all complicity in
preparing the plot, he cannot be exonerated from all suspicion
of exploiting it to his own ends once it had broken out over
his head. His open opposition to Dollfuss had been mounting,
together with his own ambitions, ever since February, when
the Civil War had made him the temporary 'man of the hour'.
His personal resentment at having been badly treated by his
Chancellor had also been growing like a cancer during these
months. Their relations had been at breaking point since
mid-June when Dollfuss had accused him of storing more
weapons than permissible in his Vienna Headquarters, and had
kept him sitting like a naughty schoolboy in front of him at

the Chancellery while the gendarmerie were sent round the corner to count the *Heimwehr* arms stock.[32] In fact, the charge proved false and Dollfuss was forced to retract it; but Fey never forgave his Chancellor for this humiliation, nor for his demotion which followed shortly afterwards.

This was, in all probability, the account which Fey sought to settle on July 25, 1934. He did not on that day commit premeditated robbery with violence against his country. But it is hard to clear him of the lesser crime of 'stealing by finding'.

*   *   *

The failure, one after the other, of the Austrian police, the Army, the SA and the *Heimwehr* to respond to the rebels' pleas for help struck the foundering operation amidships like successive torpedoes. At 5.30 Schuschnigg finally moved over to the offensive. Two of his Ministers, Neustädter-Stürmer and General Zehner, were despatched to the Ballhausplatz with an ultimatum to the rebels to evacuate the Chancellery within fifteen minutes, or force would be used to re-occupy it. The Nazi 'garrison' were promised safe conduct across the German border 'if no loss of life had been caused among the imprisoned Ministers', an indication that Schuschnigg was still unaware that Dollfuss had been dead already for over one and a half hours.

The bargaining which now started up was far tougher than the fighting had been. For another two hours the wrangle over these safe-conduct terms went on, with Fey or Holzweber appearing on the famous stone balcony above or at one of the ground-floor iron-barred windows below to negotiate on the rebels' behalf. And all the while, throughout the heavy, overcast afternoon, the serried ranks of Austria's Army, police force and *Heimwehr* stood idly in the square outside and just watched, like unemployed costumed stage 'extras', awaiting a summons that never came.

This almost universal passivity, which must be mentioned

yet again, is one of the most unflattering aspects of the whole affair. Inside the building everyone, from the great Major Fey with his loaded revolver down to the humblest clerk or office cleaner, with nothing but his brief-case or sweeping brush to flourish, had submitted without the faintest show of resistance to the invaders. Indeed, there had been several prudent shouts of 'Heil Hitler' among the 150 captive bureaucrats when the bogus proclamation of Rintelen's appointment as Chancellor was read out to them in the courtyard. And outside, the heavily armed force several thousand strong, which represented the free, legal government of the day, rested patiently on its arms while a small gang of desperadoes bargained for their lives, and only moved into the building when the parley was solemnly ended and the gates were opened for them. This was despite the fact that the news of Dollfuss's murder, though late in trickling through, was certainly known to the besiegers well before the final surrender. Weydenhammer even claims that Neustädter-Stürmer was 'fully aware' of the Chancellor's death when he made his first safe-conduct promise. If the 25th of July was not one of Hitler's great days, neither was it one of Austria's.

In the last half-hour of the revolt, Dr. Rieth, Hitler's envoy in Vienna, makes a brief appearance on the scene — like that busy little Moor who flits across the stage in the final moments of *Der Rosenkavalier*, when the action is already settled and the great curtain has just begun to fall. At midnight that night, the German Minister sent an urgent telegram to Berlin on the long day's tumult which explained how this disastrous intervention had come about.[33] Using his code-name of 'Captain Friedrich', Holzweber had rung him from the surrounded Chancellery 'at about 7.30 P.M.' asking that Dr. Rieth should come to the Ballhausplatz and be a personal witness to the safe-conduct pact 'since it concerned passage to the German frontier'. Rieth hesitated, but was finally persuaded to agree by Fey who, with Holzweber standing next to him, rang the German envoy immediately afterwards and repeated the rebels' plea. Somewhat pathetically, the Minister added for his Führer : 'I thereupon said I was prepared to receive the requisite statements from Neustädter-Stürmer emphasizing at the same time that I would not do so in my official but in my private capacity only'.

Rarely has this time-honoured formula of diplomatic evasion looked and sounded more hollow. The mere fact of public contact between Hitler's Minister in Vienna and the Nazi 'putschists' on any pretext whatsoever was bound to have a damning effect in the eyes of the world. Weyden-hammer, probably in an attempt to put himself on the right side of the fence after the fiasco, claimed later that he made a special visit to the German Legation in the late afternoon of the 25th precisely in order to warn Rieth and his Military Attaché, General Muff, against this step.[34] But, if any such warning were issued, the harassed envoy (whom Schuschnigg had wisely cut off from all telephone communication with Berlin) decided to ignore it. Taking his hat and stick as if to pay a formal call, he drove from his Legation in the Metternich-gasse into the Inner City and onto the crowded Ballhausplatz. He describes what happened then in the following words : [35]

'Outside the Federal Chancellery in the Ballhausplatz Neustädter-Stürmer, who said he had parleyed with the party as a representative of the Government, confirmed to me that the whole party had at their own request been promised safe conduct under military escort to Germany.

'Minister Fey, who had meanwhile been allowed to leave the Federal Chancellery, joined us and confirmed the promise which had been given. I told both Ministers once again that although the events which had taken place were in no way any concern of mine, I had, nevertheless, in my private capacity received the statement as requested since it had been represented to me that bloodshed would thereby be avoided.

'As I was about to leave the Ballhausplatz, a high-ranking

police officer came up to me to ask me on behalf of State Secretary Karwinsky, who was still being held, to come to a window and speak to him. I asked Minister Neustädter-Stürmer how he felt about this. He replied that I was free to do so and that he did not wish to express any opinion. I thereupon declined to accede to the request. State Secretary Karwinsky, who had meanwhile been allowed to leave the Federal Chancellery, hurried after me as I was about to get into my car, and, together with Minister Fey, who came up too, urgently requested me to accompany them to a door of the Federal Chancellery to inform Captain Friedrich that I had received confirmation of the Ministers' promises. Otherwise there might be danger of further bloodshed. Accompanied by Fey and Karwinsky I then went to the door, which was opened very slightly, and repeated to Herr Fischer [*sic* ? Friedrich], who was standing behind it, and to some of the other members of the party, what I had been told by the Ministers. I then left the square.'

Whether wise or not, Rieth's intervention set the seal on the rebels' surrender, as well as on his own career. Once Hitler's envoy had turned up in person, even if only to whisper something through a crack in the door, Holzweber and his band felt that their necks were safe. A few minutes after Rieth had disappeared, they accordingly opened the Chancellery gates. The attackers who had never attacked streamed through in triumph and, by 8 o'clock, the seat of Government was again in Austrian hands.

(As it happened, the rebels' confidence was misplaced. They were promptly taken prisoner and the *Heimwehr*, who had been chafing for action perhaps more than any other unit outside, suggested mowing them down with machine-guns. The ringleaders like Planetta, Holzweber, Maitzen and Leeb were in fact executed only a week later and the others imprisoned for varying terms. The Austrian Government's justifications for 'breaking the safe-conduct promise' varied from the weak argument that 'one does not keep promises to rebels' to the rather more substantial one that Schuschnigg and his Ministers had pledged their word only on the express condition that the conspirators inflicted no loss of life on their captives.)

So, as darkness was falling on the capital, this extraordinary spectacle of treachery within treachery, which had opened exactly twelve hours before with Herr Dobler's frantic coffee-house campaign of betrayal, drew to its close. We have referred more than once to its tragi-comic aspects, and perhaps we ought not to leave the Ballhausplatz for good without recording one little episode in which the Nazi drama and the Viennese operetta revolved literally within two hundred yards of each other, almost touching hands.[36]

On that 25th of July, it so happened that the well-known Austrian film actor and producer, Willy Forst, had a fitting with his tailor. The tailor had his rooms on an upper floor of a house in the Schauflergasse, a short street which links the Ballhausplatz with the Michaelerplatz and the famous wrought-iron archway which leads into the old Imperial Winter Palace. As the premises were only a stone's throw from the very heart of the hurricane, Herr Forst rang up several friends in high places to assure himself that the Inner City was calm before driving in after lunch from his house in the Vienna woods.

Calm it may have been ; but the fate of Austria was being decided within that congested and enchanted circle of yellow churches and palaces, and the whole area was cordoned off accordingly like the Holy of Holies in Mecca. However, the Viennese have healthy ideas about the priority of the arts over politics, and when the well-known actor explained through the window of his car that, *putsch* or no *putsch*, he simply had to get to his tailor, there was not a soldier or a policeman who did not wave him on. Towards the end of the afternoon, he was thus able to arrive at the Schauflergasse and to make his way through the mass of troops, gendarmerie, spies, counter-spies and curious bystanders who blocked the street almost solidly right up to the besieged Chancellery building.

Now this was no ordinary tailor's appointment. It was, in fact, the final costume fitting which Herr Forst was due to have before production started on a new Austrian historical film in which he was playing the part of the Duke of Modena. The costume in question was the resplendent ceremonial uniform of the Habsburg court : soft-fitting coat and narrow trousers cut in a cloth of dazzling white, with a braided belt just nipping the waist ; a long-plumed hat and a swinging sword ; the breast emblazoned with jewelled decorations, and the chain of the Golden Fleece dangling from the neck.

He had barely got all this finery in place when a great roar of excitement came up from the street below (it actually marked the moment when Fey made his first appearance through the windows of the nearby Chancellery). Without thinking, Forst bounded out onto the small balcony of the tailor's rooms to see what was going on — just as he was, plumed hat in hand and the Golden Fleece glinting in the dull light.

What Herr Forst saw in the next few seconds was an incredulous movement in the masses immediately beneath him ; followed by shouts and pointed fingers which rippled up the crowd like fire and started a portion of them swaying away from the Ballhausplatz in his direction. And what the Viennese saw from below was, quite simply, an Archduke of that dynasty which had kept order in the capital for $6\frac{1}{2}$ centuries, suddenly reappearing from banishment as if to rescue his people in their hour of need. For half a minute Major Fey as a Nazi spokesman and Willy Forst as the Duke of Modena stood on their stone balconies within earshot of one another : the shadow of the future and the ghost of the past. Then Herr Forst, always a passionate Monarchist, did something he was still regretting twenty-five years afterwards.

Instead of shouting a few words — any words — to remind the Austrians what they had been and who they still were, he stepped back out of sight in silent confusion. History stepped back with him, and the moment was lost.

This may seem an inconsequential episode ; even frivolous. But tucked away in it are several of those deeper reasons why the Germans had looked to the Viennese in vain on that day to do their work for them.

*   *   *

It is not until Emil Fey and Willy Forst had both left their balconies and gone home, and the Ballhausplatz itself was dark and empty again except for its doubled guards that we first hear from the Unmoved Mover of all this evil and commotion : Adolf Hitler. For just as Dr. Wächter had stood behind Planetta's pistol, and just as Theo Habicht in Munich had stood behind Wächter, so, behind Habicht, stood the Führer himself, who had chosen to watch developments on that day from the innocent setting of Bayreuth. The end of the story, like its beginning, centres around him.

The records of the German Foreign Office show that Dr. Rieth had managed to telephone two situation reports to Berlin during the afternoon of July the 25th — at 2.30 P.M. and at 5 P.M. — before Schuschnigg imposed a communications gag on him. The first of these messages said simply that a *putsch* was in progress in the Austrian capital and that Dollfuss, Fey and Karwinsky were being held prisoner in the Chancellery. The second said that the position was unchanged, except for reports that Dollfuss had been wounded and had resigned.

This later message, out of date before it was sent, was the only official news Hitler had of his first act of international piracy for another five hours. All the unofficial reports which he received at Bayreuth early on that July evening were anything but comforting : the deadlock and then the collapse of the revolt ; the proposed safe-conduct to Germany of the rebels ; and, worst of all, the blundering public intervention of his own envoy in Vienna.

At 10 P.M. the Führer could control neither his impatience nor his anxiety any longer. He rang up State Secretary von Bülow, who was on special late duty at the Foreign Office in Berlin, and demanded to know what Rieth was up to and what further messages had been received from him. Bülow's log-book of that night's events [37] shows that Hitler was already preparing his retreat before world opinion and was commanding the retreat himself. He at once declared that Rieth 'should have had nothing to do with the transport of the rebels to the German frontier, nor with playing the part of mediator at all'. Hitler told Bülow that he would reflect on what to do with the Austrian Nazi rebels who were being sent out of the country and confirmed that he would take all further action himself in this matter from Bayreuth. Only fifteen minutes before this, at 9.45 P.M., an agitated Dr. Rieth had finally got through again from Vienna. He falsely reported that the rebels were already on the way to the German frontier and offered some elaborate explanations about his own last-minute intervention. (Rieth added, incidentally, that it was Minister Fey who had secured the resumption of telephone communications for him.)

Rieth's message left no doubt that the true picture in Austria from the Nazi point of view was of complete and heavily compromised disaster. One of the biggest and most brazen back-pedalling operations in diplomatic history was now launched between Bayreuth, Munich and Berlin to save the international honour, as yet unsullied, of the young Third Reich. At 10.15 P.M. Bülow got on to the Propaganda Ministry who, having had no orders to the contrary, were still cheerfully proclaiming Rintelen as Austrian Chancellor, and told them to change their tune.

Half an hour later, the State Secretary made contact with

his chief, Foreign Minister Von Neurath, to discuss what departmental action of their own should be launched. The two men agreed that Rieth's action had been 'unwise' (a preliminary sentence of professional death on that hapless official) and decided that a telegram of condolence over Dollfuss's death had better be sent by the German President Hindenburg to the Austrian Federal President Miklas. This was duly despatched the next day,[38] and for good measure, Neurath added another one of his own to the Austrian Government.

Soon after midnight, Goebbels at last intervened himself to try and sort out the embarrassing confusion reigning in his Nazi propaganda machine. He seems to have persuaded Hitler that serious repercussions threatened to break out in world public opinion on the morrow, and that only an immediate and dramatic act of disavowal could cushion them. These were the days when Hitler still cared what the world thought about him and, at 1.10 A.M., the Führer accordingly approved the telegrams of condolence and ordered the formal recall of Dr. Rieth. An announcement put out ten minutes later by the German News Agency said this step had been taken by the German Government because it disapproved of the envoy's 'unauthorized intervention in today's happenings'.

Even this did not satisfy the anxious Goebbels. At 1.30 A.M. the Foreign Ministry were told that, as a result of another discussion between Hitler and his Propaganda Minister, there would now be an official statement stressing that the German Government denounced the agreement regarding the conspirators' deportation and would arrest them the moment they set foot on German soil. To complete this picture of guileless innocence, it was finally decided to announce that 'owing to the sad events in Austria, the Reich Chancellor had cut short his visit to Bayreuth'.

At 1.40 A.M. Bülow got through to Rieth in Vienna, who was still busy composing telegrams to Berlin, told him he could put down his pen, and informed him of his immediate recall. The Minister seems to have been half-expecting the chopper to fall on his neck. His only reaction was to enquire meekly 'whether the seven o'clock train on Thursday evening would be soon enough'.

In less than four hours Hitler had thus completed his first retreat from his first foreign failure. The Austrian Nazis did not help him by breaking out into delayed 'Prize-Shooting' actions at widely scattered points all over Carinthia, Styria, Salzburg, Upper Austria and the Tyrol. As with the Austro-Marxists five months before, the Nazi rank-and-file in fact only exploded properly into revolt after their Vienna leaders had failed, fallen or fled. It was not until the 28th of July that complete order was restored ; but these provincial clashes, bloody though they were in part, had no significance once the battle for Vienna had been fought, lost and disavowed by its instigators.

In the next few days, while the Nazi sabotage experts argued among themselves in secret as to what had gone wrong (a special report [39] sent to Hitler from Vienna on July 31 by one Steinacher, Head of the 'Peoples Germanic League Abroad', blamed the failure on hasty, over-optimistic preparation and commented that the uprising should have been launched, as first suggested, 'in about two months' time'), the great whitewashing process in public continued steadily from Berlin.

The very day after the fiasco, Hitler had nominated his Vice-Chancellor, Franz von Papen, as new German Minister and 'peacemaker' in Vienna. The Führer's letter of appointment contained the following unctuous paragraph : 'The attack on the Austrian Federal Chancellor, which the Reich Government most sharply condemn and regret, has aggravated, through no fault of ours, the already unstable political situation in Europe. It is accordingly my wish to contribute to a relaxation of the tension . . . and particularly to see relations with the German-Austrian state, which have long been troubled, led back once more into normal and friendly paths.'

The Austrian Government, partly under the influence of its own shock and disgust and partly under Italian pressure, hesitated to make this formal truce with Berlin by accepting a new German Minister. It was not until August 7, after State Secretary Bülow had threatened to regard any further delay as 'a declaration of diplomatic war',⁴⁰ that Schuschnigg, perhaps still prematurely, gave Papen his *agrément*. With his entry into the Metternichgasse Legation, that long intermezzo of German 'peaceful penetration' began which ended with a return to blackmail and brute force in the *Anschluss* of 1938, this time applied with efficiency and overwhelming strength.

From the European point of view, the Nazi set-back in Vienna thus caused Hitler to rearrange his whole time-table of international violence, as well as giving Austria herself four more years of precious if uneasy life. But for those with eyes to see, the omens should have been plain enough, for all the treachery and all the cynicism which later became the hall-marks of Nazism were there in 1934. Indeed, the July *putsch* showed that, even if Hitler had not yet learned to bite as cleanly as a crocodile, he already knew how to cry like one.

*   *   *

As for Dollfuss himself, the rightness of his policy had begun to show itself only fifteen minutes after his death. We have seen how, at about 3.45, he had died in his shuttered Chancellery, tormented even more by failure than by pain. At precisely 4 P.M. Mussolini, on hearing the first firm news in Rome of the Nazi *coup*, had immediately ordered the Italian Army to advance in strength towards the Brenner Pass and the Carinthian border. On the evening of July 26 von Hassell, Hitler's envoy in Rome, rang up Berlin to say that these measures were 'only of a precautionary nature'.⁴¹ But the following day German intelligence agents reported with alarm that the Italian formations encamped on the mountain slopes around Vipiteno were being issued with battle ammunition. Nor had Mussolini confined himself to the military sphere. At the same time, he had received the British and French Ambassadors in Rome to discuss common diplomatic action in the crisis. The ultimate fruits of these contacts were the Franco-Italian and Anglo-French Protocols of January and February 1935 (later confirmed at the Stresa Conference), in which the three Governments undertook to hold 'joint consultations in the event of any threat to Austria's independence'.

More might well have been done. In 1934 the *Bersaglieri* had stopped short at the Brenner, and by 1936 the Stresa Front was already dissolving in those clouds of Italian mustard gas which hung over Addis Ababa. But the help which the murdered Dollfuss got from his Italian friend was immeasurably more than anyone else was prepared to give ; and, temporary though this umbrella of Italian protection turned out to be, it was the nearest thing to safety that the Austria of Dollfuss and Schuschnigg ever knew or could have known.

In fact, the little Chancellor had served his countrymen by the martyrdom of his dying no less than by the crusade of his life. Inside a divided and demoralized Austria, he had become the nearest thing to a national symbol since the double-headed eagle was hauled down from the Hofburg ; and his funeral, attended by over a million of his countrymen, with the middle-classes predominating but with the workers also participating, was certainly the nearest thing to a national act of mourning since the old Emperor Franz Josef had been carried down into the vaults of the Kapuzinergruft from another world eighteen years before.

Abroad, Dollfuss's death fixed him in history as the person he will always remain, despite his own errors and the calumnies of his enemies : the incorporation of an Austrian way of living and thinking and therefore of an Austrian right to independent existence. This ideal he snatched back from that

Empire which his opponents despised and gave to the Republic which those same opponents had built. He thus put into the body of the young state the soul of the ancient nation. As a great London paper wrote on July 30, 1934 : 'By his death, Dr. Dollfuss has proved that a German culture really exists that is worth saving'.

The murdered Chancellor might have hoped for greater help from Britain while he was alive. But he could not have wished for a better epitaph once he was dead.

NOTES

CHAPTER ONE

1. Kons. Rat Toifl, to whom, with Ing. Ludwig Bruckner and ex-Minister Dr. Strobl, I am indebted for most of these school-time details.

CHAPTER TWO

1. The incident is quoted in E. K. Winter's *Christentum und Zivilization*.
2. From the Bardolff papers, cited in the Introduction.
3. Account given to the author by Dr. Strobl.
4. Dr. Leo Müller, a friend and colleague of Dollfuss in the Agricultural Chamber, has supplied this and other information about the period.

CHAPTER THREE

1. Dr. Julius Deutsch, Commander of the Socialist *Schutzbund*, has described to the author how, in 1926, he opposed the use of the word 'dictatorship' in Bauer's resolution, fearing the false implications it would invoke.
2. From the Bardolff papers, *op. cit.*

CHAPTER FOUR

1. The account which follows of the build-up of the 'Fatherland Front' is largely based on the Stepan papers, cited in the Introduction.
2. In a conversation with the author, November 1960.
3. For details of the above episode I am indebted to ex-Minister Dr. Czermak himself.
4. Karwinsky papers, cited in Introduction.
5. Conversation with the author, November 1960.
6. Karwinsky papers, *op. cit.*
7. My thanks are due to Dr. Strobl for providing this document and to ex-Minister Oskar Helmer for giving many supplementary details of the whole issue.

CHAPTER FIVE

1. I am indebted to Dr. Franz Mayer-Gundhof for this anecdote.
2. Documents on German Foreign Policy, Series C, Vol. 3, Telegram No. 213. (Hereafter cited as 'Documents'.)

3. Confirmed by Dr. Krisch, now Sektionschef Krisch, then Dollfuss's secretary.

4. The former Chancellor Schuschnigg and the former State Secretary and present Provincial Governor of Upper Austria Gleissner (both then in Dollfuss's Cabinet) have expressed this view to the author.

5. Information supplied by Major Wrabel, Fey's adjutant.

6. For example, by Dr. Deutsch to the author. I am also indebted to Dr. Deutsch for several unpublished details of the action used in the following account.

7. Official Government figures issued in 1934 and largely confirmed today by Dr. Deutsch, the *Schutzbund* Commander.

8. I am indebted to Frau Dollfuss and her friend in question for the details of this unknown incident, which have been recorded in a sworn testimony in my possession.

9. Dr. Stepan, who was about to be nominated Leader of the Fatherland Front.

10. Dr. Deutsch, himself a First World War artillery officer, has confirmed that 'a high percentage' of the rounds were 'duds'.

11. Dr. Stepan : private papers and diaries.

12. Hofrat Rischanek, who described the incident to the author.

13. Minister Ludwig Strobl, to whom I am indebted for the anecdote.

14. Documents, Series C, Vol. 3, Telegram No. 308.

15. Documents, Series C, Vol. 3, Telegram No. 328.

16. Documents, Series C, Vol. 3, Telegram No. 389.

17. To Hofrat Rischanek, for example, who mentioned this to the author.

18. Dr. Stepan diary, *op. cit.*

19. The present Wage-Price Commissions of the Second Republic are, incidentally, a direct functional descendant of these mixed committees introduced by Dollfuss.

CHAPTER SIX

1. Vienna Trabrennplatz, September 11, 1933.

2. Speech on December 24, 1933.

3. In a conversation with the author in September 1960 in Salzburg.

4. In an account given to the author in Vienna in October 1960.

5. Stepan papers, *op. cit.*

6. Frau Alice Rüppel, to whom I am indebted for these and other personal details.

7. Related in the Stepan papers, *op. cit.*

8. Kons. Rat Toifl, who has provided this anecdote.

9. Minister Theodor Hornbostel, Dollfuss's principal adviser on foreign affairs, was the other passenger, and it is to him that I owe the story.

10. The incident is quoted in the papers of Dr. Stepan, *op. cit.*, who was a witness.

Notes

11. I am indebted to Hofrat Dr. Rischanek for this account.

12. Dollfuss suffered increasingly during the last eighteen months of his life from deafness.

CHAPTER SEVEN

1. Later General of Artillery, to whom I am indebted for much useful information on this period.

2. Documents, Series C, Vol. 1, No. 107.

3. Documents, Series C, Vol. 1, No. 112.

4. Documents, Series C, Vol. 1, No. 173.

5. Documents, Series C, Vol. 1, No. 346.

6. Documents, Series C, Vol. 1, No. 383.

7. Documents, Series C, Vol. 1, No. 391.

8. Quoted in *Geheimer Briefwechsel Dollfuss-Mussolini* (Wien, Volksverlag, 1949), from which all subsequent extracts are taken. The documents were originally published by Paul R. Sweet in Julius Braunthal's *The Tragedy of Austria*.

9. Quoted in *Geheimer Briefwechsel, op. cit.*

10. Dr. von Hornbostel is one of the two surviving participants in the Riccione talks, and I am greatly indebted to him for the hitherto unpublished details which follow.

11. Documents, Series C, Vol. 1, No. 416, and footnote.

12. The incident is quoted in the official Austrian *Geschichte und Vorgeschichte der Julirevolte*.

13. Documents, Series C, Vol. 1, footnote 10.

14. Documents, Series C, Vol. 1, No. 191.

15. One of them was Dollfuss's former subordinate in the Lower Austrian Agricultural Chamber, Dr. Leo Müller, to whom I am indebted for an account of the incident.

16. Occasionally large extra subsidies were negotiated, as when Dr. Rieth asked for an additional RM30,000 for the Greater Germans in February 1933 (Documents, Series C, Vol. 1, No. 25).

17. I am indebted to the then State Secretary and present Provincial Governor of Upper Austria, Dr. Heinrich Gleissner, for supplementary information on these talks, in which he often acted as the spokesman of Dollfuss. Langoth has given a detailed and reasonably balanced account of them in his book *Der Kampf um Oesterreich*.

18. Documents, Series C, Vol. 2, No. 35.

19. Documents, Series C. Vol. 2, No. 49.

20. Documents, Series C, Vol. 2, No. 126.

21. Documents, Series C, Vol. 2, No. 106.

22. Stepan papers, *op. cit.*

23. Dr. Hornbostel and Dr. Stepan, to whom I am indebted for this account.

24. Documents, Series C, Vol. 2, No. 166.
25. Documents, Series C, Vol. 2, No. 167.
26. Documents, Series C, Vol. 2, No. 229.
27. Documents, Series C, Vol. 2, No. 213.
28. Documents, Series C, Vol. 2, No. 328.
29. Documents, Series C, Vol. 2, No. 308.
30. Documents, Series C, Vol. 2, No. 225.
31. Documents, Series C, Vol. 2, Nos. 333 and 334.
32. Documents, Series C, Vol. 2, No. 299.
33. Documents, Series C, Vol. 2, No. 332.
34. Documents, Series C, Vol. 2, No. 255.
35. Documents, Series C, Vol. 3, No. 5.
36. Documents, Series C, Vol. 3, No. 26
37. Hofrat Dr. Rischanek and his family, to whom I am indebted for this anecdote.

CHAPTER EIGHT

1. Documents, Series C, Vol. 2, No. 389.
2. 'Report on the Uprising of the National Socialists on the 25th July in Vienna', submitted to Hitler after the fiasco by Dr. Rudolf Weydenhammer, then Chief of Staff to the Nazi operational Headquarters for Austria in Munich. Subsequently referred to as the Weydenhammer Report. (See Introduction for circumstances in which this became available.)
3. Weydenhammer Report, *op. cit.* p. 3.
4. Weydenhammer Report, *op. cit.* p. 4.
5. Weydenhammer Report, *op. cit.* p. 6. (Passages in square brackets inserted by the author.)
6. Weydenhammer Report, *op. cit.* p. 7.
7. Documents, Series C, Vol. 2, No. 389.
8. Documents, Series C, Vol. 2, No. 369.
9. Documents, Series C, Vol. 2, No. 459.
10. Weydenhammer Report, p. 12.
11. In letters and in a two-day discussion with the author at Salzburg, September 1959.
12. 'Contributions to the history and pre-history of the July Revolt' (Vienna, 1934). Subsequently referred to as the 'Brown Book'.
13. Brown Book, p. 61.
14. Weydenhammer Report, p. 14.
15. The following account of Dobler's movements and their effects is based on the Brown Book, pp. 62-65, supplemented by information from several eye-witnesses from different sides — such as the Karwinsky papers and an account of events given to the author by Fey's adjutant, Major (now Regierungsrat) Wrabel.

16. Karwinsky papers.

17. Karwinsky papers and Dr. Schuschnigg to the author.

18. The account of police activity, or rather inactivity, which follows, is based on the Brown Book, the Karwinsky papers, and on certain eyewitness material.

19. Karwinsky papers.

20. These originals were put with the old Austrian police file on the trial of Holzweber, one of the principal 'putschists' of July 1934, and are referred to for convenience below as the Holzweber papers. (See also Introduction.)

21. For the full text and other details of the Kollerschlag Documents, see the Brown Book, pp. 53-56.

22. Holzweber papers.

23. Brown Book, p. 74.

24. Karwinsky papers, pp. 13-14.

25. Included in the Holzweber papers, *op. cit.*

26. The following sequence of events is based on the Brown Book and on Weydenhammer's account.

27. Brown Book, p. 76.

28. Statement to the author, September 1960.

29. Karwinsky papers.

30. Statement to the author, September 1960.

31. This episode, and what immediately follows, is based largely on the Weydenhammer Report.

32. The source for this incident is the Stepan papers, *op. cit.*

33. Documents, Series C, Vol. 3, No. 119.

34. Weydenhammer Report, pp. 23-24.

35. Documents, Series C, Vol. 3, No. 119.

36. For the anecdote which follows I am indebted to Willy Forst himself.

37. Documents, Series C, Vol. 3, No. 115.

38. One of President's Hindenburg's last official acts. He died on August 2 and was succeeded by Hitler almost within the hour.

39. Documents, Series C, Vol. 3, No. 143.

40. Documents, Series C, Vol. 3, No. 146.

41. Documents, Series C, Vol. 3, No. 122.

BIBLIOGRAPHY

(Note : A five-page list of books published on Austrian and Danubian problems *since* the Second World War is appended to my *Austrian Odyssey* (Macmillan, London, 1957). The first six titles printed below are additions to this general list, which I have not thought worth while reproducing. The other titles which follow are works — most of them only brochures — by, on, or about Dollfuss himself.)

Adamovitch, Ludwig. *Die neue österreichische Verfassung.* Wien, Öst. Staatsdruckerei, 1934.

Deutsch, Julius. *Ein weiter Weg.* Amalthea Verlag, Wien, 1960.

Funder, Friedrich. *Memoirs*, Part Two. Herold Verlag, Wien, 1959.

Ludwig, Eduard. *Österreichs Sendung im Donauraum.* Wien, Öst. Staatsdruckerei, 1954.

Ingrim, Robert. *Der Griff nach Österreich.* Europa Verlag, Zürich, 1938.

Rintelen, Anton. *Erinnerungen an Österreichs Weg.* Munich, 1941.

* * *

Dollfuss, Engelbert. *Die Sozialversicherung in der Landwirtschaft Österreichs.* Mertha Verlag, Wien, 1929.

Dollfuss, Engelbert. *Rednerskizze.* Herold Verlag, Wien, 1933.

Dollfuss, Engelbert. *Führerworte.* Wien, 1935.

Dollfuss-Mussolini. *Geheimer Briefwechsel.* Wiener Volksbuchhandlung, 1949.

Eder, Julius. *Kanzler Dollfuss.* Wien, 1933.

Eder, Julius. *Zwei Jahre Dollfuss.* Wien, 1934.

Hildebrand, Dietrich. *Engelbert Dollfuss.* Salzburg, 1934.

Kanzler Kalender auf das Jahr 1935. Tyrolia Verlag, Wien, 1934.

Kittel, Franz. *1934–1954 Dollfuss.* Wien, 1954.

Knoll, August. *Von Seipel zu Dollfuss.* Wien, 1934.

Maurer, Hans. *Engelbert Dollfuss.* Graz-Wien, 1934.

Messner, Johannes. *Dollfuss.* Wien, 1934.

Rambaud, R. P. *Le Grand Petit Chancelier Dollfuss.* Emmanuel Witte, Paris, 1948.

Weber, Edmund. *Dollfuss an Österreich.* Wien, Reinhold, 1935.

Weithaler, Ludwig. *Kamerad Dollfuss.* Wien, 1934.

(See also special documentary sources listed in Introduction.)

INDEX

Ach, Hermann, Minister of Interior under Dollfuss, 89

Agriculture, Austrian, reforms by Dollfuss, 37-42, 92 ; International Agrarian Congress, 38

Anschluss, Anschluss-Protocol, 55 ; Pan-German support for, 72-3 ; supporters of, 79 ; Lausanne loan, effect on, 95 ; Italian opposition to, 197

Army, Austrian, St. Germain Treaty, effects on, 106, 132

Austro-Fascism, birth of, 99 ; Dollfuss sympathy with, 223

Austro-Marxism, 50, 53-58, 66 ; relations with Dollfuss, 93-4

Bank, Creditanstalt, collapse of, 90

Bardolff, Field-Marshal, Pro-*Anschluss*, 70

Bauer, Otto, Radical Socialist leader, 30, 50, 53-5, 66, 86, 110-16 ; comparison with Karl Renner, 58-9 ; role during Civil War and subsequent flight, 131-7

Bernaschek, Richard, Socialist *Schutzbund* Commander, 124, 130, 135

Britain, financial aid from, 94 ; Dollfuss visit to, 104 ; opposition to Nazi intervention, 192, 199, 225

Buresch, Dr., Austrian Chancellor, 47, 83, 218 ; role in Nazi *putsch*, 243

Cartell-Verband, Catholic brotherhood, 15 ; support for Dollfuss, 85

Charles, last Austrian Emperor, 25-6

Christian - Socials, Austrian Right Wing party, 50, 60-4 ; power at Dollfuss's accession, 87 ; loss of power, 108-9

Civil War, Austrian, 1934, 122-55 ; Karl-Marx-Hof, 142

Coat-of-arms, Austrian, 160

Communists, Austrian, 50-3

Constitution, May 1934, 156-78 ; Fascist influence on, 161-3 ; *Heimwehr* opposition to, 164-8 ; Mussolini's Fascism influence on, 163, 169 ; 'Quadragesimo Anno' influence on, 170-5 ; effect on Nazis, 225

Council of State, new legislative under May constitution, 158

Czechoslovakia, 75, 192

Danube Basin, 79, 194 ; Rome Protocols, 221

Dobler, Johann, informer during Nazi *putsch*, 245-7

Dollfuss, Engelbert : ancestry and birth, 2 ; early years, 3-10 ; seminary at Oberhollabrunn, 11-13 ; further studies in Vienna, 13-15 ; soldier, 16-24 ; return to Vienna, 25-7 ; Peasants' Union, 34 ; marriage, 35-6 ; agrarian reforms of, 37-41 ; Director of Lower Austrian Chamber of Agriculture, 41 ; President of Austrian Federal Railways, 43 ; Minister for Agriculture and Fisheries, 45 ; political atmosphere at his accession, 49 *et seq.* ; Chancellor, 83 *et seq.* ; formation of Cabinet, 87-9 ; economic measures, 89-92 ; 7th of March proclamation, 99, 104 ; launching of Fatherland Front, 103 *et seq.* ; visits to Mussolini, 103, 111, 193, 203 ; visit to London, 104 ; Trabrennplatz Speech, 111 ; Civil War, 118 *et seq.* ; 122 *et seq.* ;

293

Index

THE END

PRINTED BY R. & R. CLARK, LTD., EDINBURGH